MY CONFECTION

MY CONFECTION

ODYSSEY OF A SUGAR ADDICT

LISA KOTIN

BEACON PRESS
BOSTON

Beacon Press
Boston, Massachusetts
www.beacon.org

Beacon Press books
are published under the auspices of
the Unitarian Universalist Association of Congregations.

19 18 17 16   8 7 6 5 4 3 2 1

This book is printed on acid-free paper that meets the uncoated paper
ANSI/NISO specifications for permanence as revised in 1992.

Text design and composition by Kim Arney

Many names and other identifying characteristics of people mentioned
in this work have been changed to protect their identities.

Library of Congress Cataloging-in-Publication Data
Names: Kotin, Lisa
Title: My confection : odyssey of a sugar addict / Lisa Kotin.
Description: Boston : Beacon Press, 2016.
Identifiers: LCCN 2015025760
ISBN 9780807069257 (paperback)
ISBN 9780807069264 (ebook)
Subjects: LCSH: Kotin, Lisa—Health. | Eating disorders—Patients—
Biography. | Sugar-free diet. | Sugar—Physiological effect. | Self-care,
Health. | BISAC: BIOGRAPHY & AUTOBIOGRAPHY / Personal
Memoirs. | SELF-HELP / Eating Disorders.
Classification: LCC RC552.E18 K68 2016 | DDC 616.85/26—dc23
LC record available at http://lccn.loc.gov/2015025760

To my mom. And my dad.

CONTENTS

PREFACE

In a 2007 scientific experiment at the University of Bordeaux, in France, a group of rats were placed in cages with two levers, one of which delivered an intravenous dose of cocaine, the other a sip of highly sweetened water. At the end of the trial, a rat was found to be 94 percent more likely to choose saccharine over cocaine.

I am that rat.

I am three, just awakened from a nightmare and standing in my crib. I hold onto the rail and cry for my mother, who has just returned home from shopping. As she enters my room and approaches my crib, I reach for her, crying to be held. She lifts her arm and, instead of hugging me, she hands me a chocolate See's sucker. The classic, square kind. The kind that is so hard, no matter how long you lick it, it seems like it could last forever—that is, unless you can't hold out and just bite the damn thing into pieces.

But my sugar addiction started before I ever took my first bite. Before I even had teeth. Rumor has it my mother lived on chocolate éclairs throughout her four pregnancies. It must have quelled her nausea. Or something. While the sugar gene skipped over my brother, my two sisters and I inherited it in utero. Once I was born, the last of four kids in six years, my parents were so exhausted that for a short time they actually rigged a bottle of sweet formula over my crib so they wouldn't have to get up for my 3 a.m. feeding. If I got hungry I could just open my mouth and suck.

That my dad was a dentist had little influence on the amount of sweets brought into our home. And I knew every corner in which to find them: In my mother's lingerie drawer. In the dark recesses of her fine leather pocketbooks. The freezer. The pantry. The empty cottage cheese container I filled with candy and stashed in my own underwear drawer. The Mason jar stuffed with candy collected by me and my cousins for our clubhouse. As president and treasurer of our little club, I felt entitled to dip into the collection as needed. Which was often.

Growing up in the '60s, we had no idea sugar would one day be considered a toxic and addictive substance, just like tobacco and booze. Dr. Robert Lustig, a pediatric endocrinologist at the University of California, San Francisco, with a special interest in childhood obesity, and author of *Fat Chance: Beating the Odds Against Sugar, Processed Food, Obesity, and Disease*, links sugar to heart disease, hypertension, and many common cancers. In her book *Suicide by Sugar*, Nancy Appleton claims sugar can contribute to everything from eczema and Alzheimer's to impairing the structure of your DNA. It doesn't matter if it's high-fructose corn syrup or derived from an organic beet. Sugar is sugar. And my drug is everywhere. It's in everything. It can make anything taste better, Lustig claimed in a 2012 UC Berkeley lecture, even dog poop.

I don't know if what they are saying about sugar is true. All I know is what happened to me. Maybe one day I'll be able to eat a cookie. For today, one is too many, a thousand are not enough.

This is the story of where my addiction took me once I left home for college and careened into my twenties, with pieces of my early childhood and adolescence thrown into the mix. It follows my trail of cookie crumbs from macrobiotics to Overeaters Anonymous meetings to therapy to vitamins to men to more therapy to more vitamins to more men and then . . . back home. Where the fudge really hit the fan.

The story ends when I graduate eight years later (yes, eight years later). But an addiction doesn't die with a diploma, and so at the end of the book I bring you into my life now. Which, despite all I now know about the ill effects of sugar, and despite the plethora of sugar-free choices now available, still presents me with a daily struggle to stay abstinent. Or, on the other side of the coin, a daily opportunity to choose life. Because, while I never did find that one magic medicine, or mantra, or man, or menu to make me whole, what I discovered nearly three decades later is that I am not alone. That might be the greatest discovery of them all.

CHAPTER 1

MACRONEUROTICS

I awaken after yet another night of debauchery. A bag of Pepperidge Farm chocolate-filled Milano cookies, two sesame bagels with peanut butter, a bag of peanut M&M's, a pint of mint chocolate chip, and cheese. Lots and lots of cheese. Real cheese, though. Not the fake Velveeta crap. I was raised in a health-food house. I avoid junk food.

In the fall of 1978, there's little talk of eating disorders, but I know something is wrong. Nobody gets that I have a problem because I'm nowhere near fat. I'm also not anorexic. Nor am I bulimic. The only explanation for my thinness is my rocket-speed metabolism, my danceresque physique, and fasting after I binge. Plus I worry. A lot. That must burn a few calories.

I clench my jaw, swallowing repeatedly to squelch the wall of nausea that rises up the back of my head. My pupils pulsate, probably from all the fat, sugar, and shit lodged in my gut. I have a cramp in my lower right side, a pocket of pain that gurgles when I press down into it. It started after I left home three and a half years ago, at seventeen, and began sugar bingeing. The family doctor called it irritable bowel. He got that right. My bowels *must* be pissed off—and stingy, too, considering I only take a crap about once every two weeks. I don't want to have to crap. It's so menial. I don't want to have to pull down my pants and see that subtle but developing roll of womanly gut and those slightly wider thighs that didn't used to be there. I don't want to have to sleep. Or breathe. Or chew. A chiropractor told me I was full of shit—literally—and sold me a can of volcanic-ash shake mix for twenty-five bucks. I never tried it. I'll shit when I'm ready. People always say that people with eating problems have no willpower. I'm the willfullest fucker I know.

I tell myself I will quit bingeing when I get diabetes. I heard somewhere that diabetes makes you dizzy, so after a binge I always roll my eyes around inside my head to make myself dizzy so I can make sure it stops. Otherwise it might be diabetes. Of course, my biggest fear is cancer. At this time no one is talking about the cancer/sugar connection, but I have my suspicions. Or maybe I just go to the darkest place.

Actually, I don't just go to the darkest place. I live there. I own real estate.

I should be happy. I'm living my dream, rooming in an old farm house and working with a professional mime troupe in a small New England town. Well . . . semi-professional. Everybody knows there's no money in mime. My parents are supporting me. But I really should be happy. I chose to be here. I've already dropped out of two colleges, worked with three performing arts programs, lived in seven different cities, and only just turned twenty-one. For my birthday my mom sent me twenty-five dollars. Cash. I spent every dime on sugar. Before noon. Alone.

The only person who gets my problem is my sister Sarah. Fourteen months my elder, Sarah has always been my higher power. My heroine. As my Brooklynese father used to say, "If Sarah jumped owaf the Golden Gate Bridge, Leeser would follow." It's true. I would put her in a needle and shoot her into my arm if I could. Instead, I turn to sugar, and then to her to save me from it.

"I can't stop bingeing!" I cry into the phone to my sister. She recently quit sugar under the guidance of a hardcore Japanese healer. He put her on a strict diet of brown rice and some putrid smelling medicinal teas, and her bladder infections disappeared. Not a granule of sugar has crossed her lips since. "The pain in my

side won't go away! I don't know what to do!" Sarah tells me
about a macrobiotic study house in Boston. She suggests that I
check myself into sugar rehab so the food nazis can kick my ass
and cure me. It will be macrobiotic lockdown. No white flour.
No milk products. No animal fat. No caffeine. And *no sugar.*
Those macros know sugar is the devil, even more than booze or
cigarettes. It's the ultimate yin. Meat is the ultimate yang. In the
middle of the food scale is brown rice. Brown rice is like their
god. Chew your rice, balance your diet, and you can solve any
problem, cure any pain. Your lover just dumped you? You're too
yin. Eat root vegetables and red adzuki beans. Got a migraine?
Too yang. Try stewed apples with barley malt. Got heartburn?
Lost your job? Got a brain tumor? Find your balance. Chew your
rice. Chew, chew, chew. As for me, I am yin incarnate. If there
was a macrobiotic dictionary and you looked up "yin," you'd see
a picture of my face. A little frosting smeared on my lip.

It is lunchtime when I arrive in Beantown. Thank God. The
sooner I get that miraculous macrobiotic food into me, the sooner
I will find salvation. I lug my bags from the back of the cab and
peer up at the austere, ivy-covered Tudor. Good. This is just what
I need. A severe, sober setting where I'll be forced to get my shit
together. Or take a shit, with any luck.

I ring the bell and am greeted by Enid, a small, poker-faced
gal with mousey-brown hair. She's as warm as cold rice. "Hi," I
mutter. "I'm, um, Lisa?"

"I know that," she says looking slightly disgusted. "We're
expecting you."

"Oh . . . great!" I say reaching for my bags. She stops me and
points to my feet.

"Remove your boots first," she instructs. I learn it's a house
rule, to prevent tracking in dirty snow, along with the bad vibes
of the civilian, omnivore world. I remove my boots and follow
her through the dark, wood-paneled vestibule that spills into a

large, dimly lit dining room. There, about a dozen sallow-faced, scrawny men and several beefier-looking women are seated on floor pillows around a long, low, Japanese-style dining table. There is no conversation. Just the steady sound of chewing, the occasional chopstick gently tapping the side of a bowl, and the sporadic smacking of lips.

Enid leads me to the end of the table where her husband, Marty, sits crossed-legged, chewing away. When I called to reserve a space in the house, I told Marty about the sugar and the side pain. He said he was sure macrobiotics could help. I hope he's more welcoming than the wife. "This is Lisa," she flatly states, then zombies off.

"Welcome!" Marty says and motions for me to sit across from him. "Please! Sit!" He reminds me of a younger version of my dad—only with hair. And enlightened. Taking my seat, I am amused by the juxtaposition of this gruff, frizzy-headed, obviously—I assume—ex-Brooklyn Jew sitting cross-legged, chomping open-mouthed on the allegedly sacred food. He should be eating bagels and lox, wiping cream cheese from his lip with the back of his sleeve.

Enid returns to slide an empty bowl and a pair of chopsticks before me and Marty gestures to the bountiful spread. "Please! Ga-head!" There are platters of brown rice, dark-red beans, and vegetables. Squash, to be exact. Green and yellow, steamy, watery squash, the gag-worthy legume I always feel pressured to savor as a vegetarian. I loathe squash. In fact, I can't stand most vegetables. When you're full of sugar, the last thing you want are vegetables. I wish I wanted to eat them, like my sister Sarah. If I eat like her, I think, maybe I can be like her. When she went vegetarian at age ten, I followed right behind. My mom took a vegetarian cooking class to accommodate us. My dad suffered through multiple lentil-cheddar loaves and carrot-raisin salads. "This health food is killing me!" he loved to say. He never recognized my vegetarianism. Sarah got all the credit. If we went out to dinner, he'd gloat to the waitress, "My dawter's a vegetarian. It takes great discipline, you know." I wanted to put my face in his and yell, "I'm a vegetarian too, you know! I have discipline, too! Love me, too!"

"What's that?" I ask Marty, all sweet and innocent, pointing to a bowl of something stringy and black.

"That," he says between lip smacks, "is seaweed. Have some!" I smile politely and fill my bowl with some rice and beans. Then I cautiously add a few chunks of the dreaded squash along with a spoonful of the slimy seaweed for good measure. I chopstick in a mouthful of rice, then immediately dig up another bite. Marty frantically waves his paw at me. "No, no! You gotta chew every bite forty times. *Very* important. Chewing your rice is *everything*."

"Oh, okay, thanks." I nod appreciatively, then take my next bite and start chewing. Folding my hands in my lap like a good macrobiotic girl, I mentally count . . . 1, 2, 3. Chewing steadily, I casually glance down the table, perusing the lineup of munching men for potential lovers . . . 9, 10, 11. It's always a good motivation to eat healthy if there's a cute guy to work towards . . . 15, 16, 17. But the men all look sort of feeble, staring down at their bowls, chewing away. Lots of spectacles and unkempt beards. One guy even has some rice stuck to his mustache . . . 23, 24. Fortunately the house has an open-door policy for macrobiotic travelers who are just passing through. My future soulmate could arrive at *any moment*.

By the time I get to 28, there is nothing solid left in my mouth to chew. I usually don't even chew my food at all. So 28 is pretty darn good. I take another bite of rice, determined to make it to 40, and stick my chopsticks straight down into my food. "No!" Marty objects. "*Never* leave your sticks like that. The energy from the food will run up through the sticks and out into the universe."

"Oh . . . sorry." I quickly pluck them out.

"Always place your sticks on the table, facing *in, towards* you, so the energy will continue moving *into* you."

I must be in bad shape, because this actually makes sense to me.

Time to try the beans. I do like beans. Especially baked beans in a can. Yum. But these beans don't taste like that. These beans taste like dirt. And farts. Like dirty, muddy farts. That's okay. This food is going to cure me. As I mix up my beans with my rice, Marty nails me again. "Don't mix up your food. Keep each food separate. Mixed-up food means you have a mixed-up mind."

"Okay." I'm so glad he doesn't know I'm already mixed up.

After lunch Enid leads me upstairs, where I meet my roommate, an eccentric seventyish earth mama named Jean with wispy, white locks and a slender, youthful figure. I didn't see her at lunch. Maybe she's on a special plan. Or maybe she's one of those health food freaks who never really eats whole meals. They just nibble on shit all day, like a bird. Jean is seated at the corner of her futon surrounded by troughs of wheat grass. She is gnawing on a crust of bread so dense it could cause a concussion. She proudly holds the bread up for us to behold. "I just found this in the back of my van. It was there for six months. All I had to do was steam it. It's da-*licious*."

Jean clearly embraces a healthy existence. She actually *wants* to live. Good for her. It's not that I don't want to live. I mean, that's why I'm here, right? I just don't know how to live without chocolate.

My roommate is the first guest downstairs when the 5:45 a.m. *gonnnnng* summons everyone to group meditation. My sister Lauren, the Zen Buddhist, has been trying to get me to meditate to quiet my mind. But it's five fucking forty-five in the morning. Why should we have to quiet our minds when we just woke up? Isn't that what sleep is for? But maybe this is good. At this point, twenty-four sugar-free hours are all I have under my belt. Cookies, cake, and candy bounce off the walls of my brain. I sit cross-legged in the very back of the meditation room, in case I nod off.

But the scent wafting from the kitchen intrigues me. Ommm-mmm—what's that smelllll? Is that what I think it is? Why, it smells like chocolate-chip coooookies. It's not cookies. In fact, it is oatmeal. The thick, pasty, steel-cut kind that sticks to your ribs. For years. And there's more squash. Which people actually eat. *For breakfast.* At least it's baked pumpkin squash, so it's less watery. If I stick to the diet and never eat sugar again, I am sure I will learn to love squash, as well as all legumes. Not if. When. As long as I don't leave the house and venture out into the world of evil yin, I'll be safe.

Every day after breakfast there is . . . *the preparation of lunch!* Enid solicits kitchen volunteers. Helping out is part of the deal. I now have three whole sugar-free days. Three days. This is the longest I've abstained from sugar since I left home. But I'm getting antsy. I raise my hand to volunteer. It will keep me out of trouble. Besides, I want to be good. And there is so much to learn: Like, you don't need to refrigerate cooked rice; you can just keep it in a bowl covered with a damp cloth for up to three days! If you cut carrot slices on the diagonal rather than straight across, every slice will have an even mix of yin and yang in every bite! Stewed pears with just a few drops of brown rice syrup will satisfy any sweet tooth! Yeah. Right.

Several other eager macro beavers and I watch as Enid picks up a kitchen knife that probably weighs more than her and irately *whacks* the stems off a bunch of giant green kale. We're having shrubs for lunch. Excellent. She measures out several cups of brown rice so carefully you'd think it were Tiffany crystal. "One grain, ten thousand grains," she says. In other words, don't fuck with the rice. She pours the precious grain into a pressure cooker and hands it to me. "Fill this with water and then we'll rinse it. Careful." I am so nervous as I take the pot that my hand slips and I nearly drop the whole thing. She glares up at me like I am the yin devil. It's amazing how someone half my size can make me feel so small.

"Sorry," I say, grimacing exaggeratedly, then proceed to fill the pot, staring, mesmerized, at the faucet water as it flows over the multitude of treasured grain.

I want sugar. Now. Three days of pasty grains, beans, fart-inducing cabbage, kale, and other cruciferous crudités have made my gut feel like an atomic bomb factory. If I swallowed a lit match, I'd blast to the moon. I wish I could fart, but I'm so blocked up even the farts can't find their way out. The only thing that will cut through my wall of gas and shit is sugar. Pure, un-adulterated sugar.

Maybe a drop of brown rice syrup will do it. It's worth a try. I'm too afraid of Enid, so I wait until we are done and the kitchen crew disbands. Once I am sure Enid has gone upstairs, I slip into the pantry. If anyone sees me I'll just tell them I'm making notes on how to set up a proper macrobiotic pantry. In thirty seconds I manage to choke down two heaping table-spoonfuls of disgustingly sweet brown rice syrup. I grab the sesame tahini butter and spoon a big glob into my mouth, fol-lowed by another helping of the syrup, trying not to choke to death. The concoction gives me nowhere near the buzz I so desperately seek. I shouldn't be here. What am I doing? I should be on stage. I need sugar. Real sugar. Just one last big splurge. Then I'll be ready. No. Don't do it. You're three days clean. Yeah, but not really because I'm still overeating. Exercise. Yes. A brisk walk. Great idea. Who cares that it's a hundred below zero? It's been three days since I set foot outside. I don't trust myself. There's that liquor store at the bottom of the hill. We passed it my first day in the taxi. I picture all the snacks dis-played by the register. Why tempt myself? Just walk the other direction. No. I'll be fine. I haven't come this far just to blow it all on some cheap liquor store crap.

I bundle up and head out into the bitter-cold January after-noon. As I trot down the hill, I dig my hand deep into my pocket, and there it is. Probably about a buck fifty in change. I should have left it behind. But you should never leave home empty-handed,

I've always thought. Especially in a strange city. What if something happens?

Indeed, something is happening. My feet have picked up speed and I am walking briskly down the hill. It's *freezing*. Of *course* I'm walking fast. Four blocks ahead is the liquor store sign. I'll just pop in to warm up. What if someone from the macro house sees me? Maybe they'll think I'm an alcoholic. That's better than being a sugar junkie. Even Michio Kushi, the almighty leader of the macrobiotic community, drinks whiskey and smokes like a chimney. He says if your diet is clean, you can do that. Too bad I'm not a drunk instead.

There are going to be Snickers bars. My gait quickens. Slow down, honey. Maybe I could just have one. Like a normal person. I break into a light jog. Am I really doing this? Doing what? I'm just getting some exercise, but I know full well the only thing that can pry off this serpent that is strangling me from within is sugar. As I bite into the milky smooth, chocolate coating, it will crack apart, giving way to a sleek strip of caramel just below the surface. I am running at full speed down the hill. Running to satisfy a raging sugar hard-on before I implode.

The liquor store electronic bell *dings* as I enter. And there they are, lined up neatly on the shelf just below the cash register. Hershey's . . . Mars . . . Kit Kat . . . open wide for Chunky. Actually, my mother never allowed Chunky's. Something about a rat hair.

Hallelujah. I have enough change for a Snickers and a Milky Way! I procure my goods and rush back out, holding off tearing into a wrapper until I am fully outside so the clerk won't see me—just in case he knows someone at the macro house. He'd call up there and describe the crazy lady with the big nose and the dark hair who couldn't even wait to open her candy until she was out the door.

My heart flutters. My mouth fills with drool. *Rip* goes the sleek, brown Milky Way paper. And there it is. All firm. All fine. All mine. My teeth settle into my first bite and at last, I am home.

Ahhhhhhhhh . . . how I missed you. Your thick, smooth bed of chocolate, caramel, and pillow-soft nougat. Right here. Right now. This is everything I know and need and want. I could live inside this bite forever. I pull up my green parka hood to conceal my bulging cheeks from the passing cars, just in case any of the drivers are headed to the house. It's like I'm having sex out in public. Like I'm walking down the street, screwing as I go.

By the time I reach the corner, I've demolished my Milky Way. I cross the street, head up the hill, and nearly smack into a light post as I look down to tear open my Snickers. This time I will try to chew each bite forty times. Or at least ten. Oh, fuck it. I'm two blocks away. I must demolish my contraband before returning to the house. I wish this joy would last. One last bite. So sad. I wish I had more cash so I could keep going. But I am broke. And freezing. And there is the macro house, just a block away. I lick my lips, wipe away the bits of chocolate, kick off my boots, and tear inside, running into Marty in the vestibule. "Cold out there, huh?" he asks.

"Y—yeah . . . it sure is!" I try not to let out any air when I speak so he won't smell my breath. Try not to let him see my eyes in case they are *sanpaku*. That's what the macros call it when somebody is imbalanced, like from drugs or booze or sugar. The eyes have more whites below the irises than above. Macrobiotic teacher George Ohsawa predicted the deaths of Marilyn Monroe and Robert Kennedy because, he said, they were sanpaku. He said Charles Manson has it, too. Keep your eyeballs even, Lisa. *Keep them even.*

"So, how's it goin'? How you feelin'?" Marty asks.

"Pretty good," I say. Because, actually, I do. Right now I feel fan-fucking-tastic.

"Well, you look good," he says, nodding his head. I hope he's not attracted to me. Enid would find out and she'd poison my beans for sure. But Marty repels me with those hairy arms and that angry New York accent. I'm afraid he's going to start yelling at me, like my dad. I don't know if it's the sugar and caffeine from the chocolate kicking in, or if it's my fear of being taken out by Enid, but a peristaltic wave rises in my gut. Thankfully Marty moves along so I can take legitimate refuge in the john. The eagle has landed.

Back in my room, my roommate, Jean, is meditating. I lay back on my futon and stare up at the cottage-cheese ceiling, trying not to let my arms touch my body just in case it is finally fat. I grab my journal and quickly record every morsel of food I consumed today. "One bowl of oatmeal, a baked apple, some pumpkin seeds, two pieces of rice bread with tahini, a bowl of miso soup, a bunch of noodles, five rice cakes with tahini, a bunch of brown rice sprinkled with seaweed salt, some cabbage, some carrots, a few big spoonfuls of tahini with brown rice syrup, an S and an M." (That's Snickers and Milky Way recorded in code, just in case.) I should write how I hate myself for falling off the wagon, how I hate my body, and how hopeless I feel that I will ever quit sugar. Instead, I write, "In a little while I will have a wonderful healthy dinner and I will attempt to chew my rice 40 times every mouthful. That will bring me back to center. I just want to be balanced and centered. I also want to start a movement theatre company and become famous for my solo theatre pieces and fall in love, but first I must stop eating sugar forever."

There.

I'm done.

I will never eat sugar again.

Again.

CHAPTER 2

UP THE YIN YANG

I can see them from the hallway, through a crack in their third-floor bedroom door. Marty and Enid lay side by side on their bed, reading. It's a large bed. I guess this is where they have sex. Does he really have sex with her? Maybe she whips him or something. Maybe she uses one of those long seaweed ropes from the beach. She can cook it and eat it afterwards.

"Hi?" I call softly with a light knock. They both look up.

"Come in!" Marty says. He puts his book down and sits up. Enid doesn't.

I enter cautiously and hover at the foot of the bed.

"Hope I'm not bothering you guys."

"No bother," Marty says. Enid looks up with disdain. "What's goin' on?"

"Oh, it's just . . . this side pain thing is getting worse and—I was wondering if . . . well, if there's anything else you think I should be doing."

They stare at me, look at one another and then back at me.

"Well, ya know," Marty says, "you've been here now—what—two weeks or so?"

"Two and a half."

"It's gonna take time for your body to detox. Ya gotta give it some time."

Phew. He doesn't know I've slipped. Several times.

Enid sits up. "Lemme see your eyes," she says.

Uh-oh. She's going to see the sugar. Maybe I should tell them the truth. I'm pretty sure they'll kick me out if I do, though. I look at her, wide-eyed, willing my pupils to hold steady as she peers in.

"Hmmm . . . ," she says.

"What?" I ask, keeping my cool. "Do you see something?"

"Have you by any chance been tested for parasites?"

"No. I mean, I had pinworms when I was a kid. . . ."

"Well that makes sense. Pinworms *love* yin."

So Enid *does* see the yin in me. Relax. She can't prove it. What's she going to do? Give me a lie-detector test? I picture my colon as a long, curvy banquet table, where dozens of worms wearing party hats feast on birthday cake. Whooping it up.

"Wow . . . ," I say. "That *totally* makes sense." But come on. It would have to be one enormous worm to cause such discomfort in my side. I just want a quick fix, and the more deprivational, the better. Because I always feel more productive when I'm suffering.

"You could try starving them out," Enid says. "Eat nothing but raw brown rice and pumpkin seeds. See if that helps."

"And if that doesn't work," Marty says, "you should consider acupuncture. There's a guy downtown, a fifth-generation Korean acupuncturist. I'd be happy to make a call for you."

I love this idea. I'll bet he could fix me. But I should try the raw grains first. It's bound to be cheaper. My father is already paying my way here. I would dread hitting him up for more. I should be able to cure my problem with macrobiotics alone.

"Oh, wow, thank you! I think I'll try the raw grain thing first, and then I'll see. But thank you guys so much!" The less safe I feel with someone, the more compelled I feel to thank them. Beneath my politeness is a vortex of fear, distrust, and rage. But don't tell anyone.

The next morning, it's nothing but handfuls of raw brown rice and pumpkin seeds. I nearly break a tooth. By noon I am famished. I won't just starve out the alleged worms—I'll kill myself in the process. No way can I keep this up. I prod Marty to make the acupuncture call and he sets me up. But, just as I feared, it's going to cost. Like, several hundred more. I dread calling home—collect, no less. But I tell myself I must have this treatment. This treatment could be *it*.

"How are you?" my mother asks with her usual phone strain. I'm supposed to be at Juilliard or Yale, for theatre and dance. Not holed up in a dark Tudor with a bunch of "creeps" (as she'd call them) learning how to de-gas beans by cooking them with wakame seaweed. You'd think that after being raised by a woman whose bibles were Adelle Davis's *Let's Eat Right to Keep Fit* and Frances Moore Lappé's *Diet for a Small Planet*, I'd be a truly healthy person. After all the vegetarian lasagna and the homemade yogurt, my bible seems to be more *Let's Eat Wrong to Keep Sick*. Food has become my weapon against myself.

"I'm fine. I'm learning so much, Mom. This is *exactly* where I need to be. Thank you guys *so* much." Thank you . . . now can I have more?

"How are you doing on money?"

"Well, that's the thing. . . . Um . . . Marty, he's the head of the house, he's really amazing, and he thinks I might need some extra treatment. But it's going to cost a little—"

"*Bert!*" she calls out. Shit. I hate this.

My father picks up from another room, and I explain to him why I need five hundred dollars. I count on the words "fifth-generation acupuncturist" to impress him, even though I'm too stoned from a pre-phone-call Snickers to actually comprehend what the fuck those words actually *mean*.

Still mystified as to what exactly I am being treated for, my father agrees to deposit yet another chunk of dough into my Bank of America account. "Thank you guys *so* much. I just *know* I'm going to be better soon."

"Just be happy," my mother says into the phone. "Happy and healthy."

Marty insists on delivering me to my first appointment with Dr. Yon Won Suh. "It's no bother," he says. "We're going into town anyway." It's my first time going any distance from the house. I'll bet he wants to make sure I actually get there, instead of ending up in the gutter with a pint of Steve's ice-cream. As I wave good-bye to my proxy parents, I make both of my hands visible so they can see I am not crossing any fingers behind my back with an alternate sugar-getaway plan. No crossies count.

It's a typical doctor's waiting room, except that there's a little rock-garden fountain running in the corner and the air smells spicy. I fill in my new patient form, drawing X's on the outlined sketch of a body to illustrate where my pain is—the right gut, the lower back, the upper left shoulder. I picture Dr. Suh as a slight, serious Asian man. Very professional. Very disciplined. I just assume he'll be macrobiotic and hope he won't know from examining me that I have fallen off the wagon. Those Eastern doctors know everything.

In fact, Dr. Suh is a two-hundred-pounds-plus, fiftyish man with a colossal belly, pocked skin, and a jovial smile. He nods several times, looking back and forth from me to my chart, then motions for me to lie face down on a table. From this position I try to be funny and charming, even though I am not sure how much English he understands. But he does smile a lot. He seems to enjoy me. I want to be his best patient. The best girl ever. After a few sessions, he even sends me down the street one day with some cash to buy his lunch: a Quarter Pounder, jelly donut, and chocolate milk. Somehow I manage to bring back all three.

Three afternoons a week I take the bus downtown to Dr. Suh's to lie on my stomach, listen to piped-in muzak versions of the Eagles and Jimmy Buffett, and transform into a human pin-cushion. I don't understand what the needles are doing. It doesn't matter. It's a place to go. It's a schedule. With each prick I hope my side cramp and my yen for yin will subside. Actually, what I really hope for is the chance to be poked by Alex, Dr. Suh's assistant. He's small in height but sturdy in build, with a neatly shaped goatee and a cute cropped haircut. As he stands beside Dr. Suh, handing him needles, I can see from his smooth, tan wrists peeking out from his starched white lab-coat sleeves that he is boyishly hairless. And he is serious. I am drawn to serious men. It's my challenge to humor them. A serious, rational guy like Alex could use an artsy, playful girl like me to open him up. Alex could anchor me. He's a strict macrobiotic. If we become lovers, I'll *have* to get clean.

Dr. Suh pops his last needle into my spine and waddles from the room. I am lying very still when Alex steps up to the table. "So," asks my prince in a white lab coat, "how are you feeling about your progress here?" I crane my neck to look up, trying not to move a muscle so the needles won't send electric shocks up my spine.

"Good," I say, hoping I look okay from this angle. This is my opportunity. The damsel in distress. "I mean, I guess I kind of hoped my side pain would be better by now."

"Well, I wanted to mention, I know a few things, and if you ever want to try something in addition to the acupuncture, I'd be happy to give you a treatment, free of charge." A treatment. Wow. What treatment? Who cares? He wants to help me. Maybe he wants me.

"Really?" I turn my cheek to him as far as I can without moving more than an inch. "That would be great." It's not just sugar I can't stop using.

Thursday night, Alex arrives at the macro house on his white horse (aka his little blue Mazda) to gather me up and take me away. He's so cute in his khakis and blue jacket. Why is he doing this? He must want the same thing. And so I happily climb into the car of a man whose last name I don't even know and drive to a distant, seedier part of town to be healed.

Inside Alex's very orderly if somewhat rundown bachelor pad, he removes his jacket, revealing a white cotton button-down tailored shirt. I like his style. Classic but casual. He hands me a peach silk robe with Oriental birds embroidered on it. I wonder why he owns this robe. He instructs me to put it on "over my panties" and join him in the bedroom. Panties. He said "panties." A very good sign. Stay calm, I tell myself. Steady. Balanced. I drop my clothes into a tight, neat pile so he won't think I am too scattered—too yin—like keeping the beans and the rice neatly separated in my bowl. Then I slip into the robe and drift into his sanctuary of love.

Alex's futon mattress is on the floor, surrounded by rows of lit tea candles. He instructs me to lie down on my back. As he reaches over my body to part the bottom portion of my robe, I gaze up at him in the candlelight, my sexy healer. He places a thin slice of raw ginger on my bare leg, just next to my knee. "This might hurt a little," he warns matter-of-factly.

"Oh, that's okay," I reassure him. "Hey, no pain, no gain!" He places a pinch of moxa—dried leaves—onto the ginger slice and lights it with a match. My leg hairs sizzle as the heat sears a hole in my skin. An actual hole.

"You okay?" he asks.

"Y—yeah!" I cringe in silent agony. "I'm fine!" I can tolerate anything for the impending prospect of love. Burning flesh. *So* sexy.

"The moxa will warm your stomach chakra and drive out the pain," Alex explains.

"Sounds good!" He places more ginger slices with more dried moxa on my other leg, just above my belly button and on each thigh. I brace myself as he lights the moxa on fire. I am a human shish kebab. It will all be worth it once he finally skewers me.

Once I am done, or well done, Alex removes the ginger. "How do you feel?"

"Good, I mean, yeah!" I try to ignore the throbbing pain of my smoldered flesh.

"There's one more thing I could try, if you want?"

"Sure! Yes! Whatever you think." How quickly I put my life in someone else's hands. Alex says to sit up and so I do, clutching my robe. Hey, I'm no hussy. He takes out a small, narrow box neatly filled with a dozen little bottles of dark liquid. "These are Bach Flower Remedies," he says. It sounds so romantic: Bach . . . the flowers . . . "Physical ailments are sometimes caused by emotions, and they can be treated with flower essences," he goes on. "Each essence corresponds to a different emotional ailment. Like, for instance, joy, sorrow, fear." I wonder why joy is considered an ailment, but I keep it to myself so he won't think I'm superficial. "Go ahead. Pick an emotion. Something you want to improve in yourself." I look down at the row of bottles. Why not ingest the whole damn collection and cure everything at once?

"Hmmm . . . let's see . . . How about the ones for remorse and longing?" I really hope regret and desire are attractive qualities to a taciturn guy like Alex. He places a drop of remorse on my tongue and we wait. "So . . ." I ask, the temptress, "which essence corresponds to *you*?" He blushes, mumbles something inaudibly about his mother (I'm not kidding), and then, suddenly, perhaps in an attempt to deflect, he kisses me. It is a stiff, clammy kiss, but at least it's something. Some human connection in this pit of chewing and needles and rules. And that's it. The lid is off the miso jar. Off go his khakis. Off comes my robe. We jump under the white cotton covers and he is immediately, I mean immediately, on top of me. In an act of self-preservation I instantly spread my blistered gams to avoid leg-on-leg contact and thus save me from excruciating pain. My desirous groans morph from "oohhhhh" to the occasional "owwwww" to keep my wounds fresh in my lover's mind. Although he is on top of me, he keeps his torso at a slight distance, trying, I assume, to avoid contact with the other burns above and below my belly-button. Or maybe he's just not the skin-to-skin intimate type, even in bed.

My seared flesh aches and I want him to comfort me, but he is too busy trying, it seems, to get it up to concern himself with my pain. After what seems like a fair amount of rubbing and groping, our sex is never consummated. It just sort of . . . stops.

In the car, driving me home, Alex apologizes for the sex. He says he thinks maybe it was because he is too yin. I wonder if it's because he's too gay.

The moment his little blue Mazda is out of sight, I hoof it down to the liquor store. It's late, but I am relentless in my quest for sugar. And with more money on me now, I can really go to town. I know I'm pushing my luck smuggling my unfinished loot into the macro house, but it's worth the risk. My roommate is so deeply asleep she looks dead. Maybe she *is* dead. No, she's breathing. I quietly finish off my lover in bed—two small packages of chocolate cream-filled cookies, a Hershey's milk-chocolate bar, and a chocolate-coated vanilla ice-cream bar covered in chopped peanuts—and pass out. Tomorrow I'll be good.

Tomorrow arrives and I am far from good. I take a break from all the macro madness and go Greyhound for a weekend visit with some musician friends in Manhattan. From the heat wave, you'd think it was August, but it's April. When I show up at their East Village loft in shorts, they see the oozing welts on both legs from the moxa treatment and they are mortified. "Don't worry, it's good!" I say. "It just means the treatment is working!" They look at me like I am on drugs, which I should be. They offer me some antibiotic ointment and Band-Aids, but I refuse politely. "I'm good," I say, standing over the stove in their 90 degree, non-air-conditioned loft, stirring my pot of steel-cut oats, dripping with sweat, boldly refusing their offer of ice-cold lemonade because it is too yin.

━━━━━━━━━

Upon my return to the nuthouse (only, nuts aren't allowed—too yin), my spirits lift when I meet Ray, a macrobiotic chef who's moved in over the weekend to offer his cooking expertise. Ray is fortyish and a little taller than me with ultra-white, shoulder-length hair, a goatee (what is it with these macro men and their goatees?), and a noticeably buff build. With his exceptionally stiff posture marred by bowlegs, he looks like he has just dismounted from his horse. Like a seasoned cowboy who's just come in off the plains. Lookin' for a woman. That would be me.

"Food is all about intuition," he explains in his soft Southern accent to a small group gathered in the kitchen after dinner. "When you're hungry for your supper, just walk into the pantry, close your eyes, and *feel* your way through the shelves of food. Let yourself be guided to wherever your instincts lead you." How happy I am later that night when Ray's instincts lead him upstairs to my room. Luckily my cellmate, Jean, is downstairs, elbow-deep in dish duty. I'm a little worried about Enid and Marty finding out. Having hot, banging sex doesn't seem very macrobiotic. Ray makes no bones about getting down to it in my little futon bed. I figure, since he's the chef, it should be okay. I hope he won't detect the sugar radiating from my skin. He pumps away and a candy-bar wrapper emerges from the foot of my bed. I quickly bury it under the covers with my toes.

Suddenly the bedroom door bursts open and I catch a glimpse of Jean's stunned face. She gasps in shock, then quickly flees. Shit. I hope she keeps it to herself.

Ray's yang more than makes up for Alex's yin. But sadly, I am just a flash in his pan, and by the end of the week he is gone. I hole up in my futon with the Indian-print bedspread pulled up over my head, scarfing Snickers bars as I devour Marty's copy of *Sugar Blues*, the best-selling expose about the deadly effects of sugar. Five years earlier, the author, William Dufty, amazed the world by comparing the addictive quality of sugar with that of tobacco and heroin. I am addicted to this book. I gobble up every word, making sure to finger up every last fleck of chocolate bar that falls onto the page.

My pain is palpable. Marty recommends a local healer, a man with the gray hue of an undertaker and a reputation for working deep. He works deep, all right, practically touching the floor through my belly with his cold, wooden fingertips. I'm embarrassed, as he must feel my wall of poop. But he is a pro. He rubs so deeply, tears stream sideways down my face, rolling cold into my ears. The more it hurts, the more it will help. "I know what the source of your pain is," he finally says. Drum roll. Here it comes. "Your mother's mother is living in your right side." I never even met my mother's mother. She died at fifty-one. Rectal cancer. But somehow this makes perfect sense. I'll believe anybody.

The next day my body is a fresco of black and blue. Even my cheekbones are bruised. So is my checking account. If I'm going to have more sessions, I'd better contribute to my cause. I register with an employment agency to work part time, assisting older and infirm people in their homes. I need fast cash and it's the only job I can think of. Helping people worse off than me.

Indeed, I have little to complain about next to the woman I am hired to assist in the quiet Boston suburb of Newton. She's recovering from stomach-cancer surgery. They had to remove part of her stomach. I wonder which part. She uses a walker and shuffles about her tiny kitchen in slippers. There's something lumpy under the front of her faded housedress. I think I hear it sloshing a bit. Maybe it's a feeding tube. Or a colostomy bag. Or both.

I make her tea, put away her dishes, and fix her toast. Mostly, I keep her company. We sit at her small, glass kitchen table with the stained flowered placemats and chat. She feeds me bland store-bought cookies and milk. I should resist, but that would be rude. As I munch away, I can't stop thinking about her stomach.

Where does the bag connect? Is it one bag for the food and the poop? How does *that* work? How does the bag stay in place? Does she have to unhook it? Does she have to keep the little hole covered with her hand while she cleans it out so all the liquid and shit doesn't come shooting out?

"What's a nice Jewish girl like you doing in a place like this?" she asks. How does she know I'm Jewish? And yes, what exactly *is* a nice Jewish girl like me from Hillsborough, California, the pristine, serene, and very exclusive bedroom community thirty minutes south of San Francisco, doing living in a macrobiotic flophouse in Boston, working in a strange suburb making tea for a stranger? I tell her about my side pain, about my home in California and my parents. She admonishes me to return to them. "That is where you belong," she says. "You need to go to them. You should go home."

Riding the bus back into Boston that afternoon, I stare out at the bleak suburban terrain and fear having my own stomach removed one day from all the damage I've surely caused it. All the sugar and white flour will form into one big stomach mass. I'm afraid even that prospect wouldn't keep me from bingeing, though. I'll be like one of those people in the hospital dying from emphysema who sneaks out to the balcony for a cigarette when the nurse isn't looking. Smoking that cigarette right through a tracheotomy hole. I imagine shoving candy bars into my stomach tube, watching the bars go up, up, up into my belly, wrappers and all.

Maybe it was the chef who acted as my informant before moving out. Or maybe my jealous, sex-starved roommate divulged my hedonism to Enid and Marty. One week later I am seated at lunch, chewing and counting, when Marty summons me to the hallway. Still chewing, I rise up and follow him dutifully, trailed by Enid. We get to the stairwell and Marty takes a few steps up, joined by Enid, then they turn to face me, several steps below them. Marty grips the banister as if to brace himself. Enid slips behind him so that all I can see are her pin-pupil eyes peering over his shoulder. "We think your energy is toxic," Marty says. "You're polluting our space. We want you out."

"Wh—what?" I say, swallowing my last bit of millet. "I—I don't understand."

"We're sorry it didn't work out. But this place is no longer right for you. You need to leave. You can have a few days, but then we want you out." And with that, they step down past me and return to the dining room to finish their lunch.

Toxic. What a word. What a horrible, awful, *toxic* word. I want to run from myself. How can I bear to stand in my own skin? But this is me. I did this. I must be out of my mind to think I'd actually get away with sneaking candy into this place. Did I really think they wouldn't find out that I fucked the chef? Did I really think I'd have no effect on people living, eating, and sleeping just a few feet away from me? They must be right. I must be bad. I passed my evil yin into the chef and then he transmitted it into the food and tainted the whole damn house. They are right. I am toxic. Dirty from the inside out. Up-to-my-sanpaku-eyeballs-in-yin dirty.

I grab my coat and boots and bolt out into the freezing day. Where to? Down the hill. I hit the liquor store like a shot, a Snickers bar halfway down my gullet before I've even paid for it.

The house is eerily quiet upon my return an hour later. It's like a macro ghost town. I half expect a tumbleweed of dried kelp to drift by. The kitchen is deserted. I grab a jar of sesame tahini from the pantry along with a knife and race up to my room. Crouched down in the corner, I rapidly tongue knife-ful after knife-ful of the thick, bitter paste into my mouth. The room is *freezing.* I am freezing. The window above my head is ajar. My roommate must have left it open. Fuck that fucking wheatgrass murderer. Planting both hands on the window sill, I hoist myself up, then reach with one hand and carelessly *slam* the window, bringing it down on my other hand. "*Shit!*" Then come the self-hate, the tears. All the old, old tears. I'm not as good as my sister Sarah. I can't give up sugar. And I fucking despise myself for it.

I crawl into the hallway, grasp the phone, pull it back into my room, jam the door shut over the cord, and call home—collect. I don't know if it is because I am upset or because my mouth is glued shut with tahini, but when my mother answers I can hardly speak. I just choke and cry.

"*Bert!*" she shrieks for my dad. "It's Lisa! Pick *up!*"

"Hullo? Hullo?" he yells from another line. The TV drones in the background.

"Hi, Dad," I gag.

"What's the matta?" he barks. "Ah you sick?"

"No, I just, I just . . ."

"Now you listen to me," my mother breaks in with restrained hysteria. She's had it. Enough is enough. "You're getting on a plane and you're coming home *immediately.* That's all there is to it!" There will be a ticket waiting for me at the TWA counter. All I have to do is pack my bags and get the hell out.

"Do you have enough money to get to the airport?" my father asks.

"Yes," I lie, then I thank them, tell them I love them, and hang up.

Visibly relieved to be ridding the house of my noxious energy, Marty offers me a ride to the airport the following morning. As I head west on the big metal bird, I gobble my airline peanuts, not even chewing them one fucking time.

How in the world will I ever face my parents?

CHAPTER 3

BELLY OF THE BEAST

I face my parents' fridge. The freezer, actually, as I burrow deep into that frozen locker for something sweet to quiet the noise in my head and numb the anxious churning in my gut. I am numb all right, still in my nightgown at 11 a.m., shivering as I unravel my family history in the form of leftover commemorative cakes, cookies, and pastries saved over the years from various occasions. I mindlessly unearth mounds of ice-encrusted items all labeled in my mother's nearly illegible script: The chocolate cake with "Thanksgiving '73." The hazelnut cookies marked "Sarah's Bat Mitzvah '68." A slab of marble cake from "Joel's bris '54." Just kidding. But only just.

It's weird being the only child home. My brother, Joel, the pediatrician, is overseas caring for sick Cambodian refugee children. My sister Lauren, the Zen Buddhist, is getting her master's in early childhood education. My other sister, Sarah the organic horticulturalist, is apprenticing at an English castle garden. And I am twenty-one years old, having dropped out of everything and moved home to try to quit bingeing on sugar.

It's been a week and still not a word has been said by my parents about why I ended up back here. We simply don't discuss it. Nor do we discuss how I totaled Sarah's truck. See, when I left the macro house, I couldn't just move directly home. I just couldn't. So I moved to the other side of the San Francisco Bay, across from home. I rented a room in the basement of a macrobiotic woman's Berkeley home, still clinging to the hope that brown rice would save me. She was hardcore, even using her living room floor as a seaweed drying rack. My time there didn't go well. The woman was not the good, holistic mommy I'd hoped she'd be. In fact, she accused me of coming on to her scrawny, holier-than-thou boyfriend, when it was *he* who hit on *me* over the bins of adzuki beans and barley that were kept in my basement bedroom. Aggrieved, I fled into a binge that day, came back to the house, passed out in a carb and sugar coma, then awoke in the morning and headed to the health-food store for a freshly pressed carrot juice to fix my life. At the time, I was driving my sister's new truck, the one she'd asked my father not to let me use while she was gardening overseas. But hey, she had Windsor Castle. She had her skinny, sugar-free body and her Kiwi soulmate. All I had was a lack of willpower, a belly full of sugar, and my alleged potential for artistic greatness. The least she could do was lend me her fucking truck.

Guzzling my hopefully life-changing juice, I was pulling out of the Berkeley health-food store when an elderly woman tapped on my window and asked if I could drive her home. Sure! Of course! Never mind that my stomach was queasy and my head felt hazy from the previous night's food bender, and that I had no idea where I was driving and neither did she. But why shouldn't I help her? Maybe *she* would love me, especially since I listened to her financial and family woes as I drove through the bowels of Berkeley, trying to find her street, all the while pawing blindly under my seat for a few unlikely forgotten Raisinets. A little hair of the dog. But all I could feel were empty wrappers and metal seat parts.

Up ahead I saw it: a yield sign. A *yield* sign? Pshaw. Nobody stops for a yield sign. So I went through the yield sign, and a moving van went through me.

It was a roar at my left. A spray of light. We were shoved into a parked car, then pushed into a light pole. Glass showered down over me. "Are you okay?" I cried. "Are you okay?"

"Oh my Lord!" the woman shrieked, her bust heaving.

We scooted out the passenger side, and she stood there crying as I flapped my arms, squawking like a distraught seagull. I looked over at my sister's truck. The driver's side was a mess of twisted metal and shattered glass. The passenger's side was fine. Like two sides of a person. One half broken, the other perfect.

When the cop arrived, I told him I was so sorry, I'd eaten all this sugar; I was just *crazed* from all the sugar. He shot me a look. "What," he said sarcastically, "like the Twinkie defense?" He was referencing Dan White, the guy who six months earlier had killed the San Francisco mayor, George Moscone, along with City Supervisor Harvey Milk. He blamed his crimes on having eaten a Twinkie. I never thought I could almost kill someone, let alone myself, all on account of a Raisinet. But that's the thing. I never thought anything through.

I just want what I want when I want it.

My parents came to Berkeley and moved me home. My father arranged and paid for my sister's truck to be towed away, and my mother wrote to my sister explaining that her little truck was no more. I think my father also paid for the moving van and the parked car. I was never told. And I certainly never asked. And then . . . on we went, never discussing the wreckage I'd left behind.

My mom must notice a change in me, but mum's the word. Maybe if I'd gained a hundred pounds, she'd admit I am troubled. Maybe if she had to squeeze past me to get out the front door. I'm too ashamed to talk to her directly about the food, though I have asked her twice to please stop buying all those sweets. But, like the mother of a drunk who keeps replacing the empty bottles, over and over she replenishes the goods, the bads, and the uglies. The Mother's brand oatmeal cookies. The circular coffee cake with shimmering white icing and slivered toasted almonds. There's also the unnamed chocolate drawer in the wooden butcher block, which is constantly stocked with Cadbury Fruit and Nut bars. Fruit and nut—that's healthy. None of us acknowledges the drawer, but we all know it is there. Even my dentist dad frequents it for his nightly fix.

My father is oblivious to my eating—and to me in general, as long as I'm not raising a ruckus. The only ruckus I am raising is in my body. I'm not hurting anyone except myself—and that doesn't count. Along with the cramp in my gut, I have an excruciating fist of pain in my left shoulder. Probably yet another result of my yin condition. And the constipation doesn't help. Yeah, I know, the guts are a long way from the shoulder, but a backup of toxins can eventually cause all sorts of problems. "It's nothing!" my father insists when I mention the agonizing pain in my shoulder. "It's just a little knot!" Just a little knot that sometimes got so severe when I was living in the macro house that I'd hand my fellow housemates my red wooden clog and implore them to pound the crap out of it, which went over big since you had to be a fucking sadomasochist to be eating that diet in the first place.

And then, there it is. Deep in the bowels of the bottom freezer shelf: "Rosh Hashanah '71." The bag of almond mandelbrot— the classic Jewish biscotti. You could break a molar on that shit even *before* it was frozen. I should at least soften the rock-solid cookies in the toaster oven, but to hell with that. I bite down hard, unable to distinguish any sweetness through the freezer burn. But this frantic, mid-morning what-the-fuck-am-I-going-to-do-with-my-life-and-how-the-fuck-am-I-going-to-stop-eating-long-enough-to-do-it binge isn't about taste. It's about grabbing what is immediately in reach to fill the hole inside and satisfy my rampant sweet tooth, and decade-old pastries are all that remain after last night's kitchen raid—half of a pint of Rocky Road ice cream and the last third of a pound cake.

How odd it is to be back in Hillsborough. Ah, Hillsborough, home to simple folk—like the Hearsts (yeah, those Hearsts, as in

Patty) and the Crosbys (uh-huh, that's right, as in Bing). Don't get me wrong. Bluebloods we definitely weren't. We didn't vote for Nixon. We didn't celebrate happy hour. Jews don't drink. We eat. We didn't do Christmas. We went to temple for Hanukah. We had darker skin, darker hair, and hairier arms than our neighbors. In school I felt like the lone Jew, since there were only three other Jewish kids that I knew of. It was hard to concentrate on my ABC's when the kids in the lunch yard were hooting at my matzoh-and-peanut-butter sandwiches—and especially since I was a late-October baby and forced into the cold halls of kindergarten at the age of not yet five. I can't blame my mom. She was desperate with four kids at home. She needed time to breathe. Or scream.

My teeth ache as I gnaw at the frozen planks of mandelbrot. It's not even noon and here I am, at it again. The vista of the day stretching before me is terrifying. My siblings are all moving forward. Being productive. Saving the world. What am I doing with my life? Right now my parents are both hard at work—my dad at his dental office, using his borscht-belt humor to distract his beloved patients as he drills away; my mom at her unique Menlo Park paper store, probably helping some budding blonde bride-to-be pick out a fancy font for her wonderful wedding invitations. My parents toil away, earning the dough to support me while I struggle to stop bingeing—which, when I think about it, only makes me want to binge even more.

Munching my mandelbrot, I march into our sunny living room museum of folk art collected over the years by my mom, funded mainly by my dad. Many of the perfectly arranged objects are from places she had to pull his arm very hard to visit. Others are from local galleries and shops she frequented to make up for all the trips she'll never take. The Mexican Day of the Dead papier-mâché skeletons propped on hand-painted wooden chairs. The Moroccan copper pots and trays. The antique coffee samovar. And all the precious Jewish art. The international mezuzah collection. The assortment of Hanukah menorahs. And the guilt-provoking black-and-white print of the rabbis staring down at me, chastising me. "Look at you—vaisting your life! Vat is wrong vit you?" With that I fling the last third of my now-defrosted loot into the kitchen trash and head out before the day is completely lost.

Up the privileged streets of Hillsborough I jog—well, trot, really, in an oversized t-shirt and baggy sweats dug up from the give-away basket in the laundry room. Good thing my mom isn't home to see me go out in the world like this. What will all the fine snickerdoodle Hillsborough ladies think as they see me lumbering by their mansion windows? Snickerdoodles, for those of you not familiar, are the flat sugar cookies with a hint of cinnamon and a cracked, brittle surface. It's the cookie that holds back, just like the genteel Gentile ladies who bake them. These upper-crusty women return from early morning tennis in their pleated white tennis skirts and pearl-post earrings, their frosty blonde hair bobbing out from under a white visor. They sit in their breakfast nooks, sipping coffee, and browsing the *San Francisco Chronicle* society page. My mom is no snickerdoodle. She is more a cross between a fine petit four and a chunky chocolate rugulach, the imperfectly formed, rolled-up miniature pastries swirled with fruit, cheese, or chocolate and embedded with nuts. And butter. And sugar. Rugulach are oddly shaped, dense, and intense, just like the females in my family. Growing up in Hillsborough, we were a plate of rugulach in a window display of snickerdoodles.

Traipsing along, I keep my head down, hoping not to be recognized by my classmates' moms as they drive by in their Jags or their Benzes, en route to a hair appointment or lunch with the antique dealer. "Isn't that the Kotin girl?" they must wonder. Their daughters have probably all graduated college by now and are onto law, medical, or architecture school. "I remember, she was in all those plays. She was good. What's she doing back home? How sad for her poor, dear mother." Past the sprawling mansions I trot, past the fancy iron gates guarded by yapping purebreds. Our house has no gate. Just a wall of eucalyptus trees and pink bougainvillea to provide a visual shield and hopefully muffle any family combat from the ears of our well-heeled neighbors. Two stories high, our house was built into a hill, with the top floor at street level and the bottom shaded by a grand magnolia tree. It is far from being my mother's dream house, but it was what my anxious father felt he could afford without losing his shirt. At the time she begged him to grab up the next lot as well for just a few grand more, but he was no gambler. The future to him was a potpourri of potential misfortunes waiting to happen. His response to his poverty-stricken, Depression-era upbringing was to hold back. Don't spend a dime. Save for the future, so you'll be prepared when—not if—disaster strikes.

My father's mother, Grandma May, was such a nervous wreck she'd check a door six times to make sure it was locked. She'd unplug, replug, and unplug the iron several times to make sure it was really unplugged. She never stopped agonizing about where her pocketbook was—which usually was right on her lap. She passed that worry gene right on down to my dad. Years later he'd check a mailbox eight times to be sure his letter went down or ask you ten times if you took your medicine, or paid that bill, or made that call. "Your mutha and I almost got in an accident. We didn't, but we could have! But we didn't. But we could have!" Trust nothing. Then trust nothing again. Then trust nothing one more time, just in case.

It didn't help his attitude toward life that he was born on the toilet. No, really. His father was working hard at his Lower East Side clothing factory when my Grandma May thought she had to take a shit, waddled to their Brooklyn brownstone bathroom, and sat down to go. Maybe she was constipated from all the worrying and pushed too hard, but out came my dad. Right into the toilet. I don't know but I have a feeling being nearly flushed down the toilet can really mess you up.

The very next day, just a trolley car away in Queens, my mother was born. Her family was so poor her father only allowed the lights to be on in one room at a time. At night the family would move together from room to room, or else be forced to spend the evening alone in the dark—which my mother often chose to do. Crouched in a corner, her sobbing echoed through the rest of the house. But my mother's response to her Depression upbringing was the opposite of my father's. Years later, in sunny California, she made up for all the darkness by spending. Then spending more. You like those shoes? Get two more pair. You'll wear them forever. She was on a lifelong quest to soothe her inner poverty with the finest of everything. Food. Clothes. Education. More education. Her children should know no limits, no matter what the cost. Piano. Ballet. Trumpet. Flute. Drums. Theatre. Painting. Summer camp. Sak's. See's.

"The world is your oyster!" was her eternal motto.

"Let me get my bearings here!" was my dad's.

Nothing was enough for her.

Everything was too much for him.

Between the two of them it was like bingeing and fasting.

I should be running faster. At least I'm moving forward. I can do this. Clean up my act. What act? Get back on track. What track? Real artists shouldn't need a track. They should embrace the unknown. But the unknown terrifies me. Just like it did my dad.

Fear and sugar. They go way back.

The first time I noticed something odd and scary about my relationship to food was my junior year in high school. It was mid-morning snack. My school mime troupe had just returned from an early morning performance at a local elementary school. Yes,

I was a teenage mime. Mime was the perfect refuge for a pubescent girl terrified of sex or anything having to do with the body. I was a natural. A real pro. My private girls' school had a fantastic performing arts program. But it was the mime troupe that put the school on the map. Even Vicky Hearst, Patty's kid sister, was in the mime troupe. Her portrayal of a fly about to be caught in my spider's web was outstanding. But when Patty was kidnapped, the parents pulled Vicky out of school and I lost my best fly.

After the show that morning we'd returned to school and I'd rushed to math, and then it was time for snack. I didn't usually partake in snack, as my mom had always served a hearty breakfast, but I couldn't resist the smell of freshly baked granola wafting from the cafeteria kitchen. I stood at the long table in my blue-checked uniform worn over my leotard, my face still caked in white makeup, chomping on a bowl of granola. I couldn't hear the chattering of the gaggles of girls surrounding me. All I could hear was the crunching inside my head. I stared down at the thin layer of butter, honey, and sugar glistening atop the creamy white milk and wondered how I would ever get enough. I became aware of a vague anxiety rising up from my gut. Some cold, nameless fear. Something about the future. College applications loomed ominously ahead. I didn't want to go to college. I just wanted to perform. Where do you go when you just want to perform? Back to the snack table, of course, for a second bowl of granola. The faster I chewed, the more the crunching blocked out the voice in my head. What college would take me? What if it wasn't good enough? How would I ever leave home? How would I make it on my own? I hoped none of my perfectly preppy schoolmates noticed as I reached for yet a third helping.

The second time I remember not being able to stop eating was on a Sunday, senior year of high school. My classmate Buffy (okay, her name wasn't really Buffy—but it *could* have been) invited our class of twenty-five girls to her family beach house for the day to take a break from finals. I was depressed and didn't want to go, especially after all those Sunday-morning bagels I had eaten at home. Nor did I want to attend UCLA in the fall as planned. My father had said it was the perfect choice—"They have a superb ahhhts program!"—though I knew my mom wanted something better for me. More exclusive. Refined. But after three years of my father footing the bill for private high school, and with my less-than-stellar SAT scores (I gave up half way through and played dot-to-dot), I figured I should give a state school a shot. Come September I would force myself to go to UCLA, because it would be good for me, just like I forced myself to go to the beach that day, hitching a last-minute ride with a classmate.

When all the girls slipped off to change into their beach attire, I procrastinated, not quite ready to remove my gigantic pin-striped overalls. I'd started wearing them on my I-feel-fat days. They were so big I swam in them. No matter how much I ate, you could never see my stomach pooch out. Again, I wasn't fat. But I could be. *At any minute.*

Before our happy host Speedo-ed it down to the shore for a run and a dip, she turned and announced, "There's lemon cheese-cake in the fridge. Help yourselves!" I pretended to be engrossed in a sailing magazine, waited for the last girl to leave, then made a beeline for the fridge.

I didn't even take the cheesecake out. Why take it out when I was just going to have a bite? Hunkered before the open fridge, I delicately peeled off the plastic wrap, mourning the thin layer of cheesecake unavoidably wasted on the Saran, grabbed a fork, and dug in. Just a small forkful here, a fingerful there, trying to keep the buttery, graham-crackery crust from falling apart before it reached my eager tongue. I stood there watching my hand move repeatedly from the cake to my mouth, cake to mouth. What was I *doing?* In broad daylight? In someone else's kitchen? Well, she *said* it was for everyone. I was part of everyone, right?

After each bite I smoothed over my path to make it look untouched, swallowing hard to get the creamy mouthful down *fast* since someone could walk through the door *at any moment.* But it tasted so good . . . it felt so good . . . each bite would be my last. No, this one. No, this one. I cringed with shame at the thought of Buffy heading excitedly to the fridge for a delicious slice to reward herself after her day of swimming and tennis, only to discover that the entire cake was now just a crust-less sliver, lying on its side. I inhaled several more bites, then had a premonition I'd better close it up, so I did. The moment after I shut the fridge door and stepped away, in walked two of my classmates. They looked like they were leaving, so I asked for a ride. As we walked out together, I knew the girls would be equally to blame as I was for the demolition of the cheesecake. I happily volunteered to take the back seat, where I sat quietly, relieved to have dodged a bullet, trying to digest the lump in my stomach, just like I am now, trying to digest all the mandelbrot cookies as I trudge up the hill.

What *time* is it? It must be noon. I must get home. Get something done. Finish *something.* Once home, I retrieve the now-thawed remains of the mandelbrot and I do them in. Good. Done. Now I can get on with my life. Except that now I want to die.

Some protein will help. Some yang to balance out the yin. First, a few slices of Muenster cheese on a buttered bagel, and then a hunk of cold chicken—if not half the bird. Make up for all those years of protein deprivation. I still haven't told Sarah I now eat flesh. It just adds to my belief that I'm not as good as her. Not only am I a weak-willed sugar addict, I am also a slaughterer. Like she'll care. I'm the one who's competing.

Seated at the kitchen table, I quickly record in my journal a list of every morsel of food I've ingested thus far today, all the while vowing not to eat another crumb until dinner. I also jot down a few ideas for new theatre pieces, getting up to refuel with a few more slices of cheese and five Medjool dates—all added to the list, of course. Nothing fills me up. Nothing satisfies me. I *slam* my notebook shut, flee the kitchen, and escape down to the pool. The sun will center me. Bring me back to a place of calm. I will bask in the beauty of the backyard.

Fully clothed, I lie straight back onto the warm concrete. The scent of sweet jasmine wafts overhead. The eucalyptus trees tower at the far end of the yard, swaying slightly in the soft summer breeze. To my right the old oak tree stands sturdy and strong. To my left the bees buzz gaily among the Indian paintbrush and the orange and lemon trees. In the middle of all this natural beauty I lie, unable to surrender. A bathing suit is out of the question. No way can I face my body in broad daylight after the damage I've surely caused it. I may not be fat to the naked eye, but I am certainly not the string bean I once was. It's not my entire body I dislike—just my stomach, hips, and ass. I resent that my diet and my dropping out of dance has caused this bulk I feel developing around my gut. I've taken to wearing a long piece of fabric wrapped around my belly on the outside of my clothes, knotted at the front. Sort of a fashionable faux girdle to hold everything in and help contain all the pain and the eventual fat.

Back in my teenage ballet and mime days, my full-of-potential days, my belly was flat. Now, my more rounded gut represents my failure. It's like a roll of shame. Pass the cream cheese. I feared this was coming. Despite having been blessed with that "perfect" dancer body, I always feared one day my dis-ease would catch up with me. My dis-ease of wanting to eat myself to death. I must have emanated self-hate, because my sister Sarah would drag me in front of the mirror and insist I acknowledge my physical perfection. "Look in the art history books!" she'd order me. "Look at the Greek statues of women! They're round, but they're beautiful! Don't buy into the Western standards for beauty. They're completely screwed up!" Then she'd disappear into the family room to spend another hour on the exercise bike.

I was never comfortable in my body. Looking at me, you'd think the opposite. I was physically gifted. Tall, but not too. Skinny, but not too. Who would ever guess there was a person crawling around under my skin not knowing where or how to be? Unnerved in the presence of others yet terrified to be alone. Desperate to express myself but secretly mortified by the slightest sign of criticism. I have to be the very best or the very worst. I detest the in-between. Was I always like this? Is it my fault? How did this happen?

It is warm. Very warm. I should at least remove the girdle. Oh what the hell. No one's around. I'll just strip down to my bra and undies. I can handle that. Leaning back on my elbows, I stare down at my long, imperfect form. I wonder how many twigs I could hide in the extra folds of my stomach. Why do my inner thighs have to touch one another at the top, then flare out at the sides? Boys don't have to deal with their thighs. Even if they're fat, their bodies don't randomly swerve this way and that. I lean way forward to pick at an already worked-over toenail until it bleeds, wiping the red on a stray jasmine leaf. Poor leaf. Sorry, leaf. "Plenty of girls would give their right arm to have a body like yours," my mom always says. I'd give my whole body just to stop wanting to climb out of my skin.

The sun is too bright. The sky too blue. The air too peaceful. There's that gnawing in my gut, that clanging in my brain. *What am I doing with my life?* I gather my clothes and take refuge in my cool, dark, low-ceilinged bedroom downstairs. Our house is an odd reverse from your traditional, two-story layout. Upstairs are the kitchen, living and dining rooms, and master bedroom. Plus there is the biggest bedroom of all, once occupied by my brother, the eldest, the sacred penis. Meanwhile, the three young vaginas were relegated to the dank, dark depths of the downstairs with our three little, low-ceilinged rooms all in a row. I understand. Really. A penis needs room to grow. It's not easy being the

firstborn male in a Jewish family. How many times did I have to
hear my father tell that story about how, when my brother was
born, he leaned over my mother's hospital bed. "Awlright, Mim,"
he announced. "Now you can have as many girls as you want!"
So she had three. In three years. I somehow don't think this was
what my father had in mind.

It really is like a tomb down here. My little crypt is sandwiched
between my two sisters'. I always passed through Sarah's room to
get to mine. I'd loiter in her doorway, hoping to absorb some of
her cool. Awaiting my banishment. Now it is deadly quiet, except
when my father is home and on the phone. The muffled boom of
his Brooklyn accent pulsates through the vent above my bed. He
speaks on the phone, following up with dental patients, making
sure they are okay. I wish he paid attention to me like that. For
me, he had no patience.

   Lying face-down on my little bed, I notice my pillow is
damp. Is that my sweat? Or is it from my decade-old tears? Why
did I cry again? Oh, yeah. I'd gotten in trouble with my father
again. Pushing buttons again. Down to my bedroom again. Is it
normal for a five-year-old to try to suffocate herself under her
pillow? Silly me. You can't suffocate yourself under a pillow!
Eventually my mother would appear at the foot of my bed. She'd
explain to me once again how my father didn't mean it. How it
was just his nature. He really did love me. Is that how you love
someone? By screaming at them? Calling them names? Paranoid.
Sensitive. Reactionary. Please *leave* him, Mommy, I secretly
wished. Make him go away. God should strike me dead just for
thinking it.

An hour passes. I awaken from a nap, sweating in my sweats, my
mouth glued together with a sickening, post-sugar film. I glance
at the clock radio. A quarter to five. My parents will be home

from work by six. I jump off the bed, pull back my hair, and lunge up the stairs two at a time for a last-minute workout. I will be the dutiful daughter and set the table before my mother can say no. Prove to my father I am good for something. "Girls!" he would yell. "Help your mutha clean up!" But she always banished us from the kitchen, insisting we engage in more fulfilling tasks than clearing a dish. Or maybe she just wanted to be left the fuck alone.

I slowly circle the round, white Saarinen tulip kitchen table, carefully setting three places with our hand-painted Italian plates and hand-blown Mexican glasses. How will the three of us ever fill the silence? The scene of our family dinner drama from years past plays out in my head. My exhausted, pent-up father would enter after a long, hard day at the dental office. My exhausted, pent-up mother would be putting her finishing touches on yet another elaborate family dinner. A dinner prepared in between chauffeuring us to this lesson and that, helping us with homework, trying to keep the peace. She'd be fuming, ready to burst.

We'd sit down to dinner. Please pass the kasha. The salad. The roast beef. My mother would stare at my father as he talked about his day. Chewing open-mouthed. My mother would glare. The tension so thick you could bite it. It was my fault. I was to blame for the discord. Me! Me! Why is Lauren *looking* at me like that? Sarah's copying me! *She's copying me!* Joel is making a face at me! Why is everybody looking at me? *Why is no one paying attention to me?*

"Lauren, Lauren, the big fat hen!" I'd chant at my sister. She wasn't even fat then. Just a little chubby, especially next to Sarah and me. But I hated her, probably because we shared an unfortunate familial position. Dad liked us the least. It's true. Otherwise why was my mom always telling me he really did love me? Plus Joel and Sarah looked more like our mom, the love of my father's life, with their finer features and martyred dispositions. Each night as the family drama unfolded, my elegant and sophisticated mother, a devotee of *Tiffany's Table Manners*, sat perfectly poised, determined to maintain her dignity. Back then, in the '60s, people stopped her on the street to ask if she actually *was* Jackie Kennedy. She had that widow's peak. Those stylish fitted A-line dresses and matching pillbox hats. The stately cheekbones. The luscious, rose-red lips pressed tight against unspoken rage as she sat there, silently tolerating the turmoil.

Lauren was not the only object of my dinner-table taunts. I teased my brother about the random moles that dotted his handsome face, pointing to my own face from one imagined mole to the next as I blurted in a staccato chant, "Dut! Dut dut! Dut dut dut!" He countered by exaggerating a gigantic nose while he sang, "Duh duh, duh duh! Duh duh, duh duh!" My nose wasn't gigantic, but it had a bump, inspiring the grade-school nazi boys to chase me yelling, "*Nose! Nose!*" Idiots. They couldn't even come up with a rhyme for "nose," so they had to say it twice. Every night I stole my mom's pink cloth hair tape to hold up my proboscis while I slept, praying, *Dear God, make it stay this way!* I had my father's exact nose, though he'd had his fixed many years ago. He and his sister Selma had been running through an open hydrant one hot Brooklyn summer day when they crashed into each other, head first, and broke their noses. For years he dangled the offer of a nose job in my face. "Is that your nose or are you eating a banana?" he loved to tease. As much as I despised my profile, I never took him up on his offer. If he couldn't tolerate looking at me and my big nose, well that was *his* problem.

Once at dinner, I bragged about how I'd entertained my fifth-grade science classmates by popping a tadpole through an eyedropper clear across the room. How all the kids had laughed. Not Sarah. My humanitarian sister burst into sobs, and I was banished to the pantry to finish my meal. Again.

Another time, when I was five, we were having dinner when a ruckus broke out. I don't remember the details, only that my father blamed me. He was always pointing that long, bony, hairy finger at me. I stood up, straight-backed, hands on my hips, and declared, "Everyone always says I'm just like you! I'm just like you! That must mean you really hate yourself!" Mouths dropped. A great hush fell over the room. And I was exiled to the pantry yet again. There I sat, perched on the kitchen stool, eye to eye with bags of egg noodles and boxes of chocolate-pudding mix. No wonder chocolate and pasta are my favorites.

But no matter how bad the nightly bickering got, there was always dessert. Chocolate or butterscotch pudding with a dollop of homemade whipped cream. German chocolate cake. Strawberry shortcake. Brownies. Cookies. Cheesecake. Baklava. Sugar was a given. Dessert fixes everything. When a child is born, people bring dessert. When someone dies, cookies, cakes, and candy are brought to the house. In times of trouble, in times of joy, sugar is part of the ritual. Baby showers. Birthday parties. Graduations. Retirement parties. Funerals. There is sugar.

Tonight at the dinner table I keep my mouth shut—except when a forkful of food is approaching. I silently scarf my grilled salmon and baked potato, my eyes shifting nervously back and forth between my parents. To my left sits my father, dining on his nightly multicourse meal of anxiety. I fear he will admonish me at any minute to get a job or finish school. I admit, it wouldn't be an unreasonable request on his part. To my right sits my mother. Her First Lady hairdo has long since given way to a sort of shoulder-length Prince Valiant bowl cut. Her cheerful outfits have been mostly replaced by loose and fashionable linen pantsuits and long skirts, most of which are black. At first it was a fashion choice. Now it's like someone has died. Like me—or the me she thought I would one day become. She had dreams for each of my siblings, but she saved her deepest, greatest wishes for her youngest. The last child. Her final hope. She looks so angry under those bangs, that solid strip of shiny, black hair that lies coolly across her forehead and provides a barricade from behind which she views the world—and me. I strain to think of something cheerful and significant to say to lift her mood. What is she thinking under those bangs? What happened to the *other* Lisa? The dancer-thin, highly productive one, who, at age five, entertained the family with hilarious original plays. Plays I directed and starred in every Sunday afternoon when the cousins came for dinner. Plays about the family, which made everyone laugh at themselves and be entertained. Nothing excited me more than performing my creations and being well-received. For those twenty minutes I had full control of the room. I had my family eating out of my hand. They said I was good. My mother's laughter melted all my pain, like chocolate in a double boiler. I was going to be someone. Who am I now?

I watch her from the corner of my eye as she sits tight-lipped, slowly chewing, glowering as she endures my father's maddening habits. Talking as he chews. Dominating the conversation with yet another story about a dental patient he saw that day or an old friend he ran into at lunch. When he isn't talking he stares with stone-cold silence at nothing in particular, infuriatingly unaware of how his silence and his chewing irritate my mom. She looks like she wants to scream. But she is committed to etiquette and refuses to allow even a centimeter of space between her lips as she eats. This is especially challenging now that she's had a chunk of precancerous skin removed from her right nostril. The surgery has drastically limited her nasal airway, forcing her to rely on only one nostril as she chews, breathing audibly, like a furious race horse, as she stares down the smidge of spinach lasagna that has unknowingly attached itself to my father's lip. How dare he ignore that fleck of food? How dare he upset her? She motions slyly to his mouth, wherein he swipes off the food and continues talking. Staring into space. Sneezing so loud the windows rattle. Swallowing as if his throat is mic'd. As he reaches for his water glass, always with the pinkie held high, the delicate gesture on the sinking Titanic, I hold my breath to prepare for the disturbing sound of his immortal *gulp*.

Worst of all his habits is his unconscious refusal to look at me as he talks. "Yoo-hoo!" I want to call. "I'm right here, Dad! I know you wish I weren't, but here I am! I'm right here, and for the moment anyway, I'm not going anywhere!"

Poor Mom. Sorry, Mom. I know you wish I were at Juilliard, not here, back home, struggling over whether to have another piece of French bread. Why does she keep buying those fucking French breads anyway? I *told* her I couldn't handle it. Even though I should. I should be able to handle anything. She always said so. My failure eats at her. And so do I. I'm trying to tell her I just may not be the next Audrey Hepburn. Or Barbra Streisand. Or president of the United States. Because she said I could be that, too.

After dinner, after our usual dance of my father urging me to help clean up, me trying to help, and my mother forcefully dismissing me from the kitchen, she and I eventually retire to my parents' bedroom for some *Masterpiece Theatre* while my dad makes his calls from the other room. My mother reclines in the black-leather Eames chair, and I stretch out on the soft, white carpet, pretending not to notice her look of disapproval, smiling to reassure her that I am perfectly happy down here. There are few activities my mom and I can comfortably do together. Watching PBS is one of them.

A year earlier we watched the Kennedy Center Honors. Ella Fitzgerald, Henry Fonda, Martha Graham, Tennessee Williams, and Aaron Copland were being honored for their contributions to the arts. "Someday that will be you up there," she'd said. "I know it." She looked so sure. I wanted to believe her. Her words gave me such a rush. As if hanging somewhere in my future was a guarantee of greatness. A golden carrot. All hope, all possibility, all success lay just ahead. All mine for the taking.

Tonight, however, what is mine for the taking is the last half of the pint of Rocky Road, sitting on the second to the bottom shelf in the freezer. Of course, I have to wait 'til my parents go to bed. Once the hall light is turned out and their door is shut, I sneak back upstairs and stand in the spotlight of the open freezer door, performing my nightly ritual once again. "Someday that will be you up there." My mother's words lifted me up. But I can't stay up. I'll never be high enough to stay up. I fall down from knowing I cannot stay up. I fall down. I rise. I fall. I rise. Like a sugar high and crash itself.

Dear beloved siblings, if you are reading this, I am sure you disagree with most if not all of it. Write your own fucking book.

CHAPTER 4

SHRINK RAP

Two weeks home, I step out of my father's silver VW Rabbit, dust the donut crumbs and powdered sugar off the front of my shirt, lick the residue glaze from my lips, and head into the square beige medical building to lie down on the proverbial couch.

This isn't my first time in therapy, mind you. My mom took me to see a shrink when I was three because I kept walking around the house saying "I hate you! I hate you!" After one session the doctor told her I was fine, that it was normal behavior for a three-year-old, and sent me home. Well, *that* was easy.

Then, when I was five, my mom insisted we all see a family counselor. For the bickering. The back-biting. We sat in a circle while the therapist asked us questions. I knew he was looking right at me when he suggested we all try not to "press each other's buttons." I went home, stuck a button up my nose, and ended up in the ER.

Then, just before my junior year of high school, my sister Sarah moved in with Aunt Ellen and Uncle Len, thirty minutes south, in Palo Alto, so she could spend senior year at the alternative high school in their district. Sarah moved out, and depression moved in. Friday nights, when she returned home for the weekend, I skulked about, picking at her, gnawing away for a scrap. I secretly hated her for abandoning me. My mother sent me to a shrink, again. I told him how I missed my sister, how I didn't know what I would do without her. He paused, then asked me what I wanted to do after high school. "Me? Oh, well, I want to perform. I just want to write and perform." He nodded silently. What did *that* mean? Did he think I was a fool? I'd show *him*. I summoned up my finest thespian skills and told him I was fine. After two more sessions he told my mom I was good to go. I called my sister and apologized for needing her too much. That weekend when she returned home, we bonded by jogging, agreeing never to get fat, and then finishing off Mom's leftover chocolate-truffle cake. For breakfast.

This time, however, therapy was my idea. Dr. Bird had helped my sister Lauren—and *she* was a *real* fuck-up. In high school, she and her friend used to finish off the entire five-pound box of See's chocolates my mom had bought for Friday dinner—all except the crappy, cream-filled pieces, of course. They'd hole up in her bedroom blasting Neil Young and Creedence Clearwater Revival. I hated her for her music, for being overweight, for getting C's, and for eating all the chocolate.

Lauren went off to this hippie college, discovered Zen Buddhism, dropped out after freshman year, and moved to a Buddhist monastery in Denver run by a skinny, creepy self-proclaimed guru. She shaved her head, gained more weight, and was on the verge of becoming a Buddhist nun. My parents flipped out and consulted Dr. Bird, who told them to stay calm and keep the doors of communication open. Six months later Lauren woke up and realized she wanted out of the worm's lair. She moved home and started seeing Dr. Bird. After three months she was able to go back to school, now at a wonderful, accredited spiritual college in Boulder.

If the shrink helped her, maybe there was hope for me.

Dr. Bird's office is dark, plainly decorated, and smells faintly of perfume and tobacco. I wonder if she smokes. I hope so. I love it when other people have bad habits. It's like a warm blanket.

I plop down on her blue-velvet couch and she settles into the brown-leather armchair directly across. A tall, shapely woman with longish, straight brown hair, she looks classy and professional in her burgundy-paisley knee-length nylon dress and blue-leather pumps. It's quiet for a moment, then she breaks the silence, crossing her taupe-hosed legs stiffly at the knee with a *shlish* sound.

"When did you get home?" she asks.

"Oh, um, a week ago? It's a little weird," I say, running my hands down the smooth velvet beneath me. I'm in a post-donut free fall and wish I could just sleep. I probably could just lie down on zee couch, but that wouldn't be productive.

"How so?" she asks.

"I don't know. It's just, I didn't really think I'd end up back here. I just couldn't stop bingeing, so I had to come home. I think I mentioned on the phone, I have a problem with sugar?" She nods silently.

"Tell me more about the food," she says. Good. If she'd said, "But you're not fat," that would've been the end.

"It's mainly sugar. I mean, I have a problem with a lot of food, but mostly it's sweets. Dessert. Once I start bingeing, I can't stop."

"Do you ever throw up?" What a question. Why is she asking me this? Oh, yeah, that's what normal girls do to stay thin. I was probably surrounded by barfing ballerinas growing up and never even knew it. The word *bulimia* never came up. So to speak.

"Oh, no," I say, shaking my head. "I never barf." She nods with an inquisitive look. I'm not going into the whole barfing thing. How I'd rather lose a limb than lose my lunch. How no matter how much food I stuff in or how sick I get, I cannot, will not, puke.

But I don't need to tell the shrink this. It's personal. Besides, she won't get it. She looks so straight. Polished. I imagine her at a cocktail party, standing tall and conversing with other medical professionals, a glass of crisp Chardonnay in one hand, a crust-covered mini hotdog on a toothpick in the other.

Me, I abhor dressing nicely, much to my mother's chagrin. A lot of good all those Saks' and Joseph Magnin outfits did for me. If I could wear a garbage bag with two slits for the eyes and a hole for the mouth to shove cake through, I'd be happy. Actually, my daily attire since moving home isn't far from that. It's either my humongous, pin-striped overalls from high school or a floor-length Indian print muumuu. The bigger the clothes, the thinner I feel.

"Well . . . why don't you start by telling me a little about what you've been doing?"

"Okay, well, I went to Crystal Springs for high school." She nods. She knows Crystal. Everyone who's anyone in the Bay Area knows Crystal. I want her to think I am someone for going there. "Crystal was amazing. I mean, I was, like, the star of the mime troupe. I was in all the plays. It was *amazing*." I pause. "And then . . . I graduated."

"What happened?"

"I went to UCLA . . . for dance . . . and theatre. . . . That was when I really started bingeing. I felt like I was crazy. I didn't know what to do. I got into a summer dance program at Colorado College, which was great, but the bingeing got worse. I got this weird, crampy pain in my side."

"Have you seen a doctor?" She looks worried. Which worries me.

"Oh, yeah. I mean, I had a barium swallow. You know, where you drink that chalky white drink and they take pictures of your gut? He said it was nothing. Just some irritable bowel. Or something. He didn't really know." I know. It's from the bingeing. And the no shitting. But I'm *definitely* not going to talk about the constipation. *Way* too embarrassing. "Anyway, after Colorado, I dropped out of UCLA and moved to Minneapolis with some dancer friends to study dance, but that didn't work out. So I ended up at Sarah Lawrence in New York, which is a great school and everything, but then *that* didn't work out. So I joined this summer mime theatre in Maine, which was amazing except

I couldn't stop bingeing, and the pain in my side got worse, and I ended up starting a mime troupe in Amherst, but it was kind of a disaster. I mean, there were nine mimes and no real leader, and my side was really bad and so was the food, and so I ended up checking into this macrobiotic study house in Boston, where I lived for three months, but then *that* didn't work out, and so I just . . . came home. And here I am."

She nods slowly. Digesting.

Milk. I need milk. Cold, cold milk. The donuts left a lardlike coating on the roof of my mouth. The wall clock ticks. Forty minutes to go.

Dr. Bird recrosses her shapely legs. The skin on her knees is pressed tautly beneath her hose. I'll bet she enjoys sex. Mature, womanly sex with her manly shrink husband. I picture the two of them in their king-sized bed, the burgundy lampshades with the lighting just so, the burgundy satin sheets. I'll bet she has orgasms. She expects them, like any normal, healthy woman. I can't imagine letting go in that way. So embarrassing. Plus, female orgasm seems so unproductive next to a man's. How do you know for sure? Where's the proof? Men are so lucky. They know when they're done. They can relax. I don't want to relax. Maybe that's my problem. The very fact that orgasms are expected to feel good makes them incomprehensible to me, not to mention unattainable.

"How is your mother?" Dr. Bird asks. Because they always want to talk about your mother.

"She's good," I say, crossing my arms over my chest, hoping Dr. Bird didn't hear me thinking about her in bed. "Why?"

"Does she know how you've been feeling?"

"Well, yeah. I mean, I *think* so. She's definitely worried anyway." I don't want to talk about my mother. It's so *clichéd*—sitting on a therapy couch talking about my mother. This is my problem, not hers.

"Do you think your mother knows what you're going through?"

"I don't know," I say. "I shouldn't be going through *anything.*"

"What should you be doing?"

"Working! Studying! Performing! Look, my mother just wants the best for me, okay?"

"I'm sure she does. But it might be helpful to explore how your relationship with her plays into the food."

I hate this. I don't want to talk about my mother. Dr. Bird just wants me to say horrible things about her to explain my food problem. I just want to get into my car and finish off that last half of an old-fashioned donut left in the bag. Poor Mom. She sacrificed everything for us. How can I sit here and talk shit about her? Lauren must have told Dr. Bird how amazing our mom is. I'm sure she didn't sit on this couch and badmouth Mom. Why should *I*? Besides, Sarah's the one who's always so critical of Mom. She's always warning me, "Don't put Mom on a pedestal." But *Sarah's* the one I have on a pedestal!

"Look," I say to my shrink. "Even if the food *does* have something to do with my mom, I want you to know she's been nothing but supportive. *I'm* the one who messed up, not her. She supported me through *everything*, okay?" There were only two times my mother said no to me: Once when I begged to come home from dance camp because I couldn't stop secretly bingeing. And once when I begged to travel across country to Sarah Lawrence College with a boy I'd just met. Other than that, she never said no.

The birds are singing merrily outside the venetian blinds. Oh, yeah, it's spring. Fucking spring. Time for new life. New growth. New disappointment.

"Well, I look forward to talking with you more," Dr. Bird says. Because that is what they say.

"Thanks," I say, rising. "See you Wednesday?" Because I can never be sure I am wanted back. Even by a paid shrink.

CHAPTER 5

LET THE BINGEING BEGIN

The morning my parents delivered me to my UCLA dorm four years earlier, I felt the floor drop out from under me. A bitter taste of homesickness welled up in my throat. I was just seventeen, all alone in this enormous university, far from the glorious bubble of praise and perfection I'd inhabited during my years at Crystal. The fact that my dorm was a dump didn't help. Something about the term "student co-op" had led me to believe this was where the cool, artsy people would live. Instead of opting to reside in the shiny, spotless hi-rise dorms, I ended up in a crappy World War II–era building, with peeling paint, cottage-cheese ceilings, stained carpeting, and residents who smelled like dirty laundry. And strong cigarettes.

I knew I'd made a mistake the minute we opened the door. My father dropped my bags, walked over to the accordion-door closet, and forced it open, pulling it partway off its hinges. "What's this?" he demanded, pointing to a sachet hanging on the wooden clothing bar. "Mari-jew-wana?" My mother stormed over, snatched it off the clothing bar, raced across the room, thrust open the filthy window, and chucked it out.

Have fun at college.

I watched the silhouette of my father's bald head and my mother's perfectly coiffed hair as they drove off in their rented station wagon back to the airport. There went my childhood. There went the safety of home and everything familiar. I never believed this day would come. Not that I didn't want to experience the world. I just didn't want to do it away from home.

The mini-fridge sat in the corner of my dorm room like a leering midget, watching me, waiting to be filled up or emptied out. My mother had asked my father to rent it for me so I wouldn't go hungry. Every few days I made the trek down through the unbearably sunny streets of Westwood Village to load up on supplies at the corner health-food store—bags of cashews, raisins, almonds, carob chips and peanut butter, honey-carrot muffins, and wedges of Muenster cheese.

Back in my room, I could never just let the food be. I had to have it inside me. I'd start with maybe a handful of nuts. A couple bites of cheese. By the end of the day, I would have finished off most, if not all, of my supplies, leaving just a few raisins or a tiny wedge of cheese.

My roommate, Julie, seemed oblivious to my food obsession. Most nights she was with her law school boyfriend at his fancy dorm. That left me alone a lot of the time. Alone with my fridge.

One morning when Julie returned after a night away, I felt magnanimous and offered her my last whole-grain cookie. She sat propped at the edge of my little bed, dressed in a cheerful sundress, her long, brown braids hanging straight like a young girl's and her long, skinny legs twisted one around the other. She slowly picked at the poor little cookie as she relayed some silly story about something that had tickled her funny bone. As she spoke I followed the cookie with my eyes, amazed at her discipline not to simply demolish it. I could have devoured a whole package of cookies in the time it took her to finish her stupid story.

That fall my loneliness was suffocating. I was isolated, unable to connect, held back by an invisible wall of fear. How could I compete with so many confident dancers and actors? Facing my body in the wall-length mirror after a night of debauchery was especially challenging. At least in modern dance there wasn't the expectation of physical perfection, though I missed ballet's uniformity of pink leotards, pink shoes, and everyone's hair pulled into a neat bun. To me, all the various colored leotards, the bare feet, and the random hair styles were blasphemy. Many of the dancers weren't even that thin. Not that you should be skinny to dance. Anyone should be able to dance. No, they shouldn't. Dancers should be thin. That's ridiculous. It's true. Fuck me. Fuck you!

There was this one dancer. At five eleven, Suzanne was so thin her hip bones jutted out like shark fins. If she fell facedown, they'd probably leave dents in the floor. She had a cropped boy's haircut and a perpetual pout. We weren't friends. I just envied her for her apparent lack of a need to respond to me. Or anyone, really. Suzanne was so cool she left wisps of fog in her wake. Or cigarette smoke. That was the other thing I envied her for. She looked so cool with that cigarette dangling from her digits. If only I smoked instead of binged. But that's just not healthy.

I wanted to be withholding, like Suzanne. But I hungered for connection. So what do you do when you are a lonely freshman? You do what your sister Sarah would do. You join the co-op bread-baking crew. What better way to connect with fellow students than by baking bread for the masses?

The best part was every Wednesday, after finishing baking at 1 a.m., we each got to take home a loaf, fresh and hot, right out of the oven. I always polished off most of mine before I'd even crossed the dark street back to my dorm. I'd stumble along the curb like a drunk, camouflaged by the dark, shoving in fistfuls of the steaming bread, burning and blistering my mouth, but unable to stop myself. Trying to fill the hole I felt inside.

Thursday mornings it was like an atomic bomb had gone off in my gut. My nights of bread were followed by days of just an apple and a yogurt. My only goal was to make myself feel hungry all over again. Like at least I had *some* control.

Sometime in October I got sick. Nothing I could put my finger on. Just some vague illness that left me clammy, feverish, nauseous. I guess there's only so much you can stuff down before your body has something to say about it. How did I take care of myself? With chocolate. I lay in bed, secretly munching my cookies, feeling like I was falling down a well of sadness. Why was I sad? What was I scared of? Nothing should be wrong. The world was my oyster.

Something was definitely wrong.

All my life, I never thought I had enough. Of anything. No matter how much praise or opportunity I received, it was never going to fill me. I don't know if this feeling comes from my father and his fears or from my mother and her hunger. Or from being the last of four kids, always worrying I would miss out. Or all of the above. Or none of it. My life was a constant internal grind. A churning of self-doubt and worry. It ate away at me, and I just ate away.

Thanksgiving weekend, I visited Sarah at UC Santa Cruz as my parents were out of town on a long-planned trip. She took me to this amazing hole-in-the-wall vegetarian Mexican joint, sat me down, and loaded me up. "Where's yours?" I asked. I always watched what she ate, hoping to be just like her. She was the best.

"I'm not hungry," she said. "You want some guacamole?" Before I could say no, she disappeared, returning moments later with a bowl of creamy guacamole and a basketful of chips. "Wait'll you try it," she said. I began to eat.

"Wow, it's amazing!"

"I'm so glad," she said. "I really want you to enjoy it. It's so good for you." I devoured my food, watching her take tiny sips of ice water. I was the all-consuming monster. She was the ethereal, self-martyring goddess who would not allow herself to be comforted by simple pleasures like melted cheese or a buttered tortilla.

"I—I can't believe how skinny you got," I said in between mouthfuls.

"I'm not *trying* to be skinny," she said. "When I see fat on a person's body, it just reminds me of all the excess in this country. It's a *political* thing."

"Oh," I nodded, shoving in my burrito. "I totally agree." I looked at her face. If only I were her, with her great willpower and poet boyfriend. She always got the boys. It's not like she was some classic beauty. But she was cute. A little shorter than me, with a mop of thick, black hair. Tiny breasts. Tiny nose. And she had an edge. An intensity. She knew who she was and she didn't give a shit what you thought of her. She didn't need me. But man, I needed her. I yearned for her. If she was feeding me like this, she must love me.

Afterwards Sarah watched me devour a vanilla sundae with hot fudge, whipped cream, and nuts. No cherry, though. The red dye #5 will kill you. I wanted to tell her how homesick I was, but I couldn't find the word. Homesick.

"Do you ever wish you'd never left home?" I finally asked.

"Oh, God, no," she chortled. "Are you kidding?"

"I just can't believe we're never going to live there again. Don't you miss Mom?"

"You know," she said, "one of these days you're going to realize Mom is not perfect. Don't idealize her. It's deadly stuff."

I spooned up my last bit of pabulum, wishing to spoon her in as well. I couldn't get enough of her. It was my fault. I was too needy. She'd said so many times. Sarah felt obliged to care for me, and God knows I leaned on her, but she wasn't really with me. In fact, she was disappearing before my very eyes.

Having been fully fed and watered, I was delivered back to her campus suite and told to stay in the living room while she retreated to her bedroom where her poet awaited her. I curled up at the end of the communal couch, listening to Jackson Browne, my romantic idol, and polishing off the second half of a large

Toblerone chocolate bar, no doubt a gift to my sister from her lover. If I couldn't be with her, I'd be with her chocolate.

One day before modern dance class I overheard Suzanne telling another girl about a great summer dance program at Colorado College. I had to interrupt and ask her about it. "Oh," she said with her usual pout, looking both sexy and self-destructive at once, "I've never been. But it's supposed to be great. It's pretty competitive."

"Are you going?" I asked.

"Dunno," she said, glowering, then rolled over into a complete split.

My mother yelped with glee when I called to tell her about the Hanya Holm Summer Dance Program. She knew all the greats. "Hanya Holm! *What* an opportunity!" Six weeks of modern dance was the last thing I wanted to do. I'd envisioned spending the summer at home with Sarah, swimming, jogging, getting skinny and tan. But I had to apply. Just to see if I'd get in. Which I did. With a scholarship. Then I *had* to go.

Suzanne didn't even apply.

The minute I got to Colorado I wanted to leave. I mean the minute. Why was I here, deep into modern dance, eight hours a day? The make-your-own-frozen-yogurt-sundae bar in the cafeteria was a daily torture. I wasn't alone in my conflict of whether or not to indulge. I'd watch my fellow dancers heading to their tables with their trays, their plates piled high with salad. They'd hesitate as they passed the frozen yogurt bar . . . then they'd move on. Or maybe take a small helping for dessert, then complain about how they shouldn't be eating it the whole time they were spooning it in.

A care package arrived from home. The timing could not have been better. It was Friday and I was headed into my first weekend with the anticipation of utter loneliness. I picked up the box on my way from class and waited to open it until I was safe inside my little room. Inside the box were two dozen chocolate-chip cookies baked by Sarah especially for me, along with several pounds of dried fruits and nuts from my mom. And I'm not just talking ordinary, everyday dried fruits and nuts. There were honey-dipped apricots so plump and moist they squirted when you bit into them. There were chocolate-covered pineapple and mango and an assortment of nuts: Brazil nuts, almonds, and cashews the size of your thumb, all dipped in chocolate as well. My mother didn't fuck around.

I chomped away for about an hour, leaving just two cookies and three honeyed apricots. I felt sick. So very, very sick. A phone call home from the booth outside my dorm would help. I would tell Sarah I'd eaten too much. She would hold my hand and talk me down. Sadly, she was out. I thanked my mom for the amazing care package. "Just enjoy," she said. "We're all so excited for you. I'll bet the program is wonderful."

"It is," I said. "I just . . . wish I could come home. . . ." I heard her "tsk" and exhale disapprovingly. "I mean, it's really great and everything. It's an amazing program. I know I'm lucky. I just—I wish I could just come home." I was weak. Literally. Like I might collapse.

"Don't be silly," she said. "You're right where you're meant to be. You have the body of a dancer. You have the talent. You'll stay where you are, and I know you'll be happy you did. I just know it." That was when it hit. A bolt of pain through my right gut. Like an electrical shock that stretched from my groin to my throat. My knees went limp and I gripped the metal phone cord, afraid to let go, all the while keeping my mouth away from the phone receiver so as not to catch anything, as per my mother's training.

I should tell her I was in pain. But what was the point? I'd brought this on myself. It's not like it was appendicitis or something I had nothing to do with. This was my doing. I should straighten up and fly right, like my mother always said. It's just that every time she said this, I pictured the birds outside our living room getting drunk on pyracantha berries and slamming into the picture window to their death.

I thanked my mom, told I loved her, hung up the phone, and went back to my room to finish off the package.

My sister Lauren knew I was suffering and invited me to Boulder for the weekend. Saturday morning I peered up from the mattress on her apartment floor to see her gazing down in her antique flowered bloomers and tank top. "How'd you sleep?" she asked kindly.

"Okay," I said. Her thighs looked like two giant pillars of flesh. Her belly stuck out. As my eyes traveled north, up her imperfect, womanly frame, I saw that the face at the top had something I'd never seen before. The face had joy. For the first time in my life I saw that she was pretty. Confident. How could she be happy when she was still overweight?

She took me to her favorite breakfast joint and insisted I have the banana-walnut pancakes. Her treat. "Mom would *love* these," she swooned. I'd never thought of my mom that way. As a separate, mortal being taking sensual pleasure in life. In between bites Lauren spoke of her spiritual journey and her search for self-acceptance. I knew she'd had several lovers. I wished I could meet someone. I felt desperate to break away. She told me I'd have to love myself before I found a man to love me. Yeah, yeah, I'd love myself once I found a man. Or an audience.

Up until that moment, the closest I'd come to being with a guy was in the spring of my senior year of high school. My mother had envisioned me spending my two-week senior project at A.C.T., the American Conservatory Theatre. But I was determined, albeit not consciously, to be deflowered, and what better place than at Ananda, a gardening and yoga community in Grass Valley, California? For two weeks I slept in a tent, pulled weeds, stretched, chanted, and choked down a raw vegan diet that, happily, gave me a massive case of the runs. I went from skinny to skinnier. I flitted about the farm in my halter top and cut-offs, enjoying the male gaze shining in my direction.

One night everyone gathered in the communal tent for a documentary film about an Indian guru who magically produced healing ash from a ceramic pot. The movie ended and Churiya, an olive-skinned, pony-tailed aspiring yogi sidled up to me. (His real name was probably something like Bernie Cohen, but who's counting?)

"Wasn't that *amazing?*" he asked, all aglow, reeking of b.o. and patchouli.

"Yes, it was!" Was he really buying into this ash thing?

"Hey," he said, "it's a beautiful night. How about a walk to the upper meadow?"

"Sure . . ." I said. "That would be nice . . ." We lay side by side on the cool, damp grass, staring up at the stars and talking about life. Or something. "You're like one of those stars," he whispered. "You're like a beautiful light shining clear and bright." It was cheesy, but I wanted to go with it. Time to let the petals fall. I wanted to trust him. I figured an enlightened guy like this would never knock up an innocent thing like me. Because the only thing that scared me more than barfing was getting knocked up. Which, of course, could lead to barfing.

Churiya lifted my little cotton top and began to fondle my breast. I lay still, preparing myself for whatever was supposed to happen next. A kiss? A hug? I suddenly became aware of a rapid beating sound, like a *thwak! Thwak! Thwak!* I peeked over and saw his hand burrowed deep in his drawstring pants. His arm was jerking up and down, up and down, in furious, fast-motion repetition. What was he *doing*? It had to have something to do with his penis. I quickly averted my eyes so he wouldn't be embarrassed. Or expect me to do something with it.

Churiya arched his back and let out a long, low *uhhhhhhhhh*. Maybe it was gas from the lentil stew we'd had for dinner. He arched further and moaned deeper with a *grooooooan*. I felt something warm and wet splash across my arm. What the *fuck*? I smiled sweetly as he wiped my wrist with his Indian batik shirt-sleeve. Then he helped me up—what a gentleman—escorted me back to my tent, said good night, and left. I curled up in my sleeping bag, wondering what I'd done wrong. Little did I know that all the men at Ananda had taken a vow of celibacy during their stay.

I should have gone to A.C.T.

After my Boulder weekend with my sister Lauren, I returned to dance camp determined to shine. The harder I ate, the harder I danced. The cramp in my side came and went. I'd see a doctor when I got home. For now I had to be great. My first choreographic assignment was a comedic solo about my various body parts battling one another. Thanks to my rubber face and my gift for isolating body parts, the piece was a hit. I was showered with praise. Wow, that went well! So well, in fact, that I decided then and there to drop out of UCLA and move with several dancer friends to Minneapolis to study at the Guild of Performing Arts. Because real artists don't need college.

When I called my parents and told them of my plans, my dad resisted but my mom backed me up. She'd never wanted me to attend UCLA, anyway. Too big. Not special enough. She knew. Now all I needed was a man to want me—even if just once. It would help me move out into the real world. But summer was nearing to a close. Time was running out to seal the deal before my big Minneapolis move. I'd spotted a student twice that summer. Blondish hair. Boyish complexion. I knew he'd noticed me as well. The very last day, I saw him at the end-of-summer-camp barbeque. He was seated across the plaza, having a beer and laughing with friends. "Go *talk* to him!" a dancer pal prodded me. "Come on, he's so *cute*!" I couldn't tell her I'd just inhaled three bowls of Carnation artificially flavored vanilla ice cream.

Some people worked up the nerve to pick someone up with a drink or a joint. I worked mine up with sugar.

"I'm just going to use the bathroom," I said, then slipped through the party crowd, furtively spooned in one more bowl of frozen courage, licked my lips, and ambled over to the boy. He was even cuter up close. He saw me and smiled. "How's it going?" he asked.

"Good," I said. "So, um, what program are you in, anyway?"

"Me? Oh, tech sciences."

"Oh, cool!" I nodded. What *were* tech sciences, anyway?

"I'm in the dance program."

"I thought so," he said. He'd *thought* so. So . . . he'd been thinking about me. That was all I needed. Ten minutes later I was following him to his dorm room. Trailing behind him, I studied the back of his head. *This is the boy I am going to fuck*, I thought. *He is going to put his penis inside me and I will never, ever, ever be the same.*

His dorm room was stuffy and warm from being closed up in the afternoon sun. I stood awkwardly, then plopped down onto the left side of his unmade, double bed. As he sat on the right, I took the initiative and slipped off my jeans. A crinkling sound made me look up. Candy? Did he have some candy? He fumbled with what I then realized was a condom package. He saw me watching and turned his back to suit up. I pictured a deflated balloon being stretched down over a cucumber and prayed that balloon would hang on for dear life and not pop off and *whoosh* away, leaving me defenseless.

We each slipped under the sheets and then met in the middle. As he reached to kiss me I held my breath so he wouldn't detect the ice cream. Soon he was on top of me, rocking his hips back and forth, grinding into me. I'd heard the first time might hurt, so I prepared myself for the pain. It didn't hurt that bad, which made me wonder if he was even inside. "Are you . . . in?" I asked, laughing a bit to sound like I might be kidding.

"Y—yeah," he said, scowling. Maybe I offended him because he came really fast after that. I watched his face at the moment of climax. His eyes rolled back and his mouth grimaced in ecstasy. A little cheer went up inside me. I didn't even care that I'd never see him again. A real, live boy had finally broken through.

But the first boy to break into my heart came the following summer. It had been a somewhat disastrous year in the Midwestern tundra for me. It wasn't just the sixty-below winter. It was the lack of daily structure. The dancing just for the sake of dancing. Let the slacker losers lollygag about and get nowhere fast. I needed to get somewhere. Fast. It was my mother's dream for me to attend the very elite Sarah Lawrence College in Bronxville, New York. Sarah Lawrence would make me worldly. Sarah Lawrence would make me great. I applied and got in, and my mother was over the moon. My father freaked about sending me to the second-most-expensive school in the country. "What was wrong with UCLA, I'd like to know?" I couldn't explain it. How I needed more. So my mom explained it for me, as she always did, behind their closed bedroom door. She broke him down, and he agreed to let me go. In a show of good faith, I promised to take a summer job at my childhood camp in the Trinity Alps of Northern California. Not just to appease my father. Being responsible for a group of young girls and forced to sit down to three squares a day would help me stop bingeing and regroup before starting my amazing new college life.

I did not intend to meet a guy at my camp job. Not consciously. But my hunger for male attention was quickly becoming on a par with my need for sugar. I wanted, no, needed a man. My longing felt insatiable. Like a bottomless pit. But I could not admit to it. I needed to be good. In my cognizant brain, all roads led to Sarah Lawrence.

Then I met Tom. Tom Lincoln. His all-American name alone legitimized me. Tom stood out from the rest of the earnest, fresh-faced camp counselors. With his clean-shaven, chiseled jaw, buzz cut, and reflective sunglasses, he had a military air about him. His unpredictable, taunting nature was sexy and scary. He was frisky and a little arrogant—sort of like my sister Sarah's poet. And Tom, too, attended UC Santa Cruz, although I couldn't quite picture him in that crunchy, laid-back, flannel-shirted setting.

Counselor orientation week, the energy between us was electric. We had to be discreet. When the counselors were given two days off before the campers arrived, a bunch of us piled into cars and pickups to spend the night in Arcata, where fellow counselor Joy White's family owned a summer home on a bluff over-looking the sea. We arrived at the house and Tom nabbed the master bedroom. He locked the door. Closed the drapes. And as the waves crashed below against the rocky shore, Tom crashed into me. The sex was passionate and hard. Finally, a man wanted me. All of me. I lost myself utterly inside him.

A week and a half into camp, Tom got his ass canned. I was mortified. "They say I'm not camp material," he said with a smirk, "whatever *that* is." I knew what that was. Camp was all about teamwork, and Tom was an obstinate ass who wouldn't take no for an answer. That was partly why I lusted for him. His drive. He wouldn't let go. In fact, he wanted me so much he rented a small room in a boarding house in the nearby town of Hyampom so that he could continue to see me the rest of the summer.

He didn't want to leave me.

This was amazing.

I admit I felt self-conscious about what the other counselors and staff thought of my continued affair with someone who'd been exiled. Especially Clive, the camp director. Clive knew my whole family. He'd even met my parents. Someone who knew my parents knew I was fucking. Not only that, I was fucking someone he didn't like. But fuck it. This was my life. And any-way, it wasn't just sex. It was love. We didn't have to say it. But we knew. And so, once every ten days on my day off, I bummed a ride to Hyampom from a fellow counselor heading that way. I always tried to be talkative and upbeat in the car, even though my shame was palpable. I knew they knew where I was headed. To fuck.

August arrived and my days with Tom were numbered. One day in bed he proposed a plan. "Let's take a train across country," he said. "I'll take you all the way to Sarah Lawrence. That way we can have two extra weeks together."

"It sounds *amazing*," I said, feeling nervous. "It's just, school starts two days after camp ends. My parents already bought my plane ticket."

"So," said my master finagler, "you'll leave camp two weeks early, I'll meet you in Frisco, and we can still make the trip!" As I composed my letter home, I tried to ignore the little voice in my head that said not to trust anyone who used that vile term "Frisco."

"Dear Mom and Dad," the letter began. "I know this might surprise you, but I've met a guy I *really* like. He wants to take me on a train to Sarah Lawrence! Can you believe it? It means I'll have to quit camp two weeks early, but I'm *sure* it'll be fine. I'm *sure* Clive won't have a problem with it." But Clive did have a problem with it. "If that's what you want," he said. "But just so you know, you'll never be invited back here to work again." I was marring the family name. So what? Someone wanted me.

Four nights later, I was seated at dinner with my fellow campers when I heard the camp pay phone ring. Before I even heard the office guy call my name, I knew it was for me.

"I beg of you," my father pleaded, "finish out the summer and fly back east as planned."

"It's your *responsibility!*" my mother cried. "How are people going to know they can depend on you if you let them down like this?" What other people? I thought it was just me.

"It'll be *fine!*" I insisted, flushed with shame as I envisioned Tom humping me while we rolled past George Washington's face on Mount Rushmore.

"You are *not* taking a train across country with some strange man from God knows where!" My mother didn't get it. Tom was no stranger. He was my soulmate.

"*Nothing's* going to *happen!*" I said. "I'm going to be *fine!*" And if I wasn't, I could always just . . . jump off the train and call home for help. Collect.

"You'll finish your job," my mother said. "Then you'll fly across country like a normal person."

"Listen to your mutha," my father said. "I beg of you."

We hung up, no promises made. But I'd heard something in their voices. A vulnerability. A shakiness. I'd been quitting things ever since I first left home. Why should this be different? Because this time, a man was involved.

"I knew you couldn't do it," Tom said when I broke it to him on the phone two days later. I couldn't see his face, but I could hear him smirking. As I gripped the receiver, I picked at a shard of wood that stuck out from the rustic phone-booth wall, trying to make my finger bleed.

"I'm sorry," I sniffled. "At least we have the rest of the summer, right? And then I'll see you at Thanksgiving!" A long, damp pause settled between us. I wasn't the bold lover he'd thought I was. I was a little girl who couldn't let go of her parents. "So, I'll see you this Thursday, right?"

"Nah," he said. "I think I might head south. Maybe hit the beach, do some surfing before school starts."

"I didn't know you surfed," I said.

"I don't."

My final two Tom-less weeks of camp were unbearable. I was a distracted wreck. Volunteering at the end-of-camp donut-making party would lift me up. But all that got lifted were dozens of giant, malformed deep-fried rings from the vat of boiling lard. In between chiding my campers to wait until we were through to take their allotted two donuts, I repeatedly turned my head to stuff in all the broken pieces. By the end of the night, I'd consumed the equivalent of about eleven colossal donuts.

We put our campers to bed, and several counselors and I headed down to the lower pasture to get high. Although I never got high. I never wanted to alter my consciousness.

Lying on the grass, someone handed me the joint and I passed it casually along, hoping not to be judged. I couldn't tell my friends what I'd just done to myself. How I could hardly breathe. How I was so nauseous I couldn't see straight. I watched them get high while I sank to the bottom of my cholesterol crater.

Summer ended. I returned home and flew Back East to college, like a good girl. I made it through that first lonely and miserable semester at Sarah Lawrence with Entenmann's pastries. That was when my side pain started again. I knew it was from the sugar and shit. But I didn't care. All I wanted was to get back to Tom for our post-Thanksgiving visit. At least that was the plan from the one letter I'd received from him that fall.

When the day finally arrived, my mother knew better than to ask me any questions as she drove me to the Greyhound station to catch a bus to Santa Cruz to see my "friend." Though I wanted to believe that Tom and I would simply pick up where we left off, I was nervous. We hadn't actually spoken since the summer. But my anxiety was soothed the moment he took me into his arms and into his bed.

It was right after sex. I was stroking his arm, telling him how much I'd missed him. When he didn't respond, I had to ask. "Did you miss me?"

"Sure," he said. "But I wasn't gonna wait around."

"What do you mean?" I started to shake.

"I slept with a few girls."

"You're kidding?" My stomach went into my throat. I half-smiled in disbelief.

"Nope. Not kidding. But Joy White, she was the best."

"Joy White? You mean, Joy White from camp?"

"Yeah," he nodded. "She came down a few times from Davis to see me." Joy White with the boyish haircut. Joy White with the family beach house, where Tom and I had consummated our love. Joy White with the practical, high-waisted jeans and the peachy-white skin. Sensible, all-American, girl-next-door Joy White. The boyish-girl I would never be. "Don't look so shocked. You could have been with me."

"No! I couldn't! Don't you understand?"

"I understand. You couldn't stand up to your parents."

"That's not *true*! I just—I knew how they felt!"

"Oh, yeah?" he cackled. "Then what are you doing here now?"

Bull's-eye.

I tried to get up, but Tom grabbed my wrists, slammed me down, and pinned my arms on either side. Suddenly his once sexy biceps seemed ugly and mean. "You could have been with me, but you couldn't stand up to Mommy and Daddy, could you? You had to fly to your rich girl's college, just like they wanted you to. Well, I did what I wanted, too. I fucked Joy White. And you know what? She was fucking *great*."

"Let me *go*!" I yelled, hoping someone would hear me. But everyone had gone home for the holiday. Everyone but Tom.

His face was in mine. "She was a *great* fucking lay, and I have you to thank for it." I let out a cry. He laughed in my mouth. Then suddenly, in a burst, he let me go. I tore naked down the fluorescent-lit hallway to the women's communal bathroom, holed up in a toilet stall, and sobbed.

I heard the bathroom door open. Then footsteps. A pair of white Adidas stopped at my stall door. "There's a bus at four," Tom's voice said. "Come on." I hesitated, then slowly swung the stall door open. He stood there, straight-faced, fully clothed. I rose cautiously from the toilet, hands cupped over my breasts, and wedged past him, trying not to make contact. Then I sprinted back to his room. I threw on my clothes and jammed my belongings into my large, tan backpack. It was the same backpack I'd used all through high school, the same one I'd packed all my books, my papers, and my mime costumes in. It still smelled of white greasepaint and Jarlsburg cheese and alfalfa-sprout sandwiches on whole-wheat bread. It was the bag that held all my hopes and dreams for the future. Nothing I'd ever carried in that bag had ever indicated anything like this ever would happen to me. *Ever.*

Tom and I were thirty minutes early for the bus. "I wanna get a cup of coffee," he said, pointing to a coffee shop at the bus stop. We sat at the counter. Everyone seemed to know him. Like a real celebrity. The sun-damaged blonde waitress was all smiles. Maybe he'd fucked her, too.

"Hiya Tom. How's it goin'?" she asked.

"Great, thanks!" He was gloating, like he hadn't just trapped me naked on his bed. I checked my watch. His red finger marks were still on my wrists.

"So! What can I get for you?" the aging, frosted waitress chirped at him. "On the house!" They laughed in unison. He ordered a coffee, then turned to me.

"Couple weeks ago," he explained, "they had a donut-eating competition. I ate twenty-five in one sitting." I nodded my head slightly, still silent since we'd left his dorm. "It's *awesome*," he said, ignoring my silence. "I get whatever I want for free, for a whole month. Coffee, donuts, juice, cocoa, anything." I listened, keeping an eye peeled for the bus. "Then, in January, they're having another contest. I'm goin' for fifty. I'll get anything I want for a whole year. Carte blanche."

"That's great," I said. Those were my only words to him. I didn't even say good-bye.

My parents were waiting for me at the seedy Market Street Greyhound station in San Francisco. As planned, we went for Mexican. We ordered, then my mom passed out the Wash'n Dri's. "Your mutha," my dad chuckled. "Awlways prepeyd." Seated between them, I fought to keep my tears inside my eyes. It wasn't just the loss of Tom that upset me. It was that I could never tell my parents what had happened. I stared down hard at the melted, orange cheddar cheese atop my enchiladas. It glistened under the harsh light of the fake Tiffany lamp overhead. One tear escaped, fell onto the cheese, and lingered there, unabsorbed. My father motioned for the check.

CHAPTER 6

I TAKE THE CAKE

The synagogue is freezing. My mother was right. I should have brought a sweater. Uncle Eli is being honored for his weighty work in medicine and Jewish thought, two topics I feel utterly detached from. Or maybe it's just the comment he made at a family gathering three years ago, just after I'd dropped out of UCLA. "*Sooo,*" said the very learned scholar, munching on a hunk of baguette smeared with baba ghanoush. "How does it feel to be a college dropout?" At the time, I just laughed. Laughed and ate. And ate and ate. Just like I am going to do today. Because now I'm not just a college dropout. I'm a double college dropout.

They say resentment is an addict's worst enemy.

The vultures descend upon two long tables displayed with finger foods and desserts. There are platters of Aunt Rena's bite-sized chocolate brownies and mini cheddar-cheese balls, both of which are easy to pop in on the sly. No one notices as I pop away. The crowd is thick and the hands are grabbing. There is also a humongous vanilla sheet cake. What's the point of *that*, I wonder. There isn't even any icing. What a rip.

I make my way down the buffet table. I'm like a quiet eating machine, like a noiseless vacuum sucking up mini spinach-ricotta pancakes, mini bagels and cream cheese, a handful of nuts, and a slice of red pepper for appearances. I keep my eyes down, praying not to be stopped by a relative and forced to relate. Sure, I'm *real* invisible, with my thick faux-girdle wrapped 'round my belly to hold it all in. "*Sooo,* Lisa . . ." I imagine a clueless relative saying.

"What are you doing with yourself these days?" What does it *look* like I'm doing? Idiot. Now could you please leave me the fuck alone so I can properly anesthetize myself? I hope my longish, lustrous hair will distract people from the rest of my body. It forms a sort of curtain behind which I can eat. The carbs and sugar kick in full force. Through my hair blockade I see the party guests' faces begin to warp like melting Chagall characters. If only I could lie down on my back under one end of the table while two suited men tip the opposite end of the table so that all the food can just slide down the length of the table and into my mouth. The men would be like my pallbearers. Pallbearers for the living.

My mother's eyes are on me. I feel them from across the temple hall. I stop chewing, suck in my gut, look up, and smile. She waves her little wave. I wonder what she tells people when they ask what I am doing home. "She's awaiting news from Yale School of Drama," she'd love to say. "It's always been her first choice." I feel huge in my tent-like Indian-print batik gown. When I wore it back in high school, I felt like a sexy hippie princess. Now I feel more like a house. Or a hotel. An empty, abandoned hotel. Like a building that needs to be torn down and rebuilt. May that a wrecking ball crashes through the synagogue wall and takes me with it.

A familiar voice cuts through my screen of sugar. "Hi, honey." I look up to see my stunning Aunt Ellen, the youngest of my mom's three sisters, with the long, dark hair, the olive skin, and the prominent cheekbones. As she reaches to hug me, I keep a good foot between our bodies, like I always do with potential mothers, to reassure her that I don't really need her. "How are you?" she asks, nibbling on a scallop-edged cookie with chocolate sprinkles. It's a loaded question. Aunt Ellen knows that I know that she knows how well I am not doing.

"I'm okay," I say, quickly inserting the rest of my brownie.

"Maybe you'll come for dinner this week?"

"That would be great," I say, burning with guilt. Something to do with my lifelong wish to be with her family instead of mine.

It always felt like a betrayal of my mother. And the shame, well, that stems back to an unfortunate doody-related incident.

I was nine when my younger cousin and I were playing in their yard. I wanted to show her what a big shot I was and so I led her under a tree, pulled down my pants, squatted down, and made a doody. Her eyes went wide with amazement. I stood up, beaming—until my guilt overcame me and I ran to turn myself in. My Aunt Ellen calmly escorted me to the bathroom for a wad of toilet paper, followed me to the scene of my crime, then gently instructed me to scoop up the evidence. Then came the humiliating poop-walk from the yard back to the toilet. I can still see that wad of t.p. with the sad little doody swirling 'round and 'round in the white toilet bowl until it finally, *finally* disappeared.

Despite my adoration of and my trust in my Aunt Ellen, despite the ten-plus years since the event, I cannot wipe this humiliating memory from my brain. I am sure she's long since let it go. As someone who's been in therapy and dealt with her own childhood guilt, she probably understood my need to be rejected by her so that I might lessen my guilt about preferring to be with her. My aunt understood shit. My mother did not.

I have no memory of being toilet trained. Who does? I mean, I'm sure I must have been, right? But by whom? Did my mother just assume I'd learn from my sisters? Maybe that's why I was compelled to make a mess. To show my mom how much I needed her.

I was five and my parents were hosting a small dinner party. My mother rarely entertained, except for her three sisters and their families. It stressed her out. The house and everything else had to be per-fect. These guests must have been dentistry-related. Or from temple. The six of them were eating, and we kids were supposed to be in bed. But I wasn't in bed. I was on the toilet, trying to push one out. I pushed and I pushed but to no avail. Finally, being a resourceful little girl, I stuck my middle finger, the longest digit, up my ass to pull it out. I reached way up, delicately working my way past the various creases and crevices of my anus, until I came upon something solid. Hello, doody! With a twist of my hand, I dug that stubborn little poop right out. Mission accomplished. Then I washed up like a good girl. Although . . . something about shit makes it hard to wash away the smell.

My mother was shocked to see me appear by her side in my feet pajamas. It was a Friday, so of course she'd had her hair done that day, set and sprayed in a Jackie Kennedy '60s bob and pulled slightly back to frame her exquisite face made up just so. "Oh!" she said with a nervous smile. "What are you doing up?" I leaned in to whisper something in her ear. The guests smiled respectfully and continued talking amongst themselves. I gently lifted her hair on one side for full aural access, leaned in close, and whispered hard.

"Mommy," I said, bursting with pride, "I had to make a doody, but it was stuck inside so I reached in with my finger and I pulled it out!" My, my. Wasn't I smart? Wouldn't she be proud of her little girl? She instantly pulled her head back, with a slight look of disgust. She looked around the table. Down at my hand. Up at me. "All right," she said, "now go back to bed," then gave me a gentle shove towards the door.

This was not what good little Jewish girls did. I must have known how she'd react. I must have wanted her to know I was shit.

I don't know *what* my mother was thinking when she offered to take home the leftover vanilla sheet cake from Uncle Eli's party. She had to chop it in half just to make it fit in the freezer. She was helping out Aunt Rena, but she wasn't doing *me* any favors. But hey, what sugar problem?

I didn't want the cake when it was fresh, why do I want it frozen? It's beyond bland. It has no icing. No cream. No fun. But all that is beside the point. It's Monday morning. I have no life. The cake is here. And so I must have it.

Using a long, serrated bread knife, I hack off a good-sized chunk of the frozen slab. I hover over the wooden island in the middle of our beautiful, bright kitchen. Williams Sonoma copper pots hang above me on a circular ceiling rack. Italian hand-painted plates rest on delicate plate stands, never to be eaten off, only to be admired. This is a kitchen that, along with the rest of the house, will never meet my mother's expectations, even though it could easily be taken from a page of *Sunset*, the quintessential magazine of beautiful California living. I stand at the wooden island like a neurotic stork, one leg bent at the knee with my foot balanced up against the other knee, gnawing away at the tasteless chunk, slicing the tip of my tongue on the icy shards as I robotically leaf through a copy of *Sunset*. Every bite will be my last—until the next, and the next, I tell myself, flipping the magazine pages faster and faster. Pictures of charming poolside furniture, refreshing and healthy fruit salads, and smooth redwood pool decks swoosh by. I should be in our pool, the shimmering pool my father pays his hard-earned money to heat. I should be swimming laps. Hundreds and hundreds of laps. But swimming would involve the terrifying task of disrobing.

What am I doing? I was going to be the next "Funny Girl." When I was twelve I believed, no, seriously, I actually believed people would mistake me for Streisand. During the movie intermission I posed nonchalantly at the lobby refreshment stand, waiting to be recognized. My imagined fans would approach cautiously, so as not to disturb me. "Excuse me," they would softly say, visibly shaking with excitement. "Aren't you—Could you be—No, you couldn't—But wait—Maybe . . . *maybe* . . . are you . . . *Barbra?*"

I *smash* the magazine shut, determined to make a new start. Make my mess disappear. Not in the trash, of course. Not going to fall for *that* old trick. I glance out the window. A tall hedge separates our house from the neighbor's long driveway, which is dark and shaded by eucalyptus trees. They'll never notice a strewn cake. If they do, they'll never suspect it was from me.

Mimi and Bert's youngest. The talented one. I gather up the remainder of the mostly melted slab, step outside, tiptoe to the edge of our property, make sure the neighbor's silver Caddy is nowhere in sight, and then I fling that sucker up and over the hedge. It hits the driveway pavement with a soggy *thud!* and splatters down the concrete.

Driving to Dr. Bird's that afternoon I implore myself *not* to tell her about the cake toss. She does not need to know. "Well," I say, plopping down onto her couch, "I threw half a sheet cake onto our neighbor's driveway this morning."

She crosses her shapely calves and stares into me, serious-like. "What was going on?" she asks.

"Nothing. I just couldn't stop eating it. It wasn't even any good. I just had to get rid of it."

She pauses. Digesting. "How's the pain in your side?"

"It's not a pain. It's a cramp. And right now it's killing me, but it's my own fault."

"How so?"

"*Because.* I ate that idiot sheet cake, *that's why.*" She still doesn't get it. I hate her for not getting it, but I can't tell her this. I don't want to be thrown out.

"Were you feeling angry about something?"

"No! Not that I know of!" I'd better at least *attempt* to pretend to be open. "I mean, the only thing I'm angry about is that I can't seem to control what I put in my fucking mouth." Oh Lord. Now I've done it. I cursed in therapy. In the professional therapist's office. Seated on her velvet couch. But hey, I *am* paying fifty-five bucks for my fifty-minute session. The *least* I should be allowed to do is curse—except, my dad is the one footing the bill. But if I think about *that*, I will never utter another goddamn fucking word in therapy ever again.

"Do you want to talk about it?" she asks.

"Talk about *what*?"

"The food."

"No," I say shaking my head. "I really don't. Besides, what is there to say?" Round and round we go, filling in our remaining thirty-something frustrating minutes with no resolution in sight. Where do my feelings end and the food begin? When does a substance become addictive? How does a harmless cookie become a whole bag and then an entire night of wanting to kill myself? If I *really* wanted to change, maybe I'd tell Dr. Bird how I never take a shit. How I sometimes have to dig out my embedded crap. How I fear I might pierce a hole in my rectum and bleed to death, and no one will ever know unless they do an autopsy and then I would *really* be embarrassed.

"Before we stop," Dr. Bird says, "I'd like to offer you a suggestion."

"Okay . . ." I sigh. Finally, some practical advice. Some direction. Some "it."

"When I want a treat, I figure out exactly how many minutes of exercise it will take to work off the calories from that treat." Is she really saying this? "For instance, I love jelly donuts. And I know it takes seventeen minutes of tennis to work off one jelly donut."

Okay, first of all, I can't ba-*leeve* this educated, seemingly sophisticated woman would choose a jelly donut over a gooey, nutty bear claw, or even just a good old-fashioned plain. I'd be very hard-pressed to eat a spongy jelly donut, stuffed with nauseatingly sweet, fake, fruity jelly.

Second, doesn't she *get* that this isn't about calories, pounds, and scales? This is about life and death. Exercise always *sounds* great—in theory. Sure. Exercise. Great idea. Self-restraint. Of course! Why didn't *I* think of that? But exercise makes you feel. I can't tell my therapist I don't want to feel. Why am I even here if I don't want to feel? But I should be perfect. I shouldn't have to feel.

"Okay, well, thanks," I say, forcing a smile, wishing she hadn't offered that asinine advice. Then I head out the door.

Maybe now that I've spent fifty minutes in therapy I can spend fifty minutes in self-destruction.

The kitchen clock reads 3:15 when I get home. In about three hours my parents will return and I will have to pretend I am normal. I don't know what to do with myself. So I start in on the second half of the frozen cake.

I chop away, feeding the monster inside me. The mental spinning begins. *Fuck* Uncle Eli and his college drop-out comment. *Fuck* my shrink. She's just another clueless asshole. Yeah, I know, a junkie's mind plays host to a million excuses. Blame her! Blame him! Yeah, I know, food is different from drugs and booze. You have to eat. But sheet cake isn't food. Sheet cake is sheet cake. And the only thing this shit cake has going for it, health-wise, is the bit of hydration it offers from having been frozen. I've probably taken in more water with the melting ice than I drank all year.

I hack away, gobbling handfuls of the icy hunk. My tongue aches. I want to stop. I keep going. Stop! Cradling the melting slab in both hands, I rush downstairs to my room and pace back and forth across my rattan bedroom rug. Perched on the edge of my little bed, the cake in my hands, my eyes flit across my bookshelves cluttered with childhood crap. They focus on the framed gold seal hanging on the wall. I earned that seal in fourth grade after Mrs. Rodriguez called my mother to tell her I wasn't "working up to my potential." I remember it was a Friday, because my mom had her hair done that morning. She looked so elegant but so sad. Like she might cry. All because of me. In that moment I decided I would never just do better. Fuck better. I would be exceptional or nothing. I went ahead and earned that goddamn gold seal, the one given only to top students.

I chomp off one more bite of cake just in case it suddenly tastes good. Stop it. Stop it now. I run to the toilet and spit out the mouthful. Then I shove the rest of the cake in as well. What do I have to be so angry about? The cake is too wide to fit, so I use my bare foot to push it down, trying to break it in half with my big toe. It begins to fall apart into smaller chunks. I remove my foot and flush the toilet, hoping to accelerate the process, then watch the whirlpool of cake-muddied water swirl 'round and 'round. The toilet gurgles. Like the cramp in my side. The water begins to rise. I stand watching, fingernails to teeth. The water fills up, and up, then it spills over the toilet seat, flowing down onto the ancient, green-tiled bathroom floor. My mother *cannot* come home to this. I dash to the laundry room for a plunger. Gripping the long wooden stick, I thrust that black-rubber sucker smack into the eye of my hurri-cake with all the strength I can muster. I thrust it down. *Slish, slush.* Soiled water and swollen chunks of cake spatter about as I work that porcelain bowl. After all the schools, the tuitions, the positive feedback, and the endless cheering on of my unlimited potential, this is where I've ended up. Holding a shit stick dripping with cake.

CHAPTER 7

COOKIE MONSTER

Before things can get any messier at home, I call my Aunt Ellen to ask about coming to dinner. Then I ask if I can come to live. Just until I feel better. The guilt is enormous. I'm choosing my younger, thinner, hipper aunt and uncle over my own parents. But as long as I'm home I won't have a rat's chance of keeping my head out of the cookie jar. Besides, my parents should be relieved to be rid of me.

My aunt and uncle throw out the welcome mat and I move into my cousin Ronna's bedroom while she is off at college doing pre-med. Her younger sister, Karen, a moody adolescent, is either at school, in her bedroom, or out with friends. Living here, I am the only child I always wanted to be, with the fantasized mother I always wanted to have.

My aunt asks me to make a list of any special foods I'd like to have in the house. "Oh, I'm fine," I reassure her. "Maybe just some fruit, or some carrots." *Riiight.* Better yet, how 'bout just some water. That'll be fine. Really. Seriously, don't mind me. Just pretend I don't exist while I sack your entire pantry. That is where they keep the good stuff, in a tall, narrow cabinet next to the fridge. It's a spot I've patrolled for years. It always amazes me how people can live peacefully alongside peanut-butter cups and Italian biscotti. I can barely coexist with bread and butter, let alone chocolate-covered pretzel twists and red-licorice whips.

Normal people go to the store, buy food, bring it home, and put it away, and when they are hungry, they take it out and they eat it. Then go on with their lives. I've gotten very good at mooching off other people's supplies, then rearranging the leftovers to disguise my tracks. At least I'd like to think so. If it's not my food I am eating, then I'm not really eating it. Whenever I *do* grocery shop, I am compelled to eat everything right away for fear the food will just sit there, lonely, waiting, or maybe go rotten and have to be tossed out. Poor food.

Aunt Ellen and Uncle Len trust me. They are good to me. And yet, here I am on a Tuesday night, standing before their cupboard double-fisted with biscotti cookies spread with peanut butter. It's not really stealing. It's not like I'm a heroin addict taking their money to buy junk. I'm just eating their junk. It's okay with them. But sneaking makes me feel so shitty.

My mom calls a couple of times a week, usually at dinner. I try to sound happy but not too. I don't want her to feel rejected. It's too much to think about. I'll eat over it later. She knows I love her. She's just calling to hear my voice and see how I am. Really what I think she's calling about is to make sure I am still welcome in her sister's home. I wonder if my aunt tells her how I am doing. I wonder if she tells her about the sudden space in her cupboard. But Aunt Ellen is cool. Besides, she could never talk openly to my mom about how I finished off three-quarters of a box of Oreos. My mom is her older sister. Their generation doesn't talk like that. Anyway I'll bet my mom slips her money for all the damage she knows I am incurring.

I hope my aunt never told her about the backyard doody.

A job will set me straight. I need structure. I put in for a sales position at the cavernous Books, Inc. and am surprised when the straight-laced manager hires me right off the bat. Doesn't he see I am a raving maniac? But this is good. Working in a bookstore will ground me. The bookstore is safe, at least until lunchtime. For just beyond all the books lies . . . *the Stanford Mall!* The Stanford Mall, where there is so much sugar in the air you can run your finger along a building wall and use it to sweeten your coffee. Where classical music piped in through speakers hidden in potted ferns accompanies yuppie moms and lanky high school girls as they parade about the mall, their bright futures dangling ahead of them, just as mine once did.

I am bored, so mind-*fuckingly* bored in that bookstore my eyeballs swell with the tedium. I watch the big hand on the clock, waiting for it to strike the one, when I can make my break for lunch. I sit in the mall plaza, usually at one of the wrought-iron tables, eating my little Muenster-cheese sandwich on wheat bread that I have brought from my aunt's. After finishing every crumb I follow it up with a crisp apple or a juicy tangerine. There. What a nice lunch. Perfect. Time to get back. The thought of returning to three and a half more hours at my dead-end job is too much to bear. I clamp my jaw, priming myself as I make my way back, step by sugarless step. "I'll get a snack after work," I reassure myself, "like a normal person would do," then walk as if I am headed back to my job. I know where I am headed. To good ole Mrs. Fields. Just for two. Two nice, warm, innocuous cookies. That's what any regular person would have. This is the cookie of cookies. The perfect mix of sweet, chewy, crunchy, and crispy. The gooey, buttery cookie melts away, leaving caramelized brown-sugar crystals on my quivering tongue. Like the core of heaven has landed in my mouth. In a second the sugar begins its rapid course and bliss surges in. It saddens me to have to swallow. That's one bite less. So sad. But wait! A whole other cookie awaits me! Two cookies quickly become six, my daily wage inhaled practically all at once as I scurry back, the beast in my belly now placated. Sort of.

With less than five minutes left on my break, it's one last rapid detour to the Yogurt Shack. I wait on line, stuck behind a cluster of bubbly teenage girls clutching each other's arms in adolescent giddiness as they decide what toppings to get. I do my best to look like a regular person. God forbid the girls think I am some kind of freak. A flasher. A scary Semitic ogress.

Hmmm . . . I cock my head . . . What to have? A small vanilla? Yes. Perfect. Plain, no toppings.

"May I help you?" asks the gangly, pimply teenage boy behind the register, staring off indifferently.

"Yes . . . let's see . . . gosh . . ." I fight to appear calm. Harmless. Don't worry, young man, I want to say. I'm not crazy. I swear! As if everyone is watching me, wondering when I will flip out. My mother appears in the back of my mind, shaking her head. "I'll have a medium vanilla—actually, could you make that chocolate? Thanks! Oh, and with carob chips, please. Wait. On second thought, make that chocolate chips. Hey, live it up, right? And with peanuts. Great. Thanks!" The sales boy could care less what I eat. I'm just the anxious Jewishy lady, just one customer closer to clocking out, when he can pound cheeseburgers and fries and get home to math, meatloaf, and pounding his other meat as he thinks about the cute girl from English. Some sweet, naive schoolgirl who still believes the world is her oyster.

With three minutes left, I fast-walk through the mall, spooning in my cup of frozen heroin at a rapid-fire pace. It makes my throat freeze and my head ache, but my physical discomfort is eclipsed by the instantaneous blissful effect of the creamy manna. I am carried immediately to that place. That *anything is possible* place. Everything will be okay once I quit sugar. I'll get the dress in the Saks window. And the boots. I'll look amazing. As soon as I quit sugar I'll start wearing cool clothes, just like I did before I left home. I will quit, I say, frantically spooning in my last few bites. I will get back to the stage. I'll look awesome opening night when I greet my fans afterwards. "*You*," they will say, "are what the theatre is *meant* to be!" I'll fall in love. I'll have it all. Every last wish. Once I stop eating sugar.

The large outdoor clock by the lingerie shop reads seven minutes past two. Crap! I tear through the mall, averting my eyes from the hideous monster reflected in the windows of the Crabtree and

Evelyn bath shop and Ralph Lauren for Kids, where perky blonde mothers chat between strollers as they pick out flowery sundresses and athletic t-shirts for their perfect Palo Alto children.

Back at work, I attempt to rise above my self-loathing to be the perfect bookstore employee, especially since I am now nine minutes late. But alas, what goes up must, sadly, come down. By three thirty the bookstore air is thick and still. The only customers are a prim elderly woman dressed in a pastel suit and pearls and a couple of thirtyish moms in mini tennis skirts and visors. They chat as they wander through, picking up books they have no intention of buying, probably just killing time before school lets out. That's when it hits. The full-on blood-sugar free fall.

I weave down the aisles, trying to look busy, then steal into the ladies room and plop down on the toilet. Forehead in my hands. Eyes shut. Brain beating. Ears buzzing. Heavy pulse thumping up my belly. Head bobbing like a true junkie. If I could just . . . *lie down*. Lethargy and despair tug at my brow. I sink deeper, passing out cold over the toilet-paper holder. This might be worrisome if it weren't part of my everyday afternoon routine, but I've been here before. Many times. My secret, sick siesta.

Several minutes into the blackout, I jolt upright. Where am I? The bookstore. I'm on the bookstore toilet. I'm working at the bookstore. Get up! Get out! Fast! How long have I been in here? Five minutes? An hour? I have no idea. It was after three thirty when I came in. What time is it now? *What time is it?* It's got to be late. Maybe four. What is that on my chin? Drool? Oh no. That's bad. I wipe it off. Don't look in the mirror. I don't want to see. Just flip my hair so it looks nice. Pinch my cheeks. Wake up! Wake up! They're not paying you to sleep in the toilet! Okay, now straighten up, stand up, and slowly, quietly, open the door leading into the bookstore. Look around. Where's my boss? Where is he? Where *is* he? Shit. There he is. By the register. Does he know? Please don't notice me. Look down. Keep your head down. Meander down the aisle. Grab a few books. Straighten up a shelf. I'm good. I'm good. A good employee.

There you go. Breathe. I'm just a normal bookstore employee. Just doing my job. Atta girl. Oh, and there's a book about tennis—in the fiction section? What's *that* doing here? I'll fix that! I grab the book and walk purposefully back to the sports section. Let's see . . . by author . . . S . . . Se . . . *There* we go. Got it. Everything in its place. Uh-oh. He's looking at me. The boss. Look sharp. Smile and wave.

"Hey! Lemme know if you want me at the register, 'K?" A model employee. "What *time* is it, anyway?" I ask. That's what a normal employee would ask. Like I'm just so casual and together.

"It's—ah—four," he says.

"Cool! Thanks!" Oh my God. I was in there forever. Take a deep breath. Look alert. I wish I had a stick of gum or a mint to help me stay awake. Once I leave for the day, I'll scrape up enough change from the floor of my car for one last cookie. My run from the mall, out to my car, back to Mrs. Field's, then back to my car will do me good. 'Til then it's just a matter of forcing my eyeballs to stay open.

And then, something happens. My aunt and uncle have a dinner guest. It's Mr. Knoll, a friend of theirs. Mr. Knoll was also the only liberal, free-thinking teacher in my ultra-conservative right-wing elementary school. My sister Sarah had him in fifth grade at South Hillsborough Elementary School. She still talks about him. How she hated school until she had him. How he changed her way of learning. My mom loved him, too. He was a real humanitarian. A radical thinker. A real left-winger. He was also huge. Like, three-hundred-plus-pounds huge. But I never thought of him as being fat. That would be mean.

The doorbell rings and we all go to greet our guest. Mr. Knoll stands at the threshold as my aunt, uncle, and I stare in amazement. He is literally half the size of his former self.

"Wow!" exclaims my uncle. "Look at you!"

"You look wonderful!" says my aunt, laughing giddily.

"It's all right," Mr. Knoll says, chuckling. "Everybody has the same response." He gives my aunt a hug. My uncle reaches to shake his hand, and Mr. Knoll embraces him as well.

"You remember my niece, Lisa Kotin?" says my aunt. "Her sister Sarah was in your class at South."

"Of course!" says Mr. Knoll. And I get a hug, too. It's hugs all around.

It's not just his body that's changed. It's his whole demeanor. He once looked like he carried the weight of the world. Now he walks with a swagger, appearing festive in a bright-yellow, cashmere V-neck sweater. I wonder what Sarah would think of her altruistic mentor now, the gold chain resting on his exposed, hairy chest, spicy cologne wafting in his wake. He oozes positivity. Like he's been born again.

Over dinner he tells the story of how he lost the weight. The three of us sit chewing, fully engrossed. "I tried *everything*," he says. "Every diet, every plan. I even went so far as to sit naked in a bathtub filled, I mean *filled*, with donuts. I thought if I surrounded myself with donuts, I'd get over my obsession."

We all laugh. Even Mr. Knoll. I wonder if he filled the tub with donuts and then somehow crawled under them. Or did he climb in first and then dump bag after bag over himself? Was it a variety of donuts, or just one type? Glazed? Glazed with jimmies? Plain? I feel cruel picturing him reclining in a large porcelain tub, his colossal gut protruding up through the pastries as he recklessly inserts one deep-fried circle after another into his bearded maw. Maybe he got so excited his own eager cruller popped up through the hole of a powdered-sugar donut. I feel cruel because I get it. I really, really get it. Except now all I want are donuts. "But as I lay there," Mr. Knoll continues, "I started eating them. I couldn't stop. That's when I knew I was powerless." Powerless? What does he mean, *powerless*?

"So, what did you *do*?" my aunt asks, fully fascinated, crunching a radish. A quiet calm comes over Mr. Knoll's face.

"I found out about this wonderful organization: Overeaters Anonymous. OA. It's based on the twelve steps of Alcoholics Anonymous." Huh? What does alcohol have to do with donuts? "I went to a meeting and these beautiful, loving people welcomed me in. I sat there and I listened, and I found something out." He pauses—for dramatic effect, I suppose—and then he proudly proclaims: "*I* am a compulsive overeater!"

Wait.

Stop.

What did he say? *Compulsive overeater?* Those words. Those two words. I can't believe someone actually put those two words together. That's—that's me. Those words are me. *I* overeat compulsively. That's what I do. Was this a set-up? Did my aunt invite him to dinner so he could tell me about OA? No way. She's not like that. She would have told me. Anyway, who cares? This is exactly what I've been waiting for. A term. A diagnosis. This is amazing!

"So . . . how does it work?" I ask. "Just out of curiosity."

"I follow the program. Every morning I wake up and admit I'm powerless over food." There's that word again. I hate that word. I am not powerless. "Every day I turn my will and my life over to a higher power." Shit. So it's a God thing. I should have known. "It's about believing in a power greater than myself. Greater than my will. I go to OA meetings. The bottom line is I can't do it on my own. I tried and I tried with every single diet in the book. But as soon as I surrendered, I became abstinent." Wait. What?

"What do you mean, abstinent?" I pray he doesn't know why I ask. "I mean, you *have* to eat."

"Of course! I eat three weighed and measured meals a day and nothing in between. Not even a bite. Thanks to OA I've been abstinent a year and thirty-seven days, one day at a time. I feel alive again. I feel *sexual* again." Now, that's a little embarrassing. My uncle laughs nervously and shoves a wad of bread in his mouth. "But, most importantly, I have faith again." It's a little creepy. He sounds like such a Bible-thumper. But I've never heard anyone talk about food like this. Like it's a drug. Maybe I can just avoid the God part. That part is for the people who really need help. I just need to get my food in control.

"So . . . how do you find out about it?" I ask. "Again, just out of curiosity!"

"You just look up OA in the Yellow Pages and you call and get a recording of the meeting schedule. I go into the city because it's closer to my home. As far as I know, the closest meeting to here is Sunnyvale."

"Oh, okay," I say, like I'm blowing it off. But I can't wait until my aunt and uncle go to bed so I can pull out that phone book. Intervention or no intervention, God or no God, I am ecstatic to finally realize who I am. *I* am a compulsive overeater. *I exist.*

CHAPTER 8

THE FIRST BITE

"You have reached the Peninsula office for Overeaters Anonymous." Wow. They really *do* exist. The woman on the recording talks in a monotone. "Overeaters Anonymous is a program of recovery based on the twelve steps of Alcoholics Anonymous." I feel nervous. Like I'm a criminal, hovering in a corner of my aunt's kitchen, my ear pressed to the receiver. "Following is a list of OA meetings located in the San Francisco Peninsula. Wednesday at 7 p.m. there is a newcomer's meeting at First Presbyterian Church, 122 South Main Street, in Sunnyvale." Wednesday. That's tomorrow. I can do that. I should. I will. I hang up and help myself to a generous portion of the tiramisu I passed up at dinner. My last supper.

The seven o'clock meeting is just getting started as I enter the basement of the Sunnyvale church. There's a musty, stale, churchy smell. Can I really do this? Come on. I always do this. I jump right in. Maybe this time it's not such a great idea. Maybe I should have thought it through. No. I'm here. This is good. I need help. I keep my head down and slip into a brown-metal folding chair in the second tier of a large circle of large women. I feel bad noticing that facing me is a row of very large behinds. They bulge out through the backs of their folding chairs. That's a lot of tushie. I scan the room and see it is all women. Not that I'd expect to see men here. Maybe in the city, where Mr. Knoll goes. But not here in small-town Sunnyvale. It's all women, and they're all—can I say this—can I really say this—fat. Am I a fattist? One of those despicable assholes who judges fat people? I feel faint. Take a breath. It smells like bodies. Perfumed flesh against flesh. I feel claustrophobic and want to leave. My mother would be so ashamed if she knew I was here. She'd never be caught dead here.

Then it hits me.

My mother.

Her body.

My mother is—has always been—as long as I can remember—overweight.

Shit.

I mean, she's not *nearly* this fat. Please. She'd never *dream* of wearing sweats out in public. But what about all her dark, loose-fitting clothing? Or the fact that I can't remember the last time I saw her wear a bathing suit or go in the pool? Kinda . . . like . . . me. Me in my giant overalls that cover everything up. Me who hates wearing a bathing suit. *Hates it.* I always wondered why she never went in the pool. Never shows her arms, legs, stomach, or any part of her body other than her face—and even that is partially shielded by that great helmet of hair. But, there's no *way* she could have an eating problem—*is there?* How can someone so poised, so elegant, so sophisticated, have an eating problem? *Especially when none of us ever see her eat?*

Oh.

My.

My mother eats.

I've never seen her, I've never noticed, but she must. Of course she does. It makes perfect sense. I'm scared. There's a pit in my stomach. A great emptiness. I want to cry.

My mom. My poor mom. I had no idea. Don't think about it. Hurts too much. Way too scary. Put it out of my mind.

"Hi, I'm Marcie and I'm a compulsive overeater!" an energetic, robust fiftyish woman in stonewashed jeans and a baby-pink t-shirt says. The group resounds with a hearty "Hi, Marcie!"

Forced friendliness makes me squirm. And groups. I get this grinding feeling in my gut. "May I see the hands of any newcomers?" Marcie asks, gazing in my direction. All heads turn. All eyes on me. The new girl. The new, thinnish girl. What's *she* doing here? They have no idea how heavy I am inside. I creep my arm into the air and smile shakily. "Welcome!" Marcie says. "What's your name? First names only, please."

"I'm . . . Lisa?" I mutter, lowering my arm and slumping slightly in my chair to try and look more portly. The group responds with a "Hi, Lisa! Welcome!" I hope they don't devour me.

"Feel free to stick around after the meeting to ask questions," Marcie says. "In the meantime, keep coming back. It works if you work it." I nod and mouth the words "thank you." I abhor slogans and the lemmings who recite them. Come on. She's just trying to help. "Now everyone, please give a warm welcome to our speaker for this evening, Sandy M." Everyone applauds as a profoundly plump, pretty-faced, thirty-something gal waves from her chair, red-faced, beaming, taking in the approval.

"Hi, I'm Sandy and I'm a compulsive overeater!"

"Hi, Sandy!" the room belts out. This is *so* embarrassing. Oh, the shame.

"Thank you *so* much Marcie for asking me to share. I am so excited to be here and to tell you that today, thanks to all of you and my higher power and OA, I am celebrating one year of abstinence!" Everyone applauds. They hoot and holler. "And . . . ," she says, barely able to contain her excitement, "I've lost fifty-two pounds!" There is an audible gasp and then the room goes wild with applause and cheers. I don't get it. If it's a higher power thing, why are they applauding *her*? Shouldn't they be yelling, "Yay, God! Go God!" How could she have lost fifty-two pounds? Where did she even put those extra fifty-two pounds? Stop it. Stop it now. I can't help it. Her body is like my mom's. Yeah, but my mom was *never* fifty-two pounds fatter than that. *Ever.*

Shut up. Fattist. Elitist fattist.

Sandy proceeds to tell her tale. How she came to OA full of despair. How she'd sneak off from the hubby and kids to binge her way across town from one fast-food joint to the next. Well that's *definitely* not me. I've never even *tasted* fast food. Never even been to a drive-through. That's, like, serious overeating. Sandy tells how she'd hit three or four drive-throughs (*three or four?*), then continue to gorge on what she calls "deep-fried, round carbohydrates with a hole in the middle" and "soft, frozen carbohydrates." What the fuck is she talking about? Oh, I get it. You're not supposed to name specific foods. If she said *donuts* and *ice cream*, people would have to run out after the meeting and binge on those foods. But what about their higher power? If he's so powerful, can't he just erase the pictures of food from their brains? Some higher power.

I picture Sandy driving around with a passenger seat full of cheeseburgers, French fries, and milkshakes. Wrappers and empty bags litter the floor. As long as she's driving, she's not really eating. Too bad she has to actually get out of the car to buy those round carbohydrates with the hole in the middle and the soft, frozen carbohydrates. That's where the dark glasses come in handy. I picture her trudging from the car into her house, slipping off her sneakers, and crawling under a brightly colored zigzag afghan on the couch. She flips on the boob tube for *Days of Our Lives* and digs into a pound cake, alternating bites of the moist, buttery cake with spoonfuls of frozen Cool Whip and chocolate-fudge sauce straight from the jar.

I wonder what my mother did after dropping us off at school. One, two, three, four of us. I don't want to think about it. I don't want to picture her eating, shopping, and eating. I'm sure she never ate in the car. She's way too sophisticated for that. Or watched daytime TV. She'd never sink that low . . . would she?

"OA saved my life," Sandy says. "I'm just so grateful for my sponsor and my Grey Sheet food plan." Food plan? That's what I need. A food plan! I know I don't have a ton of weight to lose, but I *have* to get control of my food. "I know I'm one bite away from my next binge, so I try to take it a day at a time." Again with the slogans. Let's hear more about that Grey Sheet. "I try to let go and let God," she says. Good for her. Now *she* needs a God. I'm happy for her. "I just know that I'm powerless over food, and I pray to stay abstinent, one day at a time." I just pray for that Grey Sheet.

The meeting ends and everyone joins hands and recites a prayer. I just mouth the words to be safe; besides, I don't know them anyway. Afterwards I stand there awkwardly when a chipper, mannish woman in a navy-blue suit approaches me and sticks out her hand to shake. "I'm Barbara. Welcome."

"Thanks," I say. She gives me the once-over. I know what she's thinking—that I'm not heavy enough to be at this meeting—but I resist the urge to justify my presence, how I really do have an eating problem.

"This is what I tell all the newcomers," Barbara says. "The program works if you work it. I've been abstinent eighteen months and four days, a day at a time."

"Wow, that's so great!" Again, shouldn't I be congratulating her higher power?

"So, do you have any questions?" she asks.

"Well, actually, I *was* kind of wondering about that whole Grey Sheet thing."

"Oh, that's just a food plan. You'll get to that. First things first, I encourage you to take the first step. It says, 'We admitted we were powerless over food and that our lives had become unmanageable.'"

"Sounds about right!" I say.

"There are twelve steps of recovery. It's all in 'The Big Book' of Alcoholics Anonymous. We're like their sister organization. You just replace the word *alcohol* with *food*. Once you take the twelve steps, the obsession will be lifted. It works. It really does." Yeah, yeah, yeah. Just gimme the frickin' Grey Sheet.

"It sounds *amazing!*" I say. "So . . . do you think I could just see it?"

"Of course! Marcie has copies to buy over at the table."

"No, I mean, that Grey Sheet thing."

Barbara exhales, looking distressed. She isn't making this easy. I'm probably going to have to buy that frickin' book before she'll give me the diet. "I mean, I definitely want to get the book. I just don't have the money right now. Can I . . . get it next time?"

"Sure," she says.

"Oh, that's great. In the meantime, I'd love to get started with something. . . ."

Barbara scowls and walks over to the literature table, then returns and hands me a printed white page.

"Oh, thank you *so* much," I say, wondering why it isn't gray. I want to read it so bad, but that would be rude. She'll know that all I care about is the diet.

"Well, anyway, here's my number," Barbara says, handing me a scrap of paper. "Remember to call before you take the first bite. Keep coming back."

"Thank you so much. I will!"

I'm so paranoid, I don't even let myself read the Grey Sheet when I get in my car in the church parking lot. One of the ladies might see me and they'll know that's what I really came here for. Like I'm some kind of swindler. I drive several blocks, then park the car along the El Camino to have a look. And there it is. Plain and simple. My new cure. Breakfast: 1 protein, 1 fruit. Lunch: 1 protein, 1 vegetable, 1 finger salad, sugar-free dressing optional. Dinner: 1 protein, 1 vegetable, 1 salad, sugar-free dressing optional. Black coffee or tea, diet soda, or water anytime. And that's it. No carby carbs. No fatty fats. And *no* sugar. It's severe. It's extreme. It's perfect. I'm going to follow this food plan for the rest of my life. Then I notice I am parked right in front of the all-night Happy Donuts.

I drive back to my aunt's with a renewed sense of hope. On the seat next to me is my new savior, my Grey Sheet, tucked safely beneath a quickly dwindling bag of deep-fried, round carbohydrates with a hole in the middle. My last, last supper.

The following morning I awaken, nauseous and hung over from my grand-finale binge but energized with my new plan for eating. I enter the kitchen fully armed, Grey Sheet in hand. My aunt is having coffee and reading the *New York Times*. "How was the meeting, honey?" she asks. I'd told her I was going before I went out. Luckily my uncle was playing tennis so I didn't have to tell him, too. Something about telling a man I'm in OA feels embarrassing. Like he's seeing my privates.

"Good!" I say. "I'm excited. I got this new food plan. I think it's going to be perfect."

"Oh, I'm so glad," she says and again offers to shop for me if I put together a list. Then I jump right in with my first abstinent meal: one hard-boiled egg and one green apple. Great. Time to pack my lunch. Not only will I get skinny again, but think of all the money I'll save. My aunt lends me a small postage scale and a measuring cup. By the time I get to work at the bookstore, my belly is crying for something sweet, but I clench my fists and don't give in. Just some water from the Stanford Mall water fountain. Delicious.

At lunch I warm myself in the beautiful sun, savoring my quarter pound of sliced turkey and half cup of chopped carrots and celery. Eating takes about, oh, six minutes. With a whole fifty-four minutes remaining, I browse the mall, window shopping and scribbling down ideas for theatre pieces. There's a small line in the yogurt shop. Poor people. That yogurt may taste mighty good now, but they'll have to live with themselves afterwards. Not me. Never again.

Three o'clock, the bomb hits. Hunger mixed with withdrawal mixed with terror. I white-knuckle my way until five thirty, then make a beeline for my car. Don't take the first bite. Don't stop driving no matter what. Don't breathe. Don't. Don't take the first bite of creamy, cheesy risotto rice offered to me by my aunt at dinner. "Would you like some?" she asks, trying not to stare at my plate where a can of naked tuna sits atop a cup of undressed shredded lettuce, a cup of steamed, plain broccoli on the side.

"Oh, no thanks. But it looks delicious!" I feel powerful. I don't even *want* their food. I feel clean. Light. I can do this. This is easy. For the first time in months, maybe years, later that night, as I disrobe into my nightgown, I am not afraid to look down at my body. After I've been bingeing, I'm too scared to look at my body for fear it will have gone blimp. My fear of fat is like the fear of a disease. One day clean and I already feel better. I feel thinner. Clear-headed. The storm is passing.

"Good night, honey," my aunt calls from the hallway outside my room.

"G'night!"

The house is dark and quiet. I'm hungry. I should drink some water. Get it from the bathroom. Do *not* go in the kitchen. But the kitchen water tastes better. Bullshit. But it does. Besides, I'm starving. Water will fill me up. I descend the stairs and tiptoe into the kitchen so the food won't hear me, averting my eyes from the cookie, cracker, and candy cabinet. In that cabinet is a world of pain. I fill a glass and run back up to my room. If I'm asleep I can't eat. Only eight hours until my cup of plain yogurt and sliced nectarine. Head to the pillow. Lights out. Made it.

How the fuck in God's name will I ever keep this up?

Day two is a full-on white-knuckler. Dinnertime, my aunt, uncle, and I have just sat down to eat (theirs: pasta pesto, garlic bread, and salad; mine: a quarter-pound roast turkey, plain, steamed cauliflower, and naked salad) when the phone rings. My aunt answers and I can tell by her voice that it's my mom. Every time she calls, which is about every five or six days, usually at dinner, I feel so guilty. I want her to think I am doing well, but

I want her to know I am suffering. I want her to know I am taken care of, but I don't want her to feel rejected. "Here she is," my aunt says, and hands me the phone.

"Hi, Mom!" I say, pulling the receiver around the corner and into the living room. "How are you guys doing?"

"Oh, we're just fine," she says. There's that strain. That silence. What is she thinking? "How are you doing?"

"Good! I'm good! Oh, hey, so, I didn't know Aunt Ellen and Uncle Len were friends with Mr. Knoll, you know, from South?" Should I really tell her about OA? Is that okay?

"Oh, yes. Yes they are."

"Well they had him over to dinner the other night. You wouldn't believe it, Mom. He's lost like a ton of weight. He's doing so well. He looks great!" I hope she feels included.

"Oh, well that's wonderful."

"I know! But anyway, he told me about this amazing program he joined. I mean, it's free and everything, but . . . it's all about dealing with food problems. It's called—" Stop. Don't do this. She'll know OA is connected to AA. Then she'll really worry. Fuck it. *Tell* her. She's my *mother.* Out with it! "It's called Overeaters Anonymous, but I thought I'd give it a try and . . . it's already helping, Mom. I mean, I feel like I'm finally doing what I need to do. I'm really excited. I really need help with this."

Silence. Her disapproval is deafening.

"How is your job at the bookstore?" she asks. What did I expect?

"Fine. I mean, it's fine for now."

"Well, I'm sure when you're ready, you'll move on."

We both know she's not just talking about the job.

"I'm sure," I say. I wonder if there is any of that pasta pesto left.

After the call, I gag down my turkey, cauliflower, and salad— hold the fucking dressing—and then I turn in early, just to be safe. Starving in my bed, the catcalls from the kitchen cabinet come fast and furious. Shut the fuck up, you cookies. Go fuck yourself, you pretzels and red licorice.

I wonder if my mom is eating.

Day three, I wolf down my hard-boiled egg and orange for breakfast, pack up my weighed-and-measured tofu, raw carrots, and an apple for lunch, and head to work. The morning is excruciating. The gut gnawing unrelenting. I feel numb. Excited. Scared. Horny. Nothing lasts. Why not destroy myself now? Hold on. Don't take the first bite. Pray for abstinence. Pray to whom? For what? The ghost of Mrs. Fields wafts in over the cash register. I gobble my lunch in less than four minutes, then take a dry-drunk stroll through the mall. Back at work I am straightening out the Performing Arts section when I come across a collection of Samuel Beckett plays. A biography of Charlie Chaplin. A Martha Graham Dance Company coffee-table picture book. I will never be these artists. Not even close. A cute guy comes into the store. He's probably gay. Or engaged. Or something. I'll never find a man. What *time* is it? Five whole minutes until my break. Am I *crazy?* I am *not* taking a break. I don't *dare* leave the store. Not unless it's for a phone call. I should call that OA Barbara woman. No way. I am not calling a stranger. Especially her. We have nothing in common. Fine. I'll just take a walk. Oh, no you don't. Come on . . . it's just a *walk.* I have to be able to walk. This is ridiculous. I should be able to control myself. I don't even want Mrs. Fields. This is nuts. Nuts. Chocolate chips. Stop it. Shut up. It's all in my head. If it's all in my head, then I should be able to decide to have just one cookie. Just one! I'll savor it. I'll use my entire break to eat it. Watch me.

I watch myself go from crystal-clear, weighed-and-measured perfection to all-out mania. Down go the cookies. One through ten. All in less than the three minutes it takes to return to work. Thank you, sugar. Thank you *so* much. I can breathe again. Feelin' great. Feelin' fine. See? No problem.

CHAPTER 9

WILL WORK FOR SUGAR
(AND SEX)

I want what I want when I want it. Especially since I have once again moved back home.

I was not kicked out of my aunt's. I kicked myself out before they could do it. Not that they would have. My cousin was returning from college for the holidays and needed her bedroom, but my aunt offered me the couch in the study. I just assumed my aunt and uncle had had enough of me.

But I can't stay home or I will die. I'd love to move to San Francisco. It's supposed to be great for theatre. If I'm going to move out, I'll need another job. But what can I possibly do?

Maybe I should finally put all that mime training to good use and stand out on a street corner like the great mime Robert Shields. *He* ended up marrying his mime partner and they got their own TV show! But working the crowd takes real guts. What if I run out of ideas? I *could* just do the robot and stand there frozen, changing poses every few minutes. People are suckers for that shit. Except . . . the last time I did that was at the Renaissance Pleasure Faire, and this creepy, tiny man in a velvet jester costume wouldn't leave me alone. He knocked me down and started humping my leg. The crowd roared. I didn't want to break the fourth wall, so I acted like it was part of my routine. I finally robot-moved my way up off the ground, took a robot bow, and robot-walked away.

Maybe I should go back to art modeling. When I did it in Minneapolis, the art teachers always praised me for my "exotic" features. Maybe someone will see me and want to cast me in a play. I just have to make sure I don't binge beforehand and fall asleep on the job. Drool streaming down my cheek. How embarrassing. Plus the pay sucks. Shit. What will I do? I will not sit behind a desk. No way. I need something active. Like dancing. Yes! I'm a trained dancer, after all. Dancing would be great. But where? How?

Driving home from an OA meeting in the city, I can't stop thinking about cannolis. I'll detour home through North Beach and stop for a latte. Just a latte. With one Sweet'N Low it's the perfect treat. But parking in North Beach is the worst. So I drive down Columbus Avenue and park at the bottom of the hill. It's a little seedy, but the walk back up will do me good.

A sign in the window of a small, black, boxy building reads "Exotic Dancers Wanted." Huh . . . I'm exotic. I'm a dancer. I could totally dance exotically. Especially if I'm getting paid. There are no windows, so I can't see in. That's okay. Theatres don't usually have windows. I should go in. I tug open the black-metal door and step inside, blinded by the contrast of the pitch-black interior after the glare outside. The music is so loud I feel it in my chest. "Ah, ha, ha, ha, stayin' alive. Stayin' alive." I can't see a thing, but I can smell. There's a yeasty, spilled-beer smell. At least I think that's beer. In a minute my eyes adjust. There are little round tables scattered about with several people seated. Mostly men, I think. There's also a smallish crowd of men seated at the bar. They stare up at the stage where half-naked girls writhe and jiggle. Oh. Shit. So *that's* what this place is. Well what did I think? That it was some kind of Martha Graham modern-dance club or something? I mean, it's not like the girls are fully naked or anything. They've got costumes on. Fishnets, lacy leopard bras, high heels. They're go-go dancing. Sure. Go-go dancing is just . . . dancing plus acting sexy. I can do that. I'm a performer. I can totally act sexy while I dance. Especially if the pay is good.

This could be my ticket.

One of the girls, or, women—she has so much makeup on I'm not sure *what* she is—wraps her leg around a pole and rubs. Now *that* I won't do. I draw the line. That's okay. They can't make me rub my crotch up that pole—can they? Besides, I've got plenty of great dance moves. This is a great opportunity. I'll show these men they can reach higher. They'll be so enthralled with my dancing, they'll forget all about the naked part.

I sidle over to the bar where a small, pock-faced man in a dark sports coat sits perched on a stool. The way he keeps looking around and talking with the bartender makes me think he runs the joint. "Hi!" I practically yell, enunciating every word so he can hear me over the racket. "Do you work here?"

"Yeah. Why?"

"I just— I saw the sign. I was wondering if you're still looking for—um—dancers?" He looks me up and down in my flowing flowered skirt and cowboy boots. What? Cowboy boots are sexy.

"You got any experience?" he asks.

"Oh, yeah, I mean, I've danced a *lot*." Modern, ballet, Yemenite, Eastern Indian . . .

"What's your name?"

"My name? Oh . . . my name—" I can't tell him my name is Lisa. It sounds so mundane. "Roxane," I say. "I'm . . . Roxane." Oh, God. Now I'm a hooker.

"Well, Roxane," he says. "It's pretty quiet today if you wanna take a turn."

"Oh. You mean . . . now?" What do I think he means? Oh well. I'm here. May as well give it a shot. "I mean—Sure! Thank you! That'd be great!"

"Leave your stuff in the dressing room and come out when you're ready. I'll signal you for a turn."

"Okay, thanks!" I say and head to the dressing room. I should be auditioning for the San Francisco Mime Troupe, not here. What would my parents say? Don't even go there. Anyway, they'll never know. They're thirty miles away. Alone in the dressing room, I empty the contents of my wallet into my purse to scatter the evidence. Not because I have any money to steal. I just want to make it harder for someone to find my license. They might see where I live, drive to Hillsborough, and tell my parents I am auditioning in a strip club in the city. That's crazy. Why would anyone do that? I don't know. But in place of my driver's license I put a scrap of paper with "Roxane Moore" and a fake phone number scribbled on it. Yes, I do that. Then I dig out a hair band and pull my mane into a high ponytail off to the side. Very sexy. I'll keep my jean jacket on until I step on stage, like it's part of my act, then remove it for the big reveal. Perfect.

I stand nervously at the edge of the bar and await my cue. It's just an act, I tell myself. I'm just a girl playing a girl auditioning as a stripper with no intention of stripping. Just a desire to dance. Donna Summer sings, "Lookin' for some hot stuff, baby, this evenin'. I need some hot stuff, baby, tonight." The boss taps me on the shoulder and motions for me to take my turn. Here goes nothing. I climb three narrow stairs at the end of the bar and step on stage. Keeping my eyes half-shut, just enough to see the lip of the bar so I don't fall off, I begin to dance. Sort of. I rock my hips right to left, writhing my arms around my torso. Still not looking at the audience, I remove my coat and toss it playfully aside. Then I really start to dance. Mostly in place. I am deep inside the music. In my head I look amazing. It's just me and Donna Summer up on that stage. I imagine the men staring up in amazement. They've never seen anyone dance like this. I am transforming them. They will never be the same.

Braving it, I open my eyes. There are the faces. Snickering. They aren't supposed to be snickering. *What* are they saying? Oh, I get it. They want me to take my clothes off. I can't take my clothes off. But apparently that's what they want. What do I do? Then it comes to me. I begin to mime-strip. Pouting sexily, I mime-outline my body with my hands as if to present my voluptuous womanly form. I mime-slither out of my shirt, swinging it 'round and 'round, then mime-fling it into the audience. They hoot and holler, jabbing each other in the ribs. I mime-remove my skirt, whipping it around and swinging it out, then mime-flaunt my imaginary rack, shimmying it from right to left. More laughter. Heads nod in approval, knees are slapped. I'm a hit! Then I see the manager. Not laughing. Shaking his greasy head, he makes a throat-cut gesture with his index finger. I scoop up my jacket and shimmy off stage, smiling and holding my head high all the way to the dressing room. I'm better than this.

I grab my stuff and head for the door, using my sleeved elbow to push it open and not touch where the customers' hands have been. I hope the two men walking out behind me don't follow me and rape me. What made me think I could do this? Who do I think I am? I'm just going to have to waitress like every other normal performer. I *hate* waitressing. I am a *terrible* waitress. In my first and only waitress job I was working the lunch shift at this Italian joint in Minneapolis. The place was mobbed. I was so distracted thinking about all the other things I should be doing—dancing, acting, writing—I wasn't watching where I was going, and as I exited the kitchen into the dining room my foot got caught on the carpet and I dropped the entire tray of ten steaming hot plates of rigatoni. I finished my shift and then I quit. No more waitressing.

What will I do? What can I do? Maybe I should just work in a health-food store. Seems like the logical choice. There's Real Foods on Polk Street. There's bound to be some cute, straight health-food guys who shop there. Because I really, really have to find a man. A man will be my motivation for leaving home and cutting the cord once and for all. I put in for a job and two days later I am called in for an interview. The manager is a kind, bearded man who appreciates the fact that I am an artist. He offers me a position. When can I start? Monday, I say. That's three days away. Just enough time to detox from sugar, clear my brain, and be ready to begin my new life.

As I exit the store I feel elated. Hey, I got a job! In a health-food store! For minimum wage! Crap. I should have at least *tried* to do theatre. But I shouldn't have to try. I should just make it on undeniable talent and charisma alone.

I want what I want when I fucking want it.

There's a butterscotch blond walking in the Polk Street crosswalk toward me. Without thinking I blurt out, "Excuse me?" as we pass. He stops. "Sorry, you just look so familiar." He really does. He looks like a guy I could instantly imagine going to bed with. That makes him familiar, right? He quickly takes me in. My long hair. My flowing, batik Indian hippie skirt. I guess I pass the test because the light turns green and he grabs my hand and pulls me to his side of the street. How gallant. "Sorry," I say, "I just thought I knew you."

"Well," he says, cocking his head, "now that you've met me, maybe you *do* know me."

"Maybe . . . ," I say, suddenly wary. But I can't walk away. He's way too cute.

His name is Jack. He's just graduated from the U of M in Ann Arbor. Says he just moved to "Frisco" two weeks ago. Oh no. Frisco again. But wait! He says he's here to study mime! "You're kidding?" I squeal. "*I'm* a mime!"

"Really?"

"Yes! I've studied and performed all over the place. I'm, like, a mime!" I don't usually flaunt this fact. But it's a good in. What if he becomes my boyfriend? A job *and* a boyfriend all in one day! We could be the next Shields and Yarnell!

"Well," he says, "maybe you can show me the ropes!" He dorkily tugs an imaginary rope. Oh well. We can't all be Marcel Marceau–worthy. "Want to take a walk?"

"Um . . . sure!"

As we stroll he chatters on. He's kind of all over the place. Kind of—can I say it?—boring. But I can't just leave. I'm in too deep.

"My sister lives here," he says, pointing to a super-fancy high-rise. "I'm crashing with her. Wanna come up?"

"S—sure!" If it's sweet, I'll eat it.

Riding the elevator to the sixth floor, I am relieved to learn his sister's place is a front unit. If I need to scream for help, pedestrians passing by will have an easier time hearing me.

In the bedroom Jack clears the multiple pillows from his sister's king-sized bed with one swift sweep of his arm. In a flurry he's down to his boxers and I've removed my skirt, and he's dry-humping me on the rococo-style bedspread. His tongue jabs into my mouth. It's too wet and too deep, but I don't want to offend him, so I pretend I like it.

Five minutes later he jumps to his feet. "Want to see my sister's gun?" he asks, dashing to the bureau.

"Um . . . wow . . . sure." Okay. *Calm down.* It's his *sister's* gun. She's probably gorgeous. She probably has men chasing her all over the city. Of *course* she has a gun. I wish *I* were so hot I needed a gun.

Jack rifles through a messy lingerie drawer and pulls out a small but honest-to-goodness gun. Should I scream? Now? He slips his finger through the trigger and hops back up on the bed, bouncing up and down and twirling the gun on his index finger like a disco porn star. I'm as good as dead. Luckily he has the attention span of a gnat, so I wait for him to bounce off the next wall and save my ass. "Want to take a ride on my hog?" I don't know what a hog is, but I'll do anything to get the fuck out of here.

"Sure!" I say. He drops the gun back in the drawer—phew—and we head out. Going down the elevator, I jokingly ask him what a hog is.

"My hog! My bike!"

"Oh . . . you have a bike?"

"My *motorcycle!*"

My father put the fear of God in us about motorcycles. They are right up there with prostitution and heroin. But if I don't ride with Jack, he may go back and get the gun and shoot me. At least if we're in public I can signal for help.

We ride up and down the streets of Frisco, then all the way up to Coit Tower. Thank God there are tourists. They'll save me if I need it. This guy is mad. I'm scared. I want to go home. I'd better cut this off in public, just in case he goes nuts. Worse comes to worse, I'll just run all the way back to my car. "You know what?" I say regretfully. Biting the bullet. "I'm so sorry but . . . I'd better get back."

"Oh, okay," he says. "I'll take ya back." I'm so relieved. Fuck him.

He bikes me back to his building and I reassure him that I can walk to my car from there. He asks for my number (oh good, he's not rejecting me), and I scribble it on a scrap of paper (even though I don't really want to hear from him again). He ends up calling me a couple of times, but I blow him off. Even *I'm* not that desperate.

Finally, back in the safety of my car, I want Chessmen. Crunchy, buttery Pepperidge Farm Chessmen shortbread cookies. I can't get to a 7-Eleven fast enough. I can't rip into the bag fast enough. Exiting the store, I am not even back at my car and I'm already three out of four tiers down. Ahhhh . . . bliss . . . sweet relief. Thank you, sugar.

I call home from the pay phone. I'm so late. It's almost dinnertime. My mother answers sounding worried. "Hello?"

"Collect call from Lisa Kotin. Will you accept the charges?" Of course she will.

"Hi, Mom," I say.

"Where are you?"

"I'm in the city. I'm fine. Sorry it's so late . . . but . . . so . . . I got a job, Mom. They want me at Real Foods."

"Oh, *congratulations!*" she exclaims, her voice so brimming with hope it embarrasses me. I mean, it's a fucking health-food-store job. "You see that? You can do anything you put your mind to."

"Thanks," I say, staring down in shame. Because all I really care about is finishing that final tier of Chessmen.

CHAPTER 10

MY ART

On Passover, I down four sheets of chocolate matzoh. I'm not talking chocolate-covered matzoh. I'm talking solid-milk-chocolate matzoh. Like I said, my mother doesn't fuck around.

The next morning I am halfway through a box of plain matzoh at the kitchen table. Plain matzoh is my version of methadone after all the chocolate. Straight from the box. I take a piece. Spread some butter. Sprinkle salt. Eat. Take a piece. Spread some butter. Sprinkle salt. Eat. There is virtually no nutritional value to matzoh. And it's also about the most constipating food on the planet. Take a piece. Spread some butter. Sprinkle salt. Eat. Butter. Salt. Eat. Butter. Salt. Eat. As long as I am crunching, I don't have to think about what I am going to do with my life.

I grab a magazine. Anything to distract. *Sunset?* Fuck *Sunset.* Fuck the beautiful life. The *Jewish Bulletin?* Hell no. Not a Jewish magazine. What kind of a Jew am I? A self-hating Jew, that's what. I am so going to hell. I'm already in hell. Oh what the hell. I flip through the *Jewish Bulletin.* It's all black and white and guilt provoking. But hold on—what's this—what's this ad? It's for a theatre festival. A Jewish theatre festival. Next month. In New York. At Marymount Manhattan College. It looks great. It sounds wonderful. I *miss* theatre. It's the only thing I ever knew I absolutely wanted. This festival can be my goal. I'll write a new solo piece. I haven't written a piece since I mimed a science lecture last summer at the Celebration Mime Theatre in Maine. I played a stern, dried-up science professor who is giving a talk on the splitting of atoms when her mind wanders and suddenly her lecture becomes interwoven with mimed flashbacks from a love affair that also went splitsville. And hey—the festival is at the same time as my New York University audition!

Yes, NYU could very well be the third stop on my college carousel. After much prodding from my mom, I've decided finishing school is the answer to everything. This time it's either California Institute of the Arts, Barnard College, or the NYU School of the Arts Experimental Theatre Program, where I imagine I'm a shoo-in. Unfortunately, I still have to audition. The good news is, if I audition during the same trip as the theatre festival and I blow the audition, I can tell myself: I don't need school. If my performance flops, I can tell myself: So what? I'm not a real working artist *yet*. I'm just a student. It's an addict thing. Always have Plan B at the ready. And never, ever commit.

"Marymount Manhattan College, may I help you?"

"Yes, I'm calling about the Jewish theatre festival. I was wondering if you are all booked. I mean, can I still submit something to perform?"

"Well, yes, we are all booked, but if you have something you'd like to perform, you're more than welcome to come set up in a corner of the theatre basement."

"Really? I could just . . . do that?"

"I don't see why not. I mean, we can't provide you with a tech crew—"

"Oh, that's fine! I can do my own tech!"

"Okay. Oh, and we can't provide any special lights."

"Hey, that's fine. As long as there's *some* light."

"Oh, and we can also provide some chairs."

"Well that is great! I mean, are you sure? Because I'm coming from California—"

"There shouldn't be a problem."

"Oh, God, that's so great!" Shit. Don't say "God" to the guy in charge of a Jewish theatre festival! "Thank you so much! What's your name anyway. I mean, just in case."

"Josh."

"Oh, well, Josh, thank you so much! I'm Lisa, by the way. Lisa Kotin. Thanks again."

"You're welcome. Good luck."

This is the other me. The me that doesn't want to die.

I call my cousin Annie, from my dad's side. Annie lives in NYC and offers me her couch when I'm in New York. I adore my cousin. She's six years older than me, but we get along great. She's a tall, dark beauty with a wicked sense of humor—especially when it comes to our family. She says she can't wait to see me, and to see me perform. Neither can my friend Samantha, who now lives in Manhattan. Samantha, too, has found OA. This is the girl who, back when we were in middle school together, was so popular even my uber-cool sister Sarah wasn't included in her posse. Back then Samantha and I had nothing in common. She was a hot cheerleader, and I was a skinny dweeb. Seven years later, I ran into her at Sarah Lawrence College when I was drowning in Entenmann's and loneliness. She'd put on weight. There was pain in her eyes. We ended up sharing our sugar-bingeing problem with one another. We also shared a love of the stage. I couldn't believe this Hillsborough untouchable also had an eating problem. If *she* had it, it *must* be real.

I am inspired. Like a kosher phoenix I rise up out of the matzoh crumbs, dump out the last three sheets of matzoh crackers, grab the scissors, and start cutting up the box to make a larger matzoh-box prop. I am hunched. I am old. I'm a little old Jewish lady. A

widow. I live alone. I'm coming home, walking up the stairs to
my tiny tenement apartment on the Lower East Side of Manhattan, schlepping my paper bag of groceries. Schlepping. See? I'm
already getting into the Jewish mood. I wear an old dress and a
black shawl wrapped around my head. A babushka. I come into
my little apartment. Put down the grocery bag. Unload the bag.
A can of soup. A bag of noodles. A carrot. The now enlarged
matzoh box. I'll have a matzoh. Just a little nosh. I open the box
and suddenly there is music. Klezmer music. Startled, I slam
down the lid and back up. What was *that?* Must have been my
imagination. Try again. I slowly lift the lid and . . . more music.
I slam it shut—but then, I must try again. I must find where this
music comes from. I have not heard music in twenty years. Not
since my Joseph died. Slowly I lift the lid. . . . The music gets
louder. Fast and joyous. The lid is open. I stand. I listen. I start
to move. Left . . . right . . . I begin to sway back and forth, transforming younger and younger. I lower my babushka onto my
shoulders like a shawl, loosen out my hair. I am a young woman.
I am dancing at my wedding. Spinning. Spinning and laughing
and full of joy. What joy, like I haven't known in decades. There
are only seven people in my Marymount Manhattan basement
corner audience, including Samantha and Annie, but it may as
well be seven hundred. My audience is with me. They laugh and
they feel me. They are with me every step. I spin and I spin and
I spin and then . . . the music stops. It ends. Silence. I am old
again. Old and alone. I rush to the box. Close and open. No
music. Again. Close and open. No music. But what is this inside
the matzoh box? A set of ancient candlesticks with two white
Sabbath candles. I draw them up and behold them. I strike a
match and light the candles. And then softly, sweetly, the music
returns. A smile creeps across my face. I freeze. Take my bow.
They rise to applaud. They love me. This is it. It's the love I feel
when you are with me on stage. You are with me as I transform
the moment with my body and my voice. I am fully present. For

a few fleeting moments, I am in control. Of myself. Of the audience. All by letting go and expressing myself. It's the only thing better than sugar.

The magic continues the following morning when I nail my NYU audition. Afterwards Samantha and I meet in Central Park for lunch. We each have the same: a green apple and a plain yogurt, with a packet of Sweet'n Low to mix in. Samantha praises me for my courage and talent. She tells me I have "it." And she's coming back to San Francisco for a summer theatre workshop in Berkeley. "You should do it!" she says. "You have to!" How can I not?

CHAPTER 11

WALKING CHOCOLATE BAR

It's hard to concentrate when there's sugar in the room. He's seated in the back of the class, watching me perform a solo improv about being stuck inside my body. Everyone's laughing. I know I'm a hit. I can feel it. I can feel him. I'm secretly showing off for him. Pulling out my best moves. It shouldn't matter if he likes me. I'm not here for him. I'm here for me.

Samantha doesn't like her stepbrother James. She hasn't come out and said it, but I know she thinks he's a jerk. She's annoyed he signed up for the performance workshop. I admit, he seems immature. He's just a year or two younger than me. But he's seriously scrumptious. A perfect mix of preppy and bohemian. Tall and lean with buttery skin, clothed in a slightly rumpled, untucked, pink, tailored Ralph Lauren shirt, faded blue jeans with the knees worn out. He has a habit of running his tongue smoothly across his front upper teeth, which always makes me shiver slightly, even though he's probably just moistening his mouth from all the cigarettes.

He also told Samantha he thinks I am "it."

Me. I am it.

He's going to be very, very hard to resist.

I finish my piece, take my seat, and sneak a glance his way. He's grinning at me, so sweet and fresh. Soon it is his turn. Please let him be good. Legitimize my crush. His work is amateurish and juvenile. He wears a relentless self-satisfied smirk even though no one else is laughing. But he's new at this. He's probably shy. Give him a break.

For the next three days I either make meal plans with Samantha for after class or I slip away fast so as not to be tempted by James. The energy between us is palpable, but I must not indulge. I am here to work. Then it is Friday, the day of the after-class potluck at our teacher's Berkeley home. Potlucks are like a food addict's invitation to binge. I wouldn't mind if I could just show up, fill a doggy bag, and go. If I didn't have to engage or interact, I'd be fine. To make matters worse, Samantha has to work, so I'll be on my own. And I'm sure there will be a certain walking chocolate bar hanging around. How will I avoid him? How will I not pick him up—or any other dessert?

I stop at a liquor store for a (very) cheap bottle of wine, then spend my last dime on a Snickers. For energy! I park the car, pop in the last bite of candy, and jam the wrapper into my already stuffed car ashtray. This will be fine, I tell myself. I'll go to the party like a normal person, have some food, drink some wine, relax, make some conversation, and then . . . go home. Just like everyone else. And if James is there, so what? We're just friends. No big deal. Meanwhile I park two blocks away in case he sees me check my teeth in the rearview mirror. Then I pinch my cheeks to make them rosy and head to the party.

Brushing past the wind chimes and the spiny cactus on my teacher's front porch, I cautiously enter the periwinkle-blue American Craftsman and glance around. I'm like a sharp shooter taking in the scene. Where's the food? Where's the boy? Is he here? There? There? Several of my fellow thespians stand around holding little paper plates with pasta salad and wedges of brie-smeared French bread, sipping red wine from plastic cups, and talking loudly over the jumping jazz. No James. Good. No, bad. No, good. If he's not here, I can eat what I want. I don't have to worry about looking sexy while I chew.

By the wall is a table laden with the usual line-up of potluck suspects: a large bowl of going-limp green salad, a tray with several mauled blocks of cheese and basket of Table Water crackers, the obligatory bowls of hummus and raw sliced veggies, a pan of half-devoured spinach quiche, and, oh yes, the plate of small, fudgy chocolate brownies. Upon closer examination I see a walnut poking its little head up through one. Good. Walnuts are a must in brownies. Not that I'm having any.

In an adjoining room to the left, our teacher is holding court with a few of my classmates, along with several unfamiliar hipsters. Friends of hers, I presume. She must have many.

I set down my wine bottle and proceed to pile up a plateful of healthy items, nonchalantly placing two brownies on the rim. Okay, three. They're small. Besides, no one will notice. It's what normal people do at parties. They eat. I amble through the living room, cocking my head and trying to look engrossed in the macramé wall hanging and the framed black-and-white landscapes of Yosemite as I clean my plate. I am invisible. I return for some fruit salad and another slice of quiche, and while I'm at it two more brownies. Just three. And oh, wow, who brought the cheesecake? I'll just try a sliver. I knife over a thick, creamy hunk and am just about to dig in when the front door opens. Don't look. Pretend you don't see. I don't want to have to stop eating if it's James, especially since I am knifing up an additional hunk of cheesecake. One eyeball up and I see it is indeed him, a six-pack under his arm. I don't think he sees me, so I dash into the kitchen to finish off my loot. I am shoveling in my last bite when he rounds the corner. "Hi!" he says, clearly excited to see me.

"Oh, hey!" I swallow hard and wipe my mouth, nodding repeatedly, tossing my plate into the trash. "How's it going?"

"Great!" God, he is beautiful.

"So, I was just . . . headed to the bathroom."

"Can I come?" he asks with a naughty grin, moving closer.

"Oh, that's okay!" I laugh. He's still smiling as I disappear into the john. I hope he doesn't notice how fat my ass feels.

I hate bathroom mirrors. I'm scared I'll see my face melting. That's how it feels when I binge in public. Like the sugary, fleshy fat is oozing off the front of my head. Eyes closed, leaning forward, I shake out my hair, then whip it back behind my head for a fresh look. Pinch my cheeks. Lick my lips. Eyes open. There I am. Still intact. I look tired. I should go. Or stay and mingle—with James, with everyone. But if I stay, I won't be able to stop eating. Besides, I'm exhausted. Good thing my wallet and keys are on me so I can just slip out the back. I cautiously exit the bathroom. His back is turned and I am out the door, down the block, in my car, and driving home. I feel sick and want only, dear God, to be horizontal. After my overload of food and sugar I just want to pass out. I somehow make it home, haul myself up the stairs to the apartment, and do a face-plant onto the futon bed, my jean jacket still on.

An hour or so later I am startled awake from my cotton candy–mouthed coma by the sharp *buzzzzzt* of the apartment bell. I stumble half blind to the front door and lean into the intercom. "Hullo?"

"Hi!" chirps a voice.

"Who's there?" I ask, knowing full well.

"It's me! James!" How did he get my address? Surely not from Samantha. Then I remember: the class roster. "Can I come up?"

"Uh . . . sure!" I buzz him in, race into the bathroom, splash cold water on my face, swish out my mouth, shake out my hair, and toss off my jacket just in time for his knock.

I unlatch the lock and open the door. I can do this.

"Where'd you go?" he says, entering without being asked. "I saw you at the party and then you were gone."

"I . . . I had a stomachache." To put it mildly.

"I'm sorry. Maybe I can help?" he says, moving into me.

"Oh, I don't know." I smile, shaking my head and reaching past him to pull the door shut. He gently backs me into the apartment. He backs me in further until we dead-end in my tiny kitchen, where he presses himself into me, full-on, against the fridge. Of all places. We are face to face. He kisses me. Hard and long. He is apparently oblivious to all the potluck I have inside of me. What am I doing? I am having him, that's what. He clearly adores me. He's amazing. He's perfect. Okay, so maybe he's a little cocky. A little arrogant. I'm a snob myself. I'm just too much of a people-pleaser to admit it.

We kiss our way down to the black-and-white-checkered linoleum floor. Upon landing, I keep my head and upper chest propped up against the bottom of the fridge so the food will have more time to settle in my stomach. I swallow hard to suppress a hummus burp as he slides a hand up my shirt. I wish my stomach were empty. I only feel desirable when I haven't eaten. Oh well. Not gonna turn this opportunity down. Warm air blows from the refrigerator vent up the back of my neck. Eyes on eyes, mouth on mouth, tongue on tongue, he draws down my skirt and panties, then he pries down his jeans. Some hardened bread crumbs pinch against my elbow. There are a few scattered uncooked macaronis to my right. So this is what it feels like. Having the guy you've wanted so much. And knowing, really knowing, he wants you just as bad.

We fuck and we fuck and we fuck and we fuck. On the kitchen floor. In the bed. Up against the living room wall, until the guy next door bangs on it and yells, "Hey! Keep it down!" Which only makes James fuck me louder, until the guy pounds on the apartment door. "Enough already! Knock it off!" I am mortified and playfully shush James for fear the guy will complain to the landlady, who will complain to the woman who leases the apartment, who will complain to her mother, who will complain to her mother's friend, my Aunt Ellen. Not that my aunt would pass judgment, but if *she* knows I'm having sex, then maybe my *mother* will somehow magically know. I am not supposed to be having sex. I am supposed to be moving forward in my career. Great artists shouldn't need sex. They have their art.

Saturday morning I open my eyes to see James smiling at me. "Hi," he says. The gorgeous college boy who wants me. How long can this last? Surely he's going back to school when summer is over. What then? Stop it. Enjoy it for what it is. What *is* it? At two he remembers he is expected to go somewhere with his dad at three, then he doesn't leave 'til four. I love that he doesn't want to go, and I'm so glad when he's gone. Alone at last, I tear the place apart for change, scouring every nook and cranny, digging frantically under all four edges of the wall-to-wall carpet and deep into the couch cushions for a quarter, a nickel, three crumb-covered pennies, finally coming up with just enough change for one chocolate-chip cookie from the coffee shop downstairs. I gobble the cookie before I am back upstairs. Then I take a long hot bath, get into bed, brace myself, and make the necessary call home to ask my mom to ask my dad to please deposit more money into my account Monday morning. And yes, I tell her, I'll be fine until then, picturing the box of Wagon Wheel pasta in the cabinet and the half stick of butter in the fridge. After the call, I cook the entire box of pasta and eat it in bed, sleep until dusk, then call Samantha to guiltily confess my deed with James. I wish she could celebrate my extraordinary connection with her stepbrother. I am afraid she will feel left out. Or judge me for wanting him. "Just be careful, okay?" she says. I wish she didn't need to say that. "I'm going to an OA meeting tomorrow. Want to come?"

"God," I say, "I'd love to, but I'm totally broke and have hardly any gas. I should probably stay put." I don't want to tell Samantha—I don't need OA. I have James.

I don't sleep. I eat like crap. I show up for class like an ambitious theatre student, show up for James like a positive, vital young woman, then turn away to self-destruct. Create. Destroy. Create. Destroy. I sense James and I need to slow down, but I can't say no, so my body says it for me. My tonsils swell so big they look like boxing gloves on either side of my throat. My fever rages. James calls and I tell him I am sick and hope he will bring me flowers and juice. After class he comes to me and crawls into bed and has sex with me. "Are you sure you want to?" I ask, seriously not up to it. "I might be contagious."

"I don't care," he says, kissing me deeper. If he wants me this bad, I'm not going to say no. Even though I can barely swallow.

So much for slowing down.

I get sicker and need medicine, but I am afraid to call home for help. Afraid my mother will hear the sex in my voice. I stay in bed and soothe my blazing throat with ice cream. I have no doctor. I have no insurance. Just a kind older brother who agrees to peer down my throat in the lobby of the nearby hospital where he is doing his medical school residency. We duck behind a pillar and he pulls out a cotton swab and a wooden stick, tells me to open wide, and cultures my throat. He sees my tears but says nothing. Joel is caring and good, but he's in a rush and also not particularly comfortable with intimacy. I want to tell him getting sick is my fault. I also want to tell him I can't stop hurting myself. He's a doctor. He should understand.

Two days later Joel calls to say I have the worst strep culture he's ever seen and prescribes a fourteen-day round of antibiotics. I choke the horse pills down religiously and feel instantly cured.

The magic of medicine.

James says he wants to drop out of college. He wants to start a theatre company with me. "We could get a place, maybe a loft, like below Market Street. What do you think?"

"I think . . . it's great!" I can't believe it. He wants to drop out of college—for me! I'd certainly ditch my own college plans for him, even though it turns out all three schools I applied to want me for next January. I won't tell my parents of my plan with James. Not yet. Anyway, they think James is just Samantha's stepbrother. Just a friend from class. I'll wait until we are definite, though I already picture our spacious loft with a large bed in the corner overlooking our creative nest. Of course, the bathroom will have a door on it, just in case I need to eat in private. Which I won't.

If James and I are going to start a theatre company, we should start working together. On an overcast Saturday afternoon we sit on the carpeted floor of his mom and stepdad's study to write our first theatre piece together for class. We haven't even kissed since I got here. I reach for his cheek and he recoils.

"We should concentrate," he says. He's right. We should. "We need to make it funny," he says, anxiously tapping the notepad with his pencil. "You're really funny. Do you have any ideas? We need to come up with something great." Something great. Shit. I usually work alone. What if I can't deliver?

"Well," I say, leaning in hungrily, "maybe we should improvise." Just then a woman's voice says "James?" We look up to see his mother poking her pretty, bob-haired head in the doorway. She sees me and smiles politely, her shiny-white teeth matching the string of pearls that rests about her delicate, Oil of Olay neck. She's a Snickerdoodle! And I am a dusty tchotchke from the Old Country that has been accidentally placed on a shelf amid the Tiffany porcelain statuettes.

"Hey, Mom," James mumbles. "This is Lisa, a friend from class." Friend? I wonder if he's told her he's dropping out of college to live with me and start a theatre company.

"Oh!" she chirps through pursed pink lips. "It's nice to meet you." But what did he *mean*, "friend"? Relax. It's just what guys say.

"Now remember, James," she says. "You're having dinner with your cousins at six."

"I know," he says, doodling mindlessly on the notepad.

She goes. James seems to have gone somewhere, too.

My fears that I am losing James are (somewhat) abated when he says he wants to visit my childhood home. Lucky for me my parents are gone for the day, at a trade show in the city buying product for my mom's paper store. I told them I might be bringing my "friend" over Saturday to see where I grew up. I left out the part about possibly having sex in my bed.

I watch nervously as James scans my bookshelves, haphazardly stuffed with juvenile memorabilia. The moldy apple dolls. The painted Mexican box filled with Polaroids from camp. My stack of LP's: Jackson Browne—my teenage crush. John Denver—hope he doesn't notice that one. Babs—my childhood idol. And Joni Mitchell—my other idol. Her album *Blue* is my favorite, a bat mitzvah gift from Aunt Ellen and Uncle Len. Too bad for the scratch I caused when I was fourteen. My mom had criticized me about my temper, and I got so mad, I *rrripped* off the stereo needle, leaving a divot clear across the vinyl. Blue, indeed.

"Have you ever had sex here before?" James asks glancing down at my little bed with the faded patchwork quilt.

"I haven't, actually," I say, feeling sheepish. I hate that he asks. It means he assumes I've had sex with other people—which I have—but the fact that he asks means *he* probably has, as well. And in the childhood homes of his lovers. We've never discussed our mutual histories. We shouldn't have to. Our love should trump all.

"Why not?" he asks, smiling.

"I don't know. I guess I just haven't been here that much."

James switches on my clock radio and Devo's "Whip It" explodes across the room. He strips down to nothing and starts rocking out, circling his hips and whipping himself wildly about. I undress as well, keeping one eye on my partly open bedroom door. My parents usually go for an early dinner after the gift show, but you never know. They just might appear at my door, decked out in their city clothes. My mother clutching her black leather Coach bag. My father's mouth in a great big O of shock.

James jumps into bed, reaches for my hand, and pulls me in. He kisses me, stroking my body and rubbing his velvety frame up and down against me. I am worried. Our workshop ends in a week. We still haven't made any plans. Not a single one. He enters me, purring his usual gravelly moan. His eyes are shut so he doesn't see me watching the door. Worrying. How will I know when he is really mine? Stop it. Be here now. But I can only be here now if I know he will be there then.

"Why do you always look sad after sex?" James asks when he is through. "Don't you enjoy it?" He knows I have issues. Shit.

"Of course I do!" I say, trying to sound . . . breezy! Carefree!

"You should be happy," he says.

"I know!" I say. "I am!"

Fuck. He's onto me. I can't let him know I'm not in it for the sex. I'm in it for the love. Whenever I am with a guy, I pretend I am in full pleasure, all the while worrying if or when I will see him again. As long as I have a man inside me, I feel desired. I don't *need* to come. I need to make *him* come. Then he will come back for more. Besides, everybody knows women don't have orgasms while they are fucking. You never see women in movies doing anything extra to orgasm. They just fuck and moan and pretend to come. You never see them run off to the bathroom to empty the sperm from their crotch or check to make sure their diaphragm is still in place, because God forbid they get pregnant and have to give up their dreams, even though the whole wide world keeps telling them they can have it all.

He doesn't call on Sunday. Why *should* he? I'll see him in class tomorrow. That would be a normal person's response. But I am not normal. And Monday is the first day of the last week of class, and *still* no future plans. Will this be the end? My faith is restored yet again when he invites me to attend the world premiere of Sam Shepard's *True West* Friday night at the Magic Theatre—*with his father.* He wouldn't want me to meet his father if he weren't serious about me. Right?

James's dad fits my image of a successful San Francisco bohemian divorcé, with shaggy brown hair, a rugged olive complexion, sock-less brown loafers, and a worn Levi's jean jacket. He's not very friendly, which makes me anxious. You'd think an older guy in a jean jacket would be warmer.

The play is amazing—I'm sure—it's just hard to concentrate while wondering what James's dad thinks of me. I'm glad we have some face-to-face time in a café afterwards. They each have a Danish and coffee. I just have tea. We talk about the play . . . the amazing acting . . . the brilliant writing . . . and then, twenty minutes in, James casually informs me that this Sunday, the day after tomorrow, he's leaving for a ten-day sailing trip with his dad, his stepmom, and stepsiblings. "Wow," I say, shaking my head in amazement. "I mean, it sounds fantastic. . . ." I clench my jaw to dam my tears. I had no idea. James also informs me he is staying at his dad's tonight. He'll see me tomorrow. Oh—not at my place. We'll meet in Golden Gate Park. He only has a little time, with the trip and all. I understand. I understand I should have had the chocolate black-out cake. To go.

Saturday afternoon we lay side by side on a large, flat rock in Golden Gate Park. James stares up at the flawless blue sky. I stare at flawless James. "I'm really gonna miss you," I say. I hope it's okay to say that. That's what normal people say to their boy-friends . . . right? He *is* my boyfriend . . . right?

"You'll be fine," he says. "You should just work on your stuff."

"You're right . . . I should . . . So, when are we going to look for a loft, anyway?" James sits up and stares across the park.

"I dunno," he says. I sit up and stare off, too, trying to out-distance him.

"What do you think we should call our theatre company anyway?" I ask.

"I'm not sure. . . ." We watch a guy throw a Frisbee across the meadow for his golden retriever.

"So," I push on, wishing I wouldn't. Knowing I shouldn't. "What'd your dad think of me, anyway?"

James pauses. He doesn't usually do that. Pause. Shit.

"He thought you were really bohemian." Bohemian. I nod and laugh, wishing I'd never asked.

James sails off, my summer sublet ends, and I move to . . . where else? For ten days I sit on my little bed or stand before the open fridge, afraid to leave the house in case he calls . . . from the middle of the ocean. My father is typically oblivious to my mood. My mother, however, must know I am waiting to hear from James. We don't talk about it, but I imagine she's figured out that he is more than a friend. That's the least of her worries, since I've broken my plans to her about forgoing college in lieu of starting a theatre company with James. After all my comings and goings the last few years, she really doesn't know *how* to react, so she keeps her distance, silently praying, no doubt, that I'll make the right decision. I'd love to lean on Samantha, but unfortunately she is gone. Back to New York. It's just me. I need to sit tight, as my father always says. Sit tight and drown.

Eight days pass. I get a letter. From somewhere in Greece. Six handwritten pages crammed with drawings and descriptions of his every waking hour. Yearning phrases like "I miss you so much . . . I see you in the mountains, your breasts, your hands sloping around my stomach, your face behind steam . . . If only you were here in body. Well, sweetie, someday . . ." He signs the letter "Love, lover, loverest." I count the days, hours, minutes.

Ten days pass. Eleven. He must be back. Don't call. He loves you. He wrote it. Wait.

Monday night the phone rings. He says he's been home since Saturday. *Saturday*? Calm down. He's probably exhausted. He wanted to rest and be in good form before he saw me. Anyhow, he wants to see me now. As in tonight. I shed my overalls, pull on my jeans, wash my face, shake out my hair, race upstairs, and grab the Rabbit keys off the front table. My dad is at a dental meeting, so I am spared his angst about me driving into the city, ending up in a fiery crash on the 101. But I can't avoid my mom's. *"Now?"*

she shakes her head. "You're going into the city *now*?" They treat me like I am fifteen. I can't blame them. I may be twenty-two, but my answer to puberty was becoming a mime. I mugged my way through all those uncomfortable teenage feelings. I left home at seventeen, but in my heart I never really left. That umbilical cord got stretched really long, until it snapped, landing me back here.

"I'm going to see Samantha!" Wow. Bald-faced.

"I don't want you taking the freeway home in the middle of the night."

"So I'll sleep over! I'll be *fine*! I *promise*!" Where will James and I sleep? In my car? Who cares? I don't care if I never sleep again.

"Hi," I say as James climbs into my car and closes the door.

"Hey."

We don't kiss. That's okay. We're saving it.

"Where should we go?" I ask.

"I don't know," he says. "Maybe we should just talk here."

I start to shake. "Okay . . ." But that's what lovers do. They talk in their cars. "So, how was your trip? Was it great?"

"It was. It was really great."

"I loved your letter. . . . Thank you so much. . . ."

"Sure . . . So . . . I had a lot of time to think on my trip. . . ."

"God, I'll bet."

"And, the thing is, I've decided to return to college after all."

Clunk.

Fuck.

"It's important to me," he goes on. "I want to finish school. So . . . I'm going back."

My eyes glaze over. I hope the 7-Eleven just before the 101 has It's-It ice-cream sandwiches. "Wow," I say. "So, I mean, what happened?"

"I talked to my dad about it." His dad. I should have known. The self-hating bohemian. "He encouraged me to go back. I've come this far. I don't want to just . . . drop out." Yeah. Like me. "So, anyway, I go back in a week."

"A week . . . wow . . . so . . . well . . . but . . . can I see you before then?"

"I don't know, I mean, I have a whole bunch of crap to do." Oh my God. Is he breaking up with me? I'm not sure. Don't ask. Don't rock the boat. What boat? There is no boat! Jump out now. Beat him to it. I start to cry—at least, I think I cry. My face is so numb. My whole body is numb. "It doesn't mean we won't be in touch," he says. *Oh really?* And then—what is that? Is that—is he—*smiling?* Why the *fuck* is he smiling? He's secretly excited about going back to school, that's why. *Whoopee!* Off he'll go. He hugs me and quickly gets out of the car. I guess this is it. I guess I am supposed to go. Drive. Blood pouring out of my heart.

I will never love again. I will be alone for the rest of my life.

In the morning my mother walks into the kitchen all crisp and fresh and elegantly clothed for work. I am half-clad in my thrift-shop extra-extra-large man's tailored shirt, hovering over the center island, one leg bent at the knee with my foot perched up against the other as I pick away at the last of the lemon poppy-seed cake. She moves swiftly and silently about the kitchen, nibbling from a bowl of cereal as she gathers her coffee makings. I feel her eyes on me. All my life, all I've wanted is her attention. I just hate it when she stares.

"Please leave some of that for your sister," she finally says. My sister Lauren is due home later today, on break from grad school. And that's all she says. That's enough. She's now seen me in action. Taking. Unable to stop. I can't stop eating. How could I have been so stupid? How could I have actually believed he would stay with me? I should have known he wouldn't last. Chocolate never does in my hands.

Standing with my mother, with one imperfect slice of cake on the counter between us, something goes off inside me. I watch myself reach for the cake. I watch my nail-bitten hand reach out and close in around that slice. I watch my arm rise up and off the elegant, white-porcelain cake plate. Everything my mother does is done right. Up into the air goes my hand, into the air, over my head, several crumbs sprinkling down on me. I am not doing this. This is something from a book. Or a movie. There is no one here to stop me. My mother stands watching from the other side of the island, frozen in shock. I must aim high or the cake will hit the Williams Sonoma circular iron pot rack that hangs from above. It is cluttered with brass pots and pans that have gone dusty now that the kids are gone and my mother has succumbed to fancy, fine takeout from the overpriced gourmet grocer. Fancy, fine takeout that she always invites me to partake in. Must be ten bucks for a skimpy wedge of salmon. Six bucks for half a pint of pasta salad with feta and pine nuts. She never asks me for a dime. Not a nickel. Yet here I am. Lifting my arm, reaching back to gain more distance, arching back some more, and then I *hurl* that slice of cake through the air, over the pot rack, smack in my mother's direction. I don't *want* to hit her. I want to hit *around* her. Just close enough for her to know how fucked up I am. She sees it coming and jumps aside as—*splat!*—the cake hits the wall to her left, bursting into a pop-art mural of yellow crumbs and black poppy seeds.

And then . . . silence.

She looks down. She looks up. And down. And up. All I hear is the steady rhythm of her gasping in horror. In. Out. In. Out. As much as she can through her one good nostril. I grit my teeth. If I grit hard enough, maybe I can believe this didn't happen.

"You *clean* that up this *instant*, young lady!" she shrieks. *Young lady?* That's DEFCON 1 in this house.

"No!" I scream. "Bitch!" I detonate. I'm going to die.

Down to my bunker I flee, three stairs at a time, through Sarah's room and into mine, where I slam the bedroom door so hard I imagine it coming off its hinges and crashing to the floor. Fine with me. Bring the whole fucking house down, for all I care.

Here I am again. Face-down on my bed again. Preparing to be cast out.

I hear the familiar click, click of my mother's pumps as she charges across the wooden living room floor above. Then muffled steps as her feet hit the carpeted stairwell down. Then a faint *swish* of her loose-fitting Norma Kamali charcoal-black pantsuit as she crosses through Sarah's Turkish-carpeted room. The click of her heels across the green-tile bathroom floor. Then the *whoosh* of my bedroom door being flung open as she bursts into my room and rushes to my bed. Peeking out from a one-inch space between my folded elbow and the now tear-soaked pillow, I see her looming over me, hands on hips, quaking with rage.

"Now you *stop* it this *instant!*" she shrieks. "*Why* you *can't* just be *happy* is *beyond me!* You have *everything* going for you! *Everything!*"

"No! I don't!" I scream, rolling onto my back. "I have nothing, Mom! *Nothing!*" I cover my face and sob. I'm so ashamed. I shouldn't be here. In this place. This is the shit you're supposed to go through when you're a teenager. But like I said, I skipped that part. She makes that desperate "*uccchhhhh!*" cry in her throat, waits another second, then marches out. I push myself up onto my elbows and freeze there as I listen hard. If she leaves the house, that will be it. I will have finally done it. Made her leave me. But I don't hear the door. I hear her descent back down the stairs and into my room. She stands over me, a half-empty glass of water in one hand and the other hand held out, clenched in a fist.

"Take it!" she says, opening her fist. I sit up, wiping my eyes, and peer into her hand. There, nestled in her bare palm is a tiny yellow pill. Wow, I think. She *must* be upset. She didn't even take the time to wrap it in a tissue.

"What is it?" I ask, sniffling.

"It's nothing. It's a Valium. Just . . . *take* it."

"A Valium?" I say. "I don't want Valium. I don't need Valium. Who takes Valium? Why do we even *have* Valium? I don't need

Valium! Why are you giving me a Valium? Valium is for crazy people! I don't need a Valium, Mom! *I don't need a Valium!*"

"Now just calm down now this *instant!*" she shrieks.

"I *can't* calm down! I *can't!*" I clench my jaw and sob through my teeth.

"*Please,*" she begs, finally sitting next to me. "*Take* it. It will *help* you." I can't stop crying. I want to tell her my heart is broken but I can't. I honestly don't know if she actually knew about me and James and I don't want to ask. I just wish she would hold me. Why won't she hold me? Take me in her arms and hold me, like a normal mother with her normal daughter. Why don't we embrace? What are we afraid of? I was inside her, for God's sake. I am her bones. Her blood. We can't even hug. I am ashamed. Ashamed I have a body that needs to be held. Ashamed the beautiful boy no longer wants me. Ashamed my mother doesn't want to touch me. Ashamed.

Reluctantly forcing the tiny pill between my lips, I take a swig of water and gulp it down. My mother exhales and folds her hands one into the other, resting them in her lap. "I just *know* you'll feel better once you're back in school. You know as well as I, that's where you belong. But Daddy and I agree, it's important for you to really finish this time." Finish. Something other than a bag of cookies. What a scary concept. "We know you can do it," she says. "You can do anything you put your mind to." And then, she leaves.

I lie back and stare up at that fucking gold seal hanging on my wall, the one I earned in the fourth grade when my mom insisted I could do better. She was right. Always is. I can do better. I will. But first I must get as far away from this house, this room, and this bed as I possibly can.

CHAPTER 12

ON BROADWAY

I wander down Broadway on the Upper West Side, trying to look like I am not eating. Like I know where I am going. Like I am actually going somewhere. It's September and the streets are packed. Everyone looks like they're back from the beach. Jumping in. Moving forward. I hope no one notices my hand reaching back and forth from the brown paper bag to my mouth, bag to mouth. A bite of sesame bagel. A nutty bear claw. A hefty oat-and-honey bar that comes three strips to a pack. One pack for now, one for later. Fuck it. Eat both packs at once. That's one way to ground myself.

New York is exciting. Intimidating. On fire. I can see why my father hated it here. The noise. The frantic, frenzied pace. The chaos. He talked about New York like it was the city that made him into a nervous wreck. It was New York's fault. The city was a perilous, out-of-control monster that could eat you alive. He told me that if my mom hadn't gotten him out of New York, he would have perished. That's what he said. "I woulda pa-rished." Twenty-five years out and he still sounds like he stepped right off Flatbush Avenue. All my life I carried his voice in my head, yelling, trying to get control. "Leeser! Please! Let me get my bearings heah!" He looked like he was going to blow, like a hydrant on a hot summer sidewalk.

Once when I was six and we returned to San Francisco from visiting his family back east, he was so happy to be home, he got down on his hands and knees in the TWA terminal and kissed the burgundy carpet. And he called *me* histrionic.

The boldest thing my father ever did was turn down his father's wish to take over his Lower East Side clothing factory, become a dentist, and move my mom and my two older siblings to California. It was an act of survival for him. The boldest thing *I* do is move to New York, to the land that made my father crazy. It's an act of survival for me, too. The city noise is a comfort. The traffic. The drama in the streets. I love the hustle and the bustle. In the early '80s, the homeless wander the streets shoulder to shoulder with Wall Street execs, artists, students, old people, moms, secretaries, junkies, drunks, dancers, actors, garment workers, nuns, everyone. Grand, ornately designed apartment buildings tower over me. Salsa and rap music spray from ghetto blasters, competing with honking cars and screaming pedestrians. The sidewalk is a fast-flowing river of shapes, sizes, colors, noses of all lengths, hair of all colors, fashion of all styles, and everywhere, from corner to corner, is food. Chinese. Korean. Jewish. Italian. Street vendors sell hotdogs, giant pretzels, and warm toffee peanuts that smell so good they make my heart palpitate. But I'd never eat food from a street vendor. That just wouldn't be healthy.

As I chomp my way down the avenue, I fantasize that people think I am a driven, young actress on my way to a rehearsal at Lincoln Center. Ah, to be young and talented in New York! In fact, I've just clocked out at my dreary minimum-wage filing job at the Columbia University Alumni Records Office. I'm afraid my boss, a tiny, butch lesbian with what looks like a harelip scar, is on to me when I return from lunch every day with that crazed, glazed look in my eye after hitting the bakery. I hope she doesn't notice me nodding off over the open file drawer. I try to position myself so it looks like I am just concentrating really hard, my head bent low, deep in the drawer, trying to catch a few z's and hoping to God I won't be caught. Or that I won't keel over into the open drawer, pulling the entire cabinet down on top of me.

I walk home, from 116th Street down to 94th. Eating. Looking for James. I know, it's ridiculous; he's not even in the same state—but he *just might* be here. One day I follow a guy who sort of looks like him from the back from 99th Street to 94th. I know it isn't him. I wish it were. At least until my bagel runs out. And I'm left with the hole.

I am alone in New York—except for my cousin Annie, who lets me stay on her Upper West Side living room fold-out couch for two hundred bucks a month. It's close quarters, but half the time she's either at work or with her lawyer-outdoorsman fiancé. When she's home we share laughs about the crazy gene in our family. How obsessive-compulsive our Grandma May is (though we don't have those words at this time). How she's always waiting for the worst to happen. I tell Annie about the time she came to visit us in California and walked off the plane looking so distraught. "The fish!" she said. "Was the fish okay?"

"The what, Grandma?"

"The fish! The fish! They served it on the plane! Was it fresh? Do you think it was okay?" There we were: the grandkids, the successful dentist son, and his beautiful wife, waiting to greet her with open arms. But what about the fish? The fish?

"They're so afraid to die, they're afraid to live," my mom used to say about my dad's parents. But never to his face. Maybe because it was him she was talking about, as well.

My cousin Annie has no idea what I do with food. And I have no intention of telling her. I only mention that I have a few issues with food and promise not to touch hers. She laughs it off and doesn't seem concerned. At this time in my bingeing career, I am deep into peanut butter. Like most normal kids, I always liked the stuff just fine. Then, once I left home for college, I crossed over from just plain liking it to being obsessed with it. It was probably the healthiest item in my vegetarian diet, but once I started eating it I couldn't stop. Peanut butter is like edible quicksand. It sucks you in, down to the bottom of the jar. And it's readily available. Pretty much everyone has a jar of it in the kitchen. I know I am betraying my cousin's trust dipping into hers. This is not how a responsible roommate acts. My guilt only feeds the monster, especially as I empty half a bag of her chocolate chips into the jar, well aware she is in the next room where we are watching TV. She thinks I've just come into the kitchen to make some herb tea. That's my go-to excuse when I need to escape for a fix. I always throw in "herb" to sound more virtuous. I squeeze a generous glob of chocolate sauce into the peanut butter as well, beat it all together into a great, thick glop, and quickly spoon it in. Well, as quickly as you are able to spoon in mud clots. The kettle starts to sing. I call out through the thick nutty clump in my throat, "Sure you don (clear throat) wanshum (swallow hard) tea?"

"No thanks!" she replies. I frantically spoon in my mortar, trying not to choke, then I tongue out any telltale bits of nuts and chocolate from between my teeth, prepare my tea, and calmly return to the couch, mug in hand, as if nothing has happened other than the pure and innocent act of boiling water for a nice, hot cup of tea . . . which I don't drink. No room.

Maybe I should go back to OA.

The room at the church on Fifth Avenue is brimming with angst-ridden women, many of them thinner (and angst-ier) than me. Like the skinny blonde who says she hides in the shower chewing up bags of candy and spitting it into a bucket. I'm surprised they are allowed to name specific food—like candy. But I am not in Sunnyvale anymore. The woman says the only reason she's here is because her boyfriend begged her to come back. She prays every day for her higher power to remove the obsession. Why does she need a higher power when she has a supportive boyfriend?

Then there is the voluptuous earth-mother type who sobs about how grateful she is to be back after losing her abstinence and gaining fifty pounds *in two weeks*! And the tiny, sweet, bookish bulimic who says she is on some kind of heart medicine for the damage she's caused with all the puking. She is warned not to eat chocolate while on the medicine, but the following Saturday she will eat a whole Entenmann's double-fudge cake, have a heart attack, and die before she can get her fingers down her throat.

I am not like these women. These women are crazy. I just need to get back on stage to get me out of sugar. Don't wait until NYU. Might as well try for something as long as I'm here. *Make it there, make it anywhere* . . . but what *is* it, anyway? I guess the obvious *it* for any performer is Broadway, but I won't even consider that fantasy. What a cliché. Or maybe I just tell myself that because I can't face the competition.

Backstage magazine is chock-full of off-off-off-off Broadway auditions. All I need is a headshot to get started. An eight-by-ten of my face. Great. My face, I can handle. A flyer at my favorite student café on Amsterdam Avenue reads "Headshots: 25 bucks." I rip off a tab with a phone number and make the call. The guy is a student. I hope he thinks I look good as I pose on a stool in his empty beer-can and ashtray-strewn dorm room. I hope he thinks I look very thin in my newly purchased, second-hand *shmata* dress. It's baggy but girlish, hopefully masking my body now that I am at my top weight: 145 pounds. That's 25 pounds more than I was in high school. The only reason I know this is because my cousin has a scale next to the toilet. So I step on it. A dozen times a day. But so what? Weight means nothing. Scales are for women with actual weight problems.

Then I get my photos back. Gazing down at myself I try to hide my shock. But there I am. In black and white. Me. At least . . . I *think* it's me. What's wrong with my face? Why's it all puffy? Where'd my neck go? I look like someone has pumped me with air. How'd this happen? When? And the mustache! Why didn't I remember to use Jolen cream bleach on my upper lip, just like I did in high school?

That's it. It's nothing but yogurt and apples for the next two days—along with a hefty helping of lip bleach. Especially since I saw an ad in *Backstage* for a show that would be perfect for me. A theatre company is looking for "physical performers" for an experimental production of the epic poem "Beowulf." If I get an audition, I'll distract them with my physicality and they won't notice how huge I am. Besides, it's "Beowulf." Maybe my hairiness will work to my advantage.

I send in my headshot and resume (which, by now, is four and a half pages long—I didn't know you're not supposed to include everything all the way back to elementary school) and land an audition. Tuesday afternoon I am on my hands and knees in a Chelsea theatre, writhing and growling on stage with a few other actors. We are the body of Beowulf. I am stationed at the head of the dragon. I go wild, gnashing my teeth, grunting and growling across the stage. The next day I get a call. They love me. They want to cast me as part of the dragon. Maybe I should have gone for Broadway.

My mom can't fly out for the show with the very busy pre-Christmas season at her store, so she sends my dad. It's sweet that he comes, though I wish it were her. My dad brings my cousin Annie, his sister Aunt Selma, and his mom, Grandma May. He seems impressed with my performance, despite the fact that his mother spends the entire show worriedly whispering into his ear that I am going to fall off the stage. It is a sunken stage with the audience rising up on all four sides. There is nowhere *to* fall. But up.

In December my cousin Annie's fiancé cheats on her and she loses him—along with her sense of humor. The mood in the apartment goes sour. I blithely ignore her hints about wanting her living room back so she can entertain new romantic prospects. She doesn't come right out and ask me to leave, so maybe she doesn't *really* want me gone. So I stay.

One snowy evening she returns after a long day's work, only to find that her roasted half-chicken in the fridge, the one she's been looking forward to all day, has flown the coop. I am sitting on the living room couch when I hear her enter the apartment, walk into the kitchenette, and open the refrigerator door. "Hey!" she says, sounding like she's about to cry. "Where's my half-chicken?"

"Huh? What?" I call out, feigning concern, peering over my shoulder and raising my eyebrows in pretend shock. She pokes her head into the living room, still in her coat and scarf.

"Did you eat my half-chicken?" she asks.

"What? No, I— I don't think so." It is obvious who the fox in the henhouse is. I guess I just thought what was hers was mine. Or I hoped so, anyway.

"I'm *so* upset!" she says. "I was *really* looking forward to that chicken! I can't *believe* you didn't ask me first." Believe it.

"I'm *sorry!*" I blurt out. "I didn't *know!*" Grabbing my coat and hat, like I'm the one who's been wronged, I escape into the freezing cold and binge my way up and down Broadway, gorging on a toxic late-night snack of sugar and shame. I am never going back there. *Ever!*

Around 11:30 p.m. I return to the quiet, dark apartment, grateful that the locks haven't been changed. I slip into my nightgown, flip on the radio to keep me company, and pass out in a fitful sleep on the pull-out couch.

In the middle of the night all the sugar streaming through my veins awakens me with a start. As I lie there, tolerating my sickness, I hear an announcement over the radio. John Lennon is dead. I tell myself it's just a sugar-induced nightmare, roll over, and go back to sleep.

But the nightmare is all over the papers the following morning as I make my way to work. John Lennon was shot and killed in front of the Dakota, that glorious, ominous Gothic-styled castle of a building just a dozen blocks away from my apartment. I'll bet I was stuffing my face just about the time he was shot. He was lying there, blood running from his mouth onto the cold, hard sidewalk, while I was shoving my rectangle of cellophane-wrapped carrot cake with cream cheese frosting into my mouth.

I picture blood bleeding through cold, white, cream-cheese frosting. I am in the deepest, darkest hole ever.

My cousin and I don't discuss the tragedy. We don't talk at all, really. She still doesn't ask me to leave outright. But the cock is crowing and I know my time is up. Besides, the Upper West Side feels extra bleak since the murder. I've never felt comfortable up here, anyway. It's too fancy, expensive, and clean cut. Everybody is so professional looking. And fuck Zabar's. I can't even afford a cookie at that place. I'm a downtown girl. The West Village is really gay, so I might have a hard time finding a guy there—but it's also really bohemian. I'll fit right in. Plus there are all those great jazz clubs—not that I'm into jazz, but it's cool to know they're there—and folk clubs where Bob Dylan and Barbra Streisand started out. Plus I can walk to NYU. And there are all those great cafés on Bleecker Street where I can sit and write and drink lattes. Maybe even smoke a cigarette. Like James.

I answer an ad in the *Village Voice* to share a small West Village apartment with Trina, a tiny, skinny, Japanese Fashion Institute student. As I load my bags into a taxi outside my cousin's brownstone, we hug good-bye as if no ill has come between us. I hope she'll smile when she finds the quarter-pound of sliced roast turkey I left in her fridge with a little note of apology taped to it.

Trina and I share a tiny top-floor, two-bedroom apartment on Bleecker and Sixth. The scent of warm pizza and roasting coffee beans drifts in through our windows day and night. Half a block down is the ever-beckoning Bleecker Street Pastry Shop, where I regularly blow through my budget on an assortment of butter cookies and cannolis. I keep a low profile so the bakery owner, a buxom Italian mama, won't say something to me, like "Hey-a, you-a! I see-a you-a every other day-a. You-a sure-a eat-a lotta cookies! Whatsa matta you?" Like the whole world is watching me. Keeping track.

Once I buy a chocolate log cake and have her inscribe "Happy Birthday, Linda" on it as a decoy. "Thanks so much!" I say. "I know my friend will really like it!" And she does.

I don't tell Trina about the food. She's so tiny and perfect in her miniskirts and her trendy Japanese thigh-high socks with not an inch of thigh flesh jutting out over the elastic top. I wonder if they even *have* compulsive overeaters in Japan? She sits on a tall stool in our miniscule living room/kitchen/dining room slurping large bowls of fat-free ramen rice noodles in miso soup, while I lay low in my single futon bed with my cookies and the door closed. I also can't deal with her oddball boyfriend in his tight, black jeans and narrow, pointy-toed, Italian 60s-era ankle boots. I wonder why he always has a beer in his hand.

When my Aunt Selma invites me to join her, Uncle Max, and Grandma May for Passover in New Jersey, I jump at the chance. Getting out of the city will do me good, even though being stuck out in the suburbs with all that matzoh terrifies me. But I agree to board the bus and then stand waiting at the leafy suburban stop for my aunt to pick me up.

I'm not sure but I think that must be Aunt Selma's silver-pink Caddy approaching. She's so hunkered down behind the wheel, it's hard to tell. As she nears the bus stop, I see her frosted-blonde set and pink lips. She waves to me as she drives up and almost hits me before putting on the brakes. Her windows are closed and I can't hear her, but I see her lips saying "Hello dahling." I climb in and give her a hug. "Good to see you," she says.

"You, too. Thanks so much for having me."

"Oh, of cowse," she says, driving off at five miles per hour. She is so slumped down behind the wheel she can barely see over the dashboard, especially since she's looking at me most of the time. "So tell me, deah, how are you liking the city? It's a great city, isn't it? Very exciting. So much to do. Awl that culcha. How ah you liking NYU? It's a terrific school. How's the acting? Ah you doing any mowa acting? You were tarrific in that Beowulf play. Just tarrific." It's a miracle we don't plow into a front lawn or a bagel storefront.

Uncle Max is upstairs in his boxers and a white v-neck t-shirt. He's lying on the bed watching two TVs at once. One has a better picture and one has better sound. Put them together and *voila.* "Leesa Koteen!" he calls from the bed.

"Hi, Uncle Max," I say from the doorway, where I still haven't removed my coat.

"Leesa Koteen! The great and talented Leesa Koteen! Have you ever heard of Maria Tallchief? What a terrific dancer she was. A real Indian and a great ballerina." Why is he talking to me about Maria Tallchief? Does he think I look like a Native American? Does he think I am a ballerina? Should I be complimented? Or offended—for the "Indians"? I always take what Uncle Max says with a block of salt. He fought in a horrific battle in WWII. Story has it, his young bride, my Aunt Selma, sent him a salami. "Send a salami to your boy in the army." But because he moved from base camp to base camp so often, it took two years for the salami to catch up with him. My father attributes Uncle Max's eccentricity to the violence he must have witnessed during the war. Personally, I think it was the salami.

Selma and Max's living room furniture is covered in plastic. Actually, it's not, though it looks like it could be. Their house is pure tchotchke-ville. Not the artsy, folksy tchotchkes my mom collects. More like cheesy, gaudy stuff with lots of gold paint from Turkey or Russia that's actually probably made in China. Grandma May is seated in a chair with her white pocketbook tucked in her lap. She sees me and lights up. "Oh, hello, Leeser deah. How are you? How's everything?" She looks suddenly worried. She looks for her pocketbook.

"It's right there, Mom." Aunt Selma laughs. "In your lap!"

"Oh." Grandma smiles nervously. "That's awlright."

We sit down to dinner—me, Aunt Selma, Grandma May, who is still in her fur coat because she's always cold (or maybe she's afraid someone will run in and steal it), her pocketbook safely tucked in her lap, and Uncle Max, still in his t-shirt and boxers. The food is all homemade and fresh—fresh from the local deli. Matzoh-ball soup. Potato salad. Cold cuts. Coleslaw. Never mind that it's Passover, the holiday with no bread. An enormous basket of rolls, rye bread, and challah bread (along with a stack of matzoh) is passed around. The prayers last—well—actually— there are no prayers. Uncle Max ad libs a tune that sounds like it could be in Hebrew at the top of his lungs, like he's channeling a great and mighty rabbi. Aunt Selma laughs—humored and a little embarrassed. What else can she do? She loves the guy.

"Lisa, dahling!" she exclaims, her eyebrows raised in exclamation, her mouth stuffed with food. "Have some mowa chicken! Don't be shy, please!" Crumbs are flying out of her mouth across the table. I should have brought my umbrella. "Do you like it, deah? Please! Don't be shy!" At the end of the meal there are cookies, honey cake, and chocolates. I take a plateful. As meshuga as these people are, I do not feel judged by them. I feel oddly accepted. Liked, even.

After dessert and coffee, and a little more dessert at Aunt Selma's urging, I tell her we should probably go. She packs me a doggie bag with bread, chicken, and cookies, and by a miracle of God we make it to the bus stop just as the bus pulls up.

Seated by a window, I stare numbly out at the dark suburban streets as we roll by the cold Tudor homes and the great, dark lawns. There's a pit in my stomach. It hurts. Am I hungry? How can I be hungry after everything I just ate? What is the feeling? I think . . . I want to cry, but I am too full. Or sad. *That's* what it is. I feel sad. I think about my dad sitting at the dinner table with these people, chewing, yelling, and trying to get control of the chaos. This is what he ran from. Not just crazy New York. But crazy family. He ran from his family, just like I ran from mine. But he *never* would have left New York if it hadn't been for my mother's insistence. He was far too guilt-ridden about leaving his parents, even though his sister happily took such good care of them. His guilt had him by the throat. No wonder he called my mother five times a day from the office just to hear her voice. She was his refuge. She was the most sane, beautiful thing that ever happened to him. She landed in his life like an angel, and he climbed on her wings and she carried him away, out of this world.

CHAPTER 13

A WOMB OF MY OWN

No school today. Not feeling well. Nothing in particular. Just my usual brand of yuck. Like the yuck I get every now and then since I first left home. A freaky classmate girl from my experimental-acting class calls me up. I tell her I am unwell and she pops by anyway after class. She has a lopsided haircut. It's shaved on one side and long on the other. I don't understand her haircut, or her, but she seems to like me—and being liked is hard to turn down. She has a fancy black camera and she takes multiple pictures from different angles of my tiny room, all the while talking incessantly about this really cute guy in class who she thinks wants her. I find her annoying. I secretly judge all my experimental-theatre colleagues for their seeming lack of discipline and classical training. They are all too cool for school. Our uber-hip acting teacher is a grim-faced Austrian for whom all the kids bow down in holy reverence. All but me. I am afraid I've made a mistake enrolling in yet another offbeat theatre program. Afraid to admit it because I thought this was me. Experimental. But maybe I don't want this. Maybe I don't want to stand in a circle making loud grunting noises and skipping backwards to avant-garde music with a paper bag over my head while reciting Shakespeare.

What *do* I want?

What do I want to do?

Not what do I think I should do?

What do I *want* to do?

And then, the answer comes.

I want . . . to write.

I remember writing. I remember the joy of writing plays as a young child. Creative book reports in fourth grade. Creative writing in junior high. It was the one place I felt happy. And safe. Alone on the page. So what happened? I turned twelve and I swallowed my words and became a mime.

I want to write.

For the stage.

On a page.

The words I lost.

I want to find my words. Not my sister's. Not my mother's. *Mine.*

But what if I am not as good of a writer as I am a performer?

I take a chance, submit a writing sample to the dramatic writing program, which is another department at the NYU School of the Arts.

I get in.

It's the first thing I get that I feel is really mine.

Where will I write? I need to be able to control my space. Maybe it's finally time to live alone. But the reality of finding a place for myself (even though reality is a place I don't usually dwell) is less than zero. There's always the Y. I could have my own room. I could be anonymous. But Y's are for transients. That's where people go when they are out of options. Then again, I do have a romantic notion of living at the Y, like a real writer. I could hole up in my room 'til all hours, drinking coffee, not eating, taking breaks to commune with other writers down the hall. It might be totally bohemian, cool, and great. I call the Midtown Y and they tell me to come by. A cranky female building manager who is smoking leads me down a dimly lit, brownish hallway. Along the way a door creaks open and a crusty looking man peeks his head out and then *slams* it shut. The room for let looks like a place where someone would either be murdered or take her own life. I thank the manager, then run all the way home down

Sixth Avenue and do not stop until I reach the Bleecker Street Pastry Shop.

"Just a half pound of the mixed butter cookies," I tell the lady. "They're for my school. Gosh, do you think they'll still be fresh tomorrow?" She nods slowly, bagging the cookies. I stare into the bakery case, afraid to look up, imagining her eyeing me suspiciously because she knows who the cookies are for and that they will never last 'til tomorrow. "Ya know what? Better make that a pound. Better too many than too little, right?" Fuck it. With any luck I'll be gone from the neighborhood soon. She'll never remember me.

Then I hear about the other Y—the *YMHA*. That stands for Young Men's Hebrew Association. Once I eliminate my two biggest obstacles—*Men's* (it's actually co-ed) and *Hebrew* (you don't have to be a practicing religious Jew—or even Jewish, for that matter—to join), only then do I confront my biggest hurdle.

It's on the Upper East Side.

The Upper East Side, where rich people live. Or, even worse, people *pretending* to be rich. There's no edge. No art. No soul. No thanks. Not for me.

Then one day I return to my apartment and find my bedroom smelling like barf. I ask my roommate, Trina, and she starts to titter. "Ooohhh, so, I think, my boyfriend may have—tee hee— drunk too much this afternoon, and I think he might have, hee hee, thrown up out your bedroom window." *Thrown up out my bedroom window?* What the *fuck*? And how does she know it's because he was drunk? He could have the stomach flu. He *could*. Those germs could be lurking everywhere. Great. I'll never be able to sleep in my room again, much less eat in there. This is a disaster. I cannot stay where someone has barfed. Time to move.

Exiting the Eighty-Sixth Street subway on my way to visit the YMHA, I am confronted with an enormous bakery window. There are black-and-white-iced cookies the size of my face. Layer cakes the size of my head. Bigger, actually. Great. So I'll have to pass *that* every morning on my way to school. And every night on my way home. Don't be so negative. Why not? It's my birthright. I see the building two blocks up. God, it looks so *institutional*. Don't say "God." Don't take his name in vain. Why *his*? I hate Judaism and its patriarchal penis. Sorry, Dad. It's not my fault I was born with a vagina. It's not my fault I was born. If only I had a boy's body. I should have been a fucking boy. Jewish boys are expected to excel, and girls are expected to support the boys. See, I'm not just a self-hating Jew. I'm just self-hating. Or just plain hating.

Just be nice. A nice Jewish girl.

Fuck it. I don't want to live here anyway.

But I have to live somewhere . . .

The manager is perfectly pleasant. He takes me on a tour. We ride with a few friendly residents up the elevator. Maybe it would be good to live with nice, normal people. Yeah, nice, normal, *boring* people. The hallways are so antiseptic, I expect to see people in hospital beds as we pass several open doors. He shows me a single room. Bland. Colorless. Nine by eleven. There's fluorescent overhead lighting and beige venetian blinds. Dreadful. But what's worse: living with a creep and her barfing boyfriend or being anonymous in a building full of friendly, albeit boring, people?

Much to my surprise, and to my delight, my little room at the YMHA calls to me. For the first time since I left home at seventeen, for the first time in my *life*, I am in a space that is truly mine. Who cares that it's a shoe box? It's mine! Every day after class, I can't wait to get back to my little womb to write. Seated on my narrow bed, surrounded by collected scraps of paper with all my writing ideas, I hunker down over my mother's ancient, gray Smith Corona manual typewriter. It's the very typewriter she bought for herself when she was nineteen and took a train from Queens to Missoula to attend the University of Montana. My mother had a romantic notion of the West. She hoped to find a community of liberal intellectuals discussing Sartre and Nabokov. Instead she found simple-minded, beer-swillin', bear-huntin' college kids who liked to party. At the end of the year she turned on her cowgirl-boot heel and headed home. Then she met my dad, and they fell in love and got married and started a family. Two kids would have been enough for my dad. But once my mom pulled him to California, two more arrived. Sarah and, then, fourteen months later, me. I was the straw that broke my family's back. I was the one to push my parents just over the edge. But I was the baby. My mother's last hope for greatness. She wanted all the things for me she couldn't have for herself, and so when I left the nest and she watched me desperately flapping my wings in a hundred directions, trying to find the best of the best of the best places to be, she pulled out that dusty, old typewriter and she wrote me a letter pleading with me to get back on track so that I could "be everything she knew I could be." I wanted to believe I *could*, in fact, be *everything*. I loved her words. I loved them like chocolate. Her approval is an addiction unto itself. But how in the world can I be everything? How will I ever complete her? Every day I live with the gnawing sensation that I will never, ever be enough.

And so I eat.

But now I have a vehicle. Now I have words. I stay up writing my solo plays and stories late into the night. I am finally having a dialogue with myself. Writing forces me to sit and listen to myself, to channel the craziness going on inside my head onto the page. More than that, it forces me to be with myself. If only for a little chunk of time. To stay in one place and finish a thought. I am forced to find beginnings, middles, and ends. I must sit with the unknown, instead of flailing about, asking the whole wide world what everyone else thinks I should do, then stuffing it all down because my choice may not be the perfect one.

Sugar is still my late-night companion, but I don't seem to want to pass out from it. I seem to want to stick around to see what comes out.

In my first one-woman play, entitled *La Maze*, a reluctant mother gets a surprise phone call from her unplanned fetus. At first all she hears is a heartbeat on the line. She is frightened. Thinks it's a prank call. But she can't hang up. She can't. The heartbeat gets louder.

"Hello?" she says. It beats louder. "*Hello?*" Feeling suddenly nauseous, she places a hand on her belly. During the course of the scene, through the magic of mime, the woman becomes nine months heavy with child. She looks at the receiver. At her belly. At the receiver. Frightened, she disconnects the receiver cord from the back of the phone—and the heartbeat stops. She cautiously reconnects the receiver cord into her belly—and the heartbeat resumes. She hears the voice of a young girl playfully humming.

"H—hello?" the woman says. The humming stops. "Hello?"

"Yeah?" says the voice from her belly.

"Who—who is this?"

"Who do you *think* it is?"

"I . . . really . . . don't know. . . ."

"It's me, Mom. I'm your girl."

"My *what?*"

"You heard me."

"Oh . . . my . . . oh . . . no . . ."

"Oh, yes."

"Well, I mean, so, when . . . are you . . . coming out?"

"I'm not."

"What . . . do you mean?"

"I mean, I've thought about it and I've decided to stay in."

The woman rises, miming an even fuller belly.

"But . . . why?"

"Listen, I got your number, lady. I got the *inside scoop.*"

"Inside scoop to what?"

"To *you*. I've heard it all. Every last thought. Every word. Every dream. I'm inside you, remember?" The woman starts to pace.

"Oh . . . well . . . listen, sweetheart—Can I . . . call you sweetheart?"

"You can call me whatever you want. I'm still not comin' out."

"Listen . . . it's going to be okay. . . ."

"Not buyin', lady."

"I . . . We . . . look forward to having you. . . . There'll be a wonderful bed waiting for you. . . ."

"No thanks. I'll keep my womb with a view."

"We have delicious healthy food. . . ."

"Screw that! I want candy. Speaking of which—could you send down a few more Hershey bars?"

By now the woman assumes the posture of a fully expectant mother. Ready to pop. She stops pacing and stands her ground.

"Now listen to me sweetheart, I want you to come out and I want you to come out now!"

"For the last time—no!"

"Please! At least give me a *chance!*"

"No way. I'm safe here. Once I exit, all bets are off. You know *damn well* what it's like out there, so *stop* pretending everything is hunky dory, because it's *not!* It's cold and it's hard, and you're not even sure you want me, so why the *hell* should I leave this place? Now leave me alone. I'm exhausted. Go have some coffee. Have a nap. But don't expect to have me."

Contractions hit. The woman starts to push. Both mother and daughter are kicking and screaming.

The reluctant fetus is born.

CHAPTER 14

AS YOU DON'T LIKE IT

Jenny is what people would call a "big girl." Jenny from screen-writing class. I watch how she lives in her own imperfect skin, recognizing her limitations but still going for what she wants and doing what she loves—writing, smoking, drinking coffee, eating cake, listening to rock 'n' roll, reading Shakespeare, and wearing cute, punky clothes, all despite being a "big girl." It's like she actually believes she has a right to be in this world.

Jenny shares an East Village First Avenue railroad flat with another NYU writer who is skinny and moody and sleeping with her playwriting professor. Their apartment always smells of coffee, cigarettes, and nail polish. My health-obsessed family would scoff at the trash piled high with empty Diet Coke cans, Cool Whip tubs, and coffee-cake boxes all covered in a day's worth of ashes, but to me it reeks of freedom.

Jenny thinks I should move downtown. It's nice to feel wanted. The East Village is gritty and grungy, but it feels like it could be home. There are all these artists just trying to do their thing. They are alienated—but they're alienated *together*. After a year of commuting to NYU from the Upper East Side, I think I am ready. I don't feel afraid of the homeless people sleeping in doorways or the spiky punks and the junkies hanging out in front of the rat-hole apartment where I move in on Seventh Street and Avenue C. I'm not even afraid of our downstairs neighbor, a celebrated jazz musician who is a heroin addict and often doubled over in the hallway, hanging onto the banister, talking garbled nonsense, his mouth white with foam. I am, however, a little afraid of my new roommate, Lucy. She's a total control freak and totally PC before the term *PC* has been invented. I get nervous every time I hear her keys in the front door—like she's going to come in and accuse me of something. At least she's not home much of the time as she's having an affair with a Catholic priest (or so she says) on the Upper West Side, so it's kind of like my own place . . . except for the rats. Ever since I saw one pop its furry head out of the kitchen garbage, I rarely eat in the apartment—which is a good thing. My roommate would not take kindly to *this* rat eating her cheese.

And so I eat out. The East Village is blessed with an abundance of amazing, cheap eats. Like Cosmopolitan Pizza for foot-wide slabs with sweet homemade tomato sauce, crusty crust, and a river of cheese that spills out onto the paper plate—for just around a buck. And Veselka, the Polish joint with deep bowls of mushroom barley soup served with enormous chunks of warm challah egg bread, all for two and a quarter. There's even a macrobiotic restaurant I like called The Cauldron. It looks like a witch's den, but their brown rice, tofu, and stringy black seaweed is cheap and tasty—shades of Beantown. Talk about coming full circle.

My favorite haunt is Dojo's Café on St. Mark's Place. When you walk in the door you are hit with a waft of spicy Asian fried something or other that makes your mouth water as you wait (and wait) for a table. For three bucks I order a homemade veggie burger, a holistic hockey-puck of deliciousness that rests atop a mound of crunchy brown rice next to a small green salad with a tangy orange-peanut dressing. The guy to my right has a mauve mohawk and twenty loops in each ear. The Japanese girl to my left has platinum-pink hair, and I can see her naked breasts through her fishnet shirt. There's a black guy with a dreadlocked ponytail that almost touches the floor, and he's wearing a Walkman and nodding to the beat while he eats. There's a young, nicely dressed white couple having polite conversation while they try not to slurp their noodles. Everybody comes here and I am part of everybody because everybody here is just as freaky as I am.

Jenny calls me up. "Hey, Kotin," she says. "Whatcha doin', Kotin? Wanna go to the gym? Wanna get a coffee? Come on, Kotex. Let's go out." Sunday nights we rock out at Danceteria 'til closing, then walk and talk all the way home from Eighteenth Street. We get to her building and stop at the tiny bakery just below her apartment to buy fresh, hot loaves of white bread through the locked gate from the little old toothless Italian lady. White bread—how dare I? Having it with Jenny makes it okay. We sit on her stoop, munching our bread and laughing about our various sexploits. The warm hunks of bread bring me back to my lonely UCLA bread-baking nights. I still have a hole inside. But I am finding something more to fill it with than bread.

And yet, how quickly that hole can be blown right back open again.

Like a sober drunk who finds herself seated at a bar ordering up a double. Like a clean junkie who finds herself standing at the cash machine at 3 a.m. emptying her savings account so she can score. Like an abstinent sugar addict who was *just* telling someone she honestly believes she will never eat sugar *ever again*, then walks into a bakery and orders two dozen chocolate-dipped leaf butter cookies. One minute you are fine. The next you are fucked.

Seated in the Dramatic Writing office, I strike up a conversation with a grad student. I've always been intimidated by her height, her snappy outfits, her makeup, and her pearl posts. We start to talk. Turns out she did her undergrad work at the same school as James. Turns out she knows him. *Him*.

"So," I say, feeling suddenly nauseous. "Do you . . . know where he is now?"

"Last I heard he was acting in a Shakespeare company," she calmly informs me. She has a quiet confidence, a power that comes from withholding.

"Oh . . . well . . . do you know *where*, by any chance?" I ask.

"Here," she says.

"*Here*? You mean, New *York* here? *He's in New York?*"

"That's what I heard," she says, staring off.

It's a punch in the gut. My legs start to shake. My ears pound. *Boom. Crash.* I feel like I am going to have a heart attack. He's *here* and he didn't *call* me? But he knows I'm in the city. He knows I'm at NYU. I called him at school and I told him. Yeah, it was two years ago. But he could have found me if he wanted to. He could have fucking found me.

"Wow, so, well, do you know what theatre company? I mean, I'd love to get back in touch."

"I don't know. Maybe in Chelsea, but I'm not sure." The chillier and more distant she grows, the harder away I hammer.

"So, how is he doing? Do you know how he's doing?"

"Last time I saw him was at school," she says, slanting her eyes all-knowingly. "He was acting pretty weird. Some people said they thought he might be gay."

"*Really!*" I smile in amused shock to disguise my distress. Now I'll *never* get him back.

"Personally, I didn't think he was gay," she says. "Maybe just bi. But I also think he got pretty into drugs." The drug part doesn't shock me. Neither does the bi part. Come to think of it, James's sexuality always did seem a little skewed. Maybe he was just on good behavior for me. I should have told him it was okay. I'd tell him now if I had the chance. Do drugs! Be bi! Shit, be gay! Just . . . be with me! "But he was really good looking," she says, rising, smoothing down her houndstooth skirt, clearly done talking to me. She seems bitter. I wonder if she ever had him for herself.

"I know," I say. "He really was."

There are several Shakespeare theatre listings in the *Village Voice*, but there is only one in Chelsea. A young-sounding female answers the phone. "Box office, can I help you?" She's probably a company apprentice. I'd better be careful. She might want to win favor with James and she'll mention how some woman called looking for him. How she sounded kind of desperate. He'll be intrigued, of course, so she'll describe my voice, and he'll know immediately it was me. He'll warn the company director, who will quickly replace James with an understudy to protect him from his mad stalker. Besides, the box-office girl is probably fucking him. And so I lower my voice.

"Thank you," I say—then drop it even further, just to be safe. "I'm wondering if you could tell me if a certain actor is in your current production?" I try to sound professional. Like an agent might sound. An agent who is calling in search of this vastly talented young man she's heard all about. I want the little artiste box-office sex-toy gal to feel intimidated. Let *other* people worry about *me*, for a change.

"Sure" she replies. "What's his name?" *His*? How does she know it's a *his*? I mean, I said "actor," but so what? People call men *and* women "actors." Have other broken-hearted women— or men—called looking for him?

"It's—um—it's James Cannon." Oh, God. I said it.

"Oh, yeah, James is in the show."

She said it. He's in the show. He's in the fucking show.

"Oh! So . . . is he . . . on every night?" Because, you know, an agent's life is just *so* busy.

"Yes," she says. "He's on every night . . . and this is actually the last weekend."

"Oh . . . *really*! So . . . do you have seats for Sunday night?" Closing night. He'll be vulnerable. He'll see me and it will all come back to him. We'll take up right where we left off.

"Yes, there's still plenty of seats."

"Well, that's great! Thanks *so* much for your help." Then I quickly hang up so she can't trace the call.

It is ten minutes 'til curtain. I am seated mid-audience, right where I imagine the actors' sightline will flow most directly from the stage. *What* play am I seeing, again? Oh, yeah, *As You Like It*. I peer around at the two dozen other audience members, making sure no one is watching, then I carefully open my program and frantically scan the page. And there it is. In black and white. *James Cannon*. My hands dampen. My mouth goes dry. *Please* let the show be raucous so the audience won't hear my throbbing heart.

This is crazy. How do I know he'll want to see me? I know. I just know. But he *dumped* me. No. It was his *father's* decision for him to go back to school. Yes, but he went. Because he felt pressured! He could have said no. And lose his college money? Well, if he loved me, yes! Why am I still feeling it? What happened to the last two and a half years? I must have devoured over two dozen chocolate bars since James. It's like I am hollow inside and no amount can fill me. I don't even know what I want. That's what sugar does. Destroys my taste for anything else.

There was the dashing Wall Street exec whose fine leather briefcase and Italian suit legitimized me—until, three dates in, he let on that I wasn't the only one. That was okay. Why should I expect to have him for myself? Then his other woman got my number from his Rolodex and called to give me a heads-up that "our" lover had infected her—as well as a friend of hers—with a nasty, stubborn bug—something about trich-a-something-or-other—and how it was a pain in the ass (or thereabouts) to get rid of. Nevertheless, I was still game, until he made the executive decision to "protect me" from his escapades and cut me off.

There was the Columbia lit major who soon revealed that he, too, was sharing his goods with another gal. Did I want to meet her? Well . . . sure. Why not? The three of us went out. Her tits were three times the size of mine. No—four. Then I found out the two of them (and her breasts) were involved with yet *another* girl and that the threesome frequented Plato's Retreat, a sex club on the Upper West Side. It sounded dirty and scary, but I was hurt they hadn't asked *me*. Not that I would go. But they could have asked.

A sexy, older, published playwright was walking his little white terrier on Bleecker Street when I engaged him in conversation about writing. He invited me up for a signed copy of his famous play from the '70s and I spent the night. He had a chronic, phlegmy cough but refused to take antibiotics. Instead, he juiced constantly and reeked of garlic. When I lay my head on his bony chest, I swear I heard the death rattle. I wanted to run but I didn't. Was I a star fucker? He wasn't even really a star. Then he requested I trim back my pubic hair and so I did, even though I was offended. Despite the trim, we both agreed we weren't well-suited. Fuck him.

There was the cute Irish tourist who spent three days in my bed before flying off to Disneyworld. I tagged along when he went to JFK, hoping that a hand job in the airport bathroom would keep him from getting on that plane. It didn't. There was my one-night stand with a chiseled blond actor from the original Broadway production of *A Chorus Line*. After that I never wanted to see the jerk's face again—except, I had to, every time I got off at the Eighth Street subway stop and there he was in the second row of that fucking *A Chorus Line* poster. There was the punk rocker Jenny introduced me to who fucked me twice, then decided to go back to his girlfriend once she got a real job in a bank. Some punk rocker. There were the half dozen recovering drunks and addicts I met at AA meetings where I went to "get program" while secretly trolling for guys. In the '80s there were almost no men in OA, and besides, I'd never want to date a guy with an eating disorder. Not sexy. I felt a little guilty telling the AA-ers that I was cross-addicted. I knew they thought I meant drugs and alcohol, when what I really meant was cookies, cake, and candy. There was the proper sober Brit who said I was lovely but that he needed to be with a *real* alcoholic, and the ex-junkie who drummed frantically on my bedroom wall after sex. There was the auto-erotic cross-dresser I picked up on line at the movies who showed me how he got off by tying himself in a chair with an orange stuck in his mouth. The sweet, kind Jewish med student who I thought I should at *least* give a try—maybe a Jewish man was what I'd always wanted, maybe I could finally be happy—until I went back to his apartment and saw how neatly he'd bagged up his pumpernickel bread and his bagels like a good little boy, and that was the end of that. There was the big, oafish intellectual from the subway in the long, black overcoat who pinned me against my bedroom wall for forty-five minutes, threatening to slap me while quoting Nietzsche and testing my knowledge of existentialism. And the Polish counter guy from Stromboli Pizza who I thought might be worldly until he showed up at my apartment in skintight, white bell-bottoms, told me what a huge cock he had, and asked, "Want to see it?" He started to take out his kielbasa, but I told him I wanted to get something to eat first, maybe I'd see it later. I feigned a headache after dinner so I could ditch him and meet up with this *other* new guy on the other side of town, but then *he* showed up in a fugly fake motorcycle jacket, and besides, he wasn't very smart. And of course, there were all the cute NYU film major-wannabe directors. One snored when we went to the movies, then left me for his editing professor. One moved back to Montana to film a documentary on some moose. One had a severe case of backwards erection. I know, it's confusing. When he got hard, it pointed down and under, and I had to fuck him upside down and backwards. I called him the next day to say hi and make sure he wanted to see me again (even though I wasn't sure *I* did), and he said he'd been up all night puking. Say no more.

Every time a short-lived romance ended, I landed in a pit of sugar. Then I'd get sick with a virus or bronchitis and drag myself to the NYU health clinic, weak and depressed, coughing up a storm. They'd treat me with antibiotics, which always worked immediately—except for the raging yeast infections left in their wake. When I was not holding a guy between my legs, I was holding an ice pack or a crotchful of Monistat. I even signed up to be part of a free "chronic yeast infection study" at Brooklyn Hospital. Every time the doctor leaned down to swab up yet another culture, I repeated my theory about how sugar might be causing this. He repeatedly denied any link and wrote me up another prescription.

I also tried a host of natural remedies: vinegar douches, plain yogurt shoved inside me with a Tampax tube, whole cloves of peeled raw garlic stuck up in me, Betadine solution squirted in with a turkey baster while I was upside down in a shoulder stand (cure my yeast *and* get in shape!), and warm baking-soda compresses. There were also the gentian violet suppositories, which only turned my white underwear purple. At least I was sticking to NYU colors.

When my family gathered in Boston for my cousin Annie's wedding, my sisters and I opted to share a hotel room. I looked forward to some good sister time. I needed them. As we entered the room I saw there were two double beds. Lauren and Sarah instantly tossed their suitcases onto the same bed as if they'd planned it all along. I looked at them in shock.

"What's wrong?" Sarah asked.

"Nothing. I just—I was hoping maybe I could share a bed with one of you."

They eyed each other sheepishly.

"We were just thinking you might want your own bed," Lauren said.

"Of *course* I don't want my own bed. You guys *know* how lonely I've been!"

"It's just," Sarah chimed in, "we know you've had all these . . . physical problems."

"You mean, the *yeast* infections?" I asked.

"Well, yes," Lauren said. "But how do you know it's really yeast?"

"Well what do you *think* it is?" I asked, trying to contain my hysteria.

"That's the *thing*," Sarah said. "We *don't* know."

"But what we *do* know," Lauren said, "is that we both want children." And then, suddenly, it all became clear. Some friend had told me about an article that had recently come out linking yeast infections to HIV. My sisters must have heard about the article, too. Knowing of my sexual exploits, and by now both attached to men they called their soulmates, they must have put two and two together and labeled me lethal. I admit the knowledge that chronic yeast infections could be a symptom of HIV had stopped me cold in my tracks. Maybe I needed to quit sugar to make sure I didn't have HIV. In 1982 the AIDS scourge had only just reared its horrific head. I never asked guys to wear condoms. I didn't want them to feel hemmed in. I did, however, wear my diaphragm religiously. I was more afraid of pregnancy than death. Still, I always breathed a deep sigh of relief whenever I saw the ex-junkie I'd screwed strutting down St. Mark's looking alive and healthy. "Hey, howya doin'!" I always said, then kept walking before he could remember who I was.

The fact that my sisters actually feared that my germs would crawl down from my crotch, onto the sheets, and into their bodies, infecting them and causing their infertility—or death—undid me. "I can't ba-*lieve* this!" I yelled, like an angry child, throwing my suitcase down onto the other bed, then locked myself in the hotel bathroom. Of course I only stayed there for five minutes because I got lonely and it was time for dinner.

But it wasn't me who slept with all those walking chocolate bars. It wasn't me who was sick all the time. Who was this person? This insatiable monster? What am I doing here now in this theatre? What am I looking for? What have I lost? What do I hope to find? Oh, yeah. James. And then, the audience lights go out. There's loud, Elizabethan music. The curtain opens and several actors leap on stage. My eyes dart from left to right—is that him? Is that? Is *that*? Is he sleeping with her? With her? With him? With all of them? And then, suddenly, he bounds on stage. Yes, that's him all right, in all his boyish glory. He looks just the same. All goofy and sexy. When he turns to address the audience, I am sure he is looking right at me. I blush in the dark. I can't stop smiling. He must see me. He must know I came to see him. Why else would I be here on a Sunday night? Well, maybe I'm just a theatre buff. A lover of Shakespeare. Oh, that he might come to me in the audience, kneel before me, beg my forgiveness, and profess his undying love!

I am the last to exit the theatre. I see him outside the lobby, smoking and chatting with a cluster of his fellow thespians. He stands with one arm folded over his belly, supporting the other arm which is bent at the elbow, held straight up with a cigarette in hand. Vintage James. I cautiously cross the lobby. Only a glass door separates us now. My eyes are pinned on him. I open the door and walk outside, stopping three feet from him. He sees me and he looks confused. And then suddenly it registers. "Oh—hi!" he says with a look of dopey surprise.

"Hey," I say, coolly. I guess he didn't see me from the stage after all. I'm so embarrassed. Wound *so* tight, if you touch me I might topple. "How's it going?"

"Good . . . wow . . ." He takes a deep, long drag off his Marlboro. There's a new crease between his eyebrows. "So, what's going on?" *What's going on? You broke my heart, you fucking fuck! That's what's going on!*

"Oh, well, I'm still at NYU," I say, nodding my head. "Dramatic Writing Program."

"Oh, that's cool," he says, taking another drag. We may as well be at a fucking business convention.

"So, how about you? Are you . . . living in New York?"

"For now!" he says, laughing with his comrades as if they share some hidden joke. Actor assholes. You loved me, you shithead. Now you act like you're embarrassed to be *seen* with me. Yeah, I know, you probably have some wild cast party/orgy to go to. That's okay. I already have long-standing plans with a pint of chocolate chocolate-chip.

"So, should we . . . exchange numbers or something?" I ask, all practical.

"Sure," he says "I don't have anything to write—"

"I do," I say, whipping out a scrap of paper and a pen. How am I doing this? Or, more importantly, why? I tear the scrap in half and we each jot our numbers down. I'm sure he'll toss mine the minute we part, but I pocket his. "Anyway, I know it's your last night . . ."

"Well hey, thanks for coming!"

"Sure!" I say. "It was great!" I pray he is watching me as I walk away and don't look back. He'll see I am fine. I am just fine without him. Everything is blurry. Keep going. Wipe the tears and keep going. Places to go. People to see. Stop at the crosswalk. Look left. Look right. Stay on straight so he can see me for as long as possible as I *walk away from him*. I can't stop the humiliation. I can't stop the pain. To be, or not to be. But I can put sugar in my mouth. My body will be happy. I walk and I walk and, only when I am 1,000 percent sure I am out of his sight, I vanish into a deli.

CHAPTER 15

ENDGAME

I am at my top weight—165 pounds—probably due to increased bingeing since my James sighting. Apparently I *am* capable of putting on weight, even though, with my height and bone structure, I wear it well (as much as I abhor that term). One more semester of school, then it's out into the real world I go. Finding my soulmate is a must.

My sisters have each found good men who love and respect them, who want to be with them. How did they *do* that? Why am I the one still struggling with food? We've all wrestled with my mom's high standards and unrealistic hopes. Why were *they* able to break away? Not to mention they are *both* now thinner than me. How did *that* happen? At least I finally have my own apartment. Yes, the floors are so slanted you'll get a blood rush if you lie in the wrong direction. The prehistoric radiator knocks and hisses. The bathtub is about two feet long. The roaches in the floorboards crawl all night, and God knows the smell of urine outside the building is a long way from the sweet scent of jasmine and eucalyptus. But for less than two hundred bucks a month, this two-room hovel is my castle. If only I could meet my prince.

I am not above picking up men. In fact, I've gotten very good at it. I just haven't picked up the right one.

Walking home from my new, part-time Tower Records job one sultry August night, I am headed east on Seventh Street when I see a waspy-looking chap in a suit and tie carrying a leather attaché case. I say "chap" because he's not your usual scrappy East Village fare. He's more of a—well—a chap! I quicken my gait, and as I stride past him in my denim miniskirt he sees me and does a double take. "Well, hello," he says in an amused, dapper sort of way.

"Hi," I say, acting surprised.

What are the chances of finding a Princeton grad, a tasty dirty-blond with a boyishly smooth, squared-off chin, a guy who lives just two blocks east of me on Sixth Street and Avenue C, a guy whose job is head of English Lit at a reputable city college, whose passion is Samuel Beckett and who reads me Rilke poems in bed after sex, who is the perfect balance between responsible, radical, and romantic, who platonically shares a two-bedroom apartment with a brainy, liberated, thank-God-not-too-attractive Jewish chick on one of the grittiest blocks in New York? Well . . . it just seems a little too good to be true. And if there's one lesson most addicts refuse to learn, it's that if something seems too good to be true, it probably fucking is.

We go to bed. And I know. Shaun is *it*. The perfect guy to ground me my last year of college. I just wish he wanted to see me more than twice a week.

"I'm sorry, dear," he says. *Dear*? "But two nights a week is all I can manage with my various literary obligations and such. And you—you've got school, young lady. Let's see some willpower, shall we?" God, if he thinks *this* is a lack of willpower, wait until he finds out about the sugar! But that'll never happen, especially since he described his roommate as being fat. She is indeed on the zaftig side, but *fat*?

September arrives. I return to school and Shaun to teaching. Then it's October. We've almost reached the two-month mark! I mean, I wish he wanted to sleep at *my* place once in a while—he won't even come over to hang out. Aren't girlfriends and boyfriends supposed to hang out? Okay, so my place isn't Shangri-la, but at least we'd have privacy. That's okay. We don't need privacy. When you have something special with someone, you can be intimate anywhere.

One afternoon I call him at his school office to cancel our dinner date. I am sick in bed with another one of my vague illnesses. Body aches. Bad taste in my mouth. Feel like crap. This is the illness I've been getting since I first left home. Whenever I get this, I think I created it. It's enmeshed with the sugar, the disappointment, the depression. I don't want to be depressed. I want to be out and alive and amazing. I also want to be in bed with sugar. I want to live. I want to die. I want Shaun to offer to come take care of me. "Maybe you could just . . . come over?" I ask.

"You rest, dear," he says. I'm not sure about this "dear" thing. "You need to be well for your schoolwork. I have a late meeting anyway. We'll talk tomorrow, all right?"

I shouldn't feel bad. I know he cares for me. . . . I think. . . . But what is that feeling . . . way deep down . . . that voice. . . . I feel . . . nervous. . . . My feelings cannot be trusted. But this guy is a catch. If I let him go, someone else will nab him. I should feel confident in what we have. I do—I just need to run to the window every five minutes to see if he is passing by on his way home.

Around twelve minutes after eight, I peek out the window and see him, strolling east on Seventh, arm-in-arm with a black-rooted tramp. He doesn't see me—thank God. Maybe she's a colleague. A friend. I get back into bed and grab the phone. Wait. Stop. Don't do anything rash. Call him. No. I pull on my jeans, race over to his place, and bang hard on his turquoise-blue door. He answers barefoot in crisp white boxers and a white undershirt. He looks like a boy. Like a little fucking boy who was just caught with his hand in the cookie jar. "Shhh," he says, guiding me out and closing the door most of the way behind him.

"I *saw* you!" I say, shaking with fear and fury. "Who *is* she?" He smiles all-knowingly, pressing his finger to his lips to *shhhhh* me.

"Calm down," he says, placing both hands on my shoulders. "She's my *cousin*. She just got to town and needed a place to stay, so I gave her my bed."

"Oh," I sniffle, feeling foolish. "Well . . . so . . . where are *you* gonna sleep?"

"On the couch! Don't *worry*! We'll see each other tomorrow night, okay? Now you, missy miss, you go home and get some rest. Get well soon!" He kisses me softly on the forehead, turns me around, and sends me off.

Walking home, I picture Shaun all curled up on the couch in his little living room and I am comforted by his chivalry. This is a great guy.

Then I remember—he doesn't have a couch.

I decide to decide it was just a misunderstanding, even though the following night when I arrive a little early, Shaun's roommate tells me he actually met the blonde on the train coming home last night. In fact, he's brought home several women since we started dating. I decide to decide the roommate is just jealous. And crazy. She wants him for herself. It's obvious.

On my birthday Shaun takes me to a trendy German bistro on East Seventh Street, then to see Samuel Beckett's *Endgame* at the Cherry Lane Theatre. The production is intimate, stunning, and deeply disturbing and I have no fucking idea what it's about. It doesn't matter. I want to bring Shaun back to my place. He wants to go to his. "Yours another time, dear." Or "darling." Or whatever he calls me. It makes me feel weird. I ignore my discomfort. That's what I do.

In his bed, I jelly up and slip in my diaphragm. It's not in right. Damn this imperfect female body of mine. It's always so hard getting that flying saucer wedged up correctly inside me. My cervix is tilted. That's what a doctor said, anyway. If you ask me, it's probably tilted as a result of all the bingeing and the constipation. I literally believe I've caused a change in my anatomy, so that now it's hard to slide in a diaphragm. But it's not in right. I can feel it. If I feel it then why don't I fix it? Why do I not take care of it? Maybe I *want* to get knocked up. That is ridiculous. If I do harbor some sick, desperate hope that getting knocked up will somehow tether this guy to me, it is buried under layers and layers and *layers* of denial. But it's easier for me to imagine having an abortion than asking him to pull out when he comes. He might lose interest. And so I let him stay inside. I let him stay, and he knocks me up.

My period is only one day late but I know. I know. There is a slight burning at the top of my stomach. I feel slightly seasick. Woozy. Unmoored. Am I just *imagining* this feeling, because I know when you are pregnant you get heartburn and nausea? Maybe. I check my underwear every thirty minutes. Is it red? No. I wipe myself. Red? No. Are you sure? Yes. Are you sure you're sure? *Yes.* No red. No blood. None. I have to wait *two whole weeks* to take that stupid pee-on-a-stick test. I barely even see Shaun. He's busy, and I'm . . . pregnant! The test is positive. Shit. Fuck. *Get it out!* Maybe I am selfish. Maybe I want to remain the baby forever. Maybe I saw my mother's unhappiness and decided I would never be a mom. Maybe a lot of things. Go ahead. Judge me. Do it. I don't care. I don't want a baby. Never did. Ever. Not with *anyone*.

I get the name of an Upper East Side clinic from NYU. Then I have to wait *another two weeks* to have the procedure. Yep. That's right. They won't take it out until I am eight weeks. I feel like I am swelling from within and just want the sickness to stop. They say it helps the nausea if you eat. "Nibble on something." Who nibbles? Who fucking nibbles? I eat. Bread. Cheese. Crackers. Cookies. Nothing helps. Nothing. My face looks pudgy. And pale. I have to call him. I have to tell him. I know it's over between us. He's a liar and a cheat, and I still fucking want him.

"Shaun? It's me."

"Oh, hello, you!"

"Hey, so, I have something to tell you."

"Oh? Well, what might that be?"

"Actually, well, I am pregnant, Shaun—but I don't want you to worry. I am going to have an abortion. I hope you don't mind."

"Oh, dear, oh, my, well—are you sure? I mean, gosh, thank you!" Gosh? Thank you?

"I am going to the clinic this Saturday. Can you come?"

"Oh, I'd love to, but, gosh, I have to go out to Long Island to see my father. I think I told you . . . he has cancer."

"I know. . . . I am sorry. . . ." His father doesn't have cancer. I know because his roommate told me. "Well . . . can I at least see you before then?"

"Well . . . goodness . . . I'm so busy with meetings and such, but I'd at least like to help you pay for this. Why don't you come over now for just a minute, dear, and I'll give you some money for Saturday. I'd like to do that." Such a gentleman. "Do you know what it will cost?" I feel dirty. Should I really take his money? Is that okay? Oh fuck him. He's the one who knocked me up. Besides I am nearly broke.

"Oh, it's, um, about, two hundred and fifty." I hear him inhale through his teeth. Fucker.

At his apartment, he hands me the money and I stare into his face, waiting for him to break down and tell me the truth about his father. About his other women. He doesn't. He just gives me 125 bucks to cover his half of the abortion and 20 bucks for a cab to the clinic. Big of him.

I lower my head and press through the cluster of irate protestors gathered outside the clinic. They try to block my entrance with giant poster boards. At first I don't know what the images on the posters are. Something gray and red, amorphous and disgusting. Then I realize—they're fetuses. Lifeless, aborted fetuses. How dare they make me look at these? That is *not* what I have inside me. Get away from me you horrid freaks! I shield my eyes but the women are up in my face. Their mouths are yelling. Their eyes are cursing. I can't hear their words. It's just noise. The clinic door opens and a woman in a blue medical outfit steps out. She sees what is happening, grabs my arm, and pulls me safely inside.

I sign in, pay my fare, and wait along with two dozen other women. Wait for the misery and the nausea to end. After an hour I am taken into a freezing cold room, given a hospital gown and a plastic bag for my clothes, and told to wait on the cold metal table. I sit shivering on the table for another hour. The doctor finally comes in and wheels me into a small windowless room. "There will be a loud sucking sound," he says. "You might experience some cramping." *Just get this fucking thing out of me.* He puts on a surgical mask and gloves, glides some sort of tube into me, and starts up the machine. I turn my head and close my eyes. I can't block out the noise. The sharp slash of pain through my womb. Or the deep, deep cramps. Let's get this womb cleaned up. Vacuum every corner. Get up every crumb. Don't look back.

The roaches scatter when I return to my darkened apartment around 2 p.m. and flip on the overhead light. I stand limply in the middle of the room, staring at the wall, then I walk into the next room, pull off my clothes, climb into my flannel nightgown, get into my unmade futon bed, pull the covers up around my throat, and pass out.

Around 6 p.m. I awaken, zombie-like, hung over. A deep, dull ache throbs down there, in my uterus, I suppose. I automatically reach for my purse, dig out my wallet, and find the crumpled scrap of paper with James's phone number. I've kept it all this time. Why am I calling him now? Do I think he will comfort me? It's not like he ever comforted me before. I pull the phone into my futon and dial. It's Saturday night. He's not going to be there. But he might. What will I say? No answer. No phone machine. Ten rings in and I hang up. I am hungry. I hobble to the fridge. My womb aches. Nothing to eat but a rubbery carrot and some brown rice. I take the rice to bed and eat it cold. I sleep. Wake up an hour later and dial James. No answer. Thirty minutes pass. I dial. No answer. Wait another ten. Dial. No answer. I can't stop. Like taking cookies. Over and over. Unstoppable. Let this be my last. Let this be. Let this be.

Around 1 a.m. I finally reach him. "Hullo?" he says. At least—I think it's him.

"James?"

"Yeah?"

"It's me. Lisa."

"Oh, *hi!*" His voice perks up. He actually sounds excited. "What's going on?"

"Oh, not much. I just . . . thought I'd call."

"Wow. So, what are you doing?" he asks.

I sit up, suddenly optimistic.

"Now? I mean . . . nothing really . . . Why?"

"You wanna come over?"

Do I want to *what?* Now? Tonight? Holy fucking mother of fucking crap.

"Um, sure," I say. "That'd be great." Why does he want to see me? Does he want to have sex with me? He might want to have sex with me. How am I going to do that? Don't worry. I'll work it out. I always work it out. "So . . . where do you live, anyway?"

"Upper East Side. Seventy-Fourth and Second."

"Okay, well, I just have to grab the bus."

"Don't take the bus, take a cab." A cab will cost at least seven bucks. I don't have seven bucks hanging around. My checking account has about forty-one dollars in it, but the cash station is a mile away, and it's one o'clock in the morning and I just had an abortion.

"I can't. I mean, I don't have enough money. I'll just take the bus. It's fine."

"No, I've got cash," he says. Of course he does. His mom lives in Pacific Heights. His dad lives in Marin. "I'll wait for you downstairs, at the corner of Seventy-Fourth and Second."

Man, he *really* wants to see me. I wonder if I am going to sleep with him. I have to wear a Kotex because I am still bleeding from the abortion. That's good. He'll see it and he'll think I'm on my period. Good. I don't want him to have to worry about getting me pregnant.

I watch myself pull on my jeans and black-leather motorcycle jacket, the one I just got with birthday money from my mom. I watch myself stuff an extra Kotex into my zippered chest pocket, then put on some lipstick and my black hi-tops. I watch myself leave my apartment at 1:40 a.m., just about twelve hours after an abortion, descend the five flights down, and venture into the night. I watch my hand rise up to flag down a taxi on First Avenue. I climb into the back of the cab and I hear my voice tell the driver where to go, then I sit back and watch the city *whoosh* by. I feel like a lady of privilege taking a limo to an event where they are expecting me. They have paid for my travel and they are waiting for me. I feel so pampered. Like royalty. Before I know it we are crossing Seventy-Fourth Street—and there he is. Leaning against a brownstone stoop in his signature untucked tailored shirt and faded jeans. Only . . . now he's got on those brown-leather Topsider boat shoes. Just like his dad. Since when did he start wearing those?

"Pull over here," I tell the driver. "Right where that guy is. He's going to pay you." We pull over and James approaches the cab, reaching for his wallet. He leans into the passenger window to pay. I climb out the back and take a few steps away, feeling sheepish. "Thanks," I say as the cab takes off.

"Sure!" he says, no kiss, no hug, then leads me into the building and up the dark stairwell to his small, messy sublet. Once inside I prepare myself for the big embrace—I cannot wait—but he walks to a small corner table and picks up a mixing bowl of what looks like a mound of mayonnaisey tuna with a fork stuck into it. Tuna. Gross. Of all the foods. Why doesn't he offer me any?

I scan the room for signs of a love life, but the decor is spare and impersonal. Good.

"So, what were you up to tonight, anyway?" I ask casually.

"Just some party," he says, suddenly seeming a bit loaded. I forgot. He was out. He was probably drinking. I hope that's not why he invited me over. Because he was drunk.

"So . . . was it any good?"

"Nah, it was just a bunch of theatre people. Just some kids from school. It was kind of lame." Well, *that's* a relief.

"Right," I say, then plop down on the couch. James flops down on the futon at my feet. His bed, I assume, this being a studio with no sign of any other bedlike surface. "So, how's living on the Upper East Side?" I ask, shivering a bit. Probably just the anesthetic still in my body. Oh, yeah. That.

He places his bowl aside and smacks his lips. "It's pretty bogus."

"I can imagine," I say. "I never really go north of Fourteenth Street." Yeah, except for an abortion. And to see you.

"It's okay for now," he says. "It's pretty cheap. This friend from school owns it." I wonder what *kind* of friend?

There is a lull, peppered by more small talk, and then, as if in a dream, he reaches up and takes my hand—he actually takes my hand in his to draw me down. I resist for a moment, and then I slide down beside him. Shoulder to shoulder. Face to face. We begin to kiss. He tastes like tuna and whiskey. I don't care. It's happening. I knew this day would come. I held my breath through all the men and all the food, just to get back to James. We kiss and we kiss. He clambers on top of me and starts grinding himself into me. This is it. We're finally together again. We're going to do it. Am I *crazy*? I could get an infection. I could bleed to fucking death. I don't care. The chemistry is here. Just like old times.

"We shouldn't do this," he says, suddenly pulling off of me and sitting up. What's going on? Has he suddenly sobered up? Has he just changed his mind, just like that?

"Do what?" I ask all innocence.

"I just don't think we should open this can of worms." I picture the posters outside the abortion clinic, now with images of slimy gray worms slithering out from open, jagged-edged cans. My head spins. My stomach swirls. "But, you do have great skin." A fine specimen. "You know," he says, "I *was* in love with you." *Was.* Past tense of *is.* He *was* in love with me. *Was. Was.* Fucking *was.*

Where does this guy get off? Spoiled little twit thinks he can play hockey with my heart. He was only in love as long as it was convenient. As long as he wasn't pissing daddy off. What an amateur. Dilettante. He won't even sleep with me. Although, I have to admit, the fucking asshole probably just saved my life.

He reaches for his bowl, licks off the last forkful of tuna, and gets up to stretch. "Aaarrrggghhh." It's 5:45 a.m. and just getting light. He puts on the Talking Heads album *Little Creatures.* Loud. I worry about the neighbors. He doesn't.

"I guess I should go," I say, hoping I have enough change for the bus ride home.

"By the way," he says. Maybe now he'll ask. Make sure I have enough change. "Do you by any chance have those records I loaned you?" I know which ones. They're sitting on my bedroom shelf in Hillsborough, six or seven LPs he loaned me that summer because he wanted me to hear them. Jimi Hendrix. Patti Smith. Meatloaf. Of course I still have them. Maybe that's why he invited me over.

"Gosh, I don't think so," I say, shaking my head regretfully. "Sorry."

"Oh well," he yawns, walking me to the door. "Thanks for coming over."

"Sure," I say, picturing my body being flattened by the Second Avenue bus when I fling myself in front of it. He opens the door and pecks me lightly on the cheek. And shuts it.

Seated in the back of the bus, I am no longer royalty. I am the lowest pauper. A slave with only two teeth digging up potatoes. My fellow passengers are obviously on their way to work. I feel ashamed for having been up all night, trying to revive a hopeless dream. We make our way down the avenue and the city comes alive. Shop doors open. Worker bees emerge from corner delis balancing briefcases with coffee cups and bagels, descending into subway entrances, ready to get the new day off to a start. Like normal people. In functional lives. And functional relationships.

The second I am back in my apartment I go straight to my turntable and put on the Talking Heads' *Little Creatures* while I climb back into my flannel nightgown. The record starts to skip on the opening song: "And She Was." It skips and skips. I glare across the room at the imperfect vinyl, nostrils flaring, mouth pursed in rage, then I stomp over and I *snatch* it off the turntable and fling it hard across the room. "*Fuck!*" I scream. The record *smacks* the wall and bounces to the floor. Blurry-eyed with tears, burning with regret, I pick up my broken record and cradle it in my arms. Was, was, fucking was. *Fuck* that asshole. Because he wasn't. And never really was.

CHAPTER 16

DRAMA OF
THE GIFTED CHILD

I am close. So close. I can see my diploma at the end of the tunnel. James, Shaun, everyone and everything is behind me now. I am twenty-seven. Time to grow up. Time to finish. All I have to do, according to the head of Dramatic Writing, is weave my seven short solo theatre pieces into a full-length script. Easy. Right? But I don't want to weave them together. I want to keep them separate. Solo. Like me. I am told that is not acceptable. I am told I must find a way for the solo plays to relate to the whole.

I hate rules.

I ask my screenwriting professor for advice. He's an eccentric middle-aged man with pasty skin and a sagging jowl. He's heavy into Jungian therapy. He believes every human being struggles with having been separated from mommy at birth. And so, instead of advising his writing students to, say, add a car chase or more sex to their script, he might suggest they consider their protagonist's secret wish to sleep with their mommy, crawl back into her vagina, or kill their daddy.

When I first started his class, my professor suggested I read a book called *The Drama of the Gifted Child*. I was so flattered. He thought I was gifted! Then I found out it's not a book about being gifted. It's a book about being fucked up. It's about the child who is so smart and so aware of the wishes of her parents and has such a strong desire to fulfill them that she loses track of herself and her own identity. Now I'm *really* flattered. He thinks I am smart and aware.

When I ask him in class for advice on how to bridge my short pieces together, I brace myself. He's going to say something shocking. I feel excited. "How old were you when you started to walk?" he asks. Everyone titters. *Here we go.*

"You mean, as a baby?" I ask. Yes, he nods. "I think, about, seven months?"

"*Seven months!*" he shrieks. It's true. My mother still raves about how I basically skipped the crawling stage and went right to running. Like that meant I was brilliant or something. "*There's* your problem," he says. "There's all *kinds* of studies that show when babies walk too soon, they skip over the most crucial steps in their brain development. The parts of the brain used for creeping and crawling are also used for reading, writing, and speech development. That's crucial stuff!" No wonder I'm such a great mime. "I bet, if you go home and crawl for fifteen minutes a day, you'll find great improvement in your writing."

That night in my apartment I get down on all fours and attempt to crawl. Only, it's so small, there's nowhere to go. There are crumbs all over the dark wood floor. Have I ever even *cleaned* this floor? I don't even own a broom. Let alone a mop. Try again. This is ridiculous. A roach scampers by. Keep trying. How long was *that*? Three minutes. Four. My knees are raw, embedded with dried-up food bits. I don't feel any more capable of writing than I did seven minutes ago when I started.

After class the next day I report back to my professor. "I tried that crawling thing."

"Oh yeah? How'd it go?"

"I'm not sure. I mean, my apartment is so small . . ."

He suggests we go to lunch. Cool. Maybe he will tell me how talented I am, how he believes in me. I just have to do X, Y, Z to make it. "You like Cuban?" he asks as we ride down the elevator.

"Sure! That sounds great!" I hope it's not too spicy.

"We'll go to my favorite place. It's a diner in Chelsea. They have fantastic noodles."

"Oh—okay!" *Chelsea,* huh? Even though there's a million places to eat around here? Wait. I know he lives in Chelsea. I hope he doesn't want to bring me back to his place. I hope he's not attracted to me. I mean, I hope he is and I hope he isn't. Truth is, I want all men to want me. Even if I don't want them. But he's married. He mentions his wife *all* the time. She's ten years older than him—and a shrink to boot. I'm sure his desire to help me is perfectly innocent. I hope so. It would be hard to say no after everything he's doing for me.

The Cuban diner is bustling. The waitress takes our orders, two bowls of their specialty soup with noodles, then rushes off. I sit up straight, hands folded in my lap, ready and waiting for my professor to impart his writerly wisdom unto me.

"I want to talk to you about the image you're projecting," he says. Huh? I don't want to talk about my image. I want to talk about my work. But this is good. Image is important. He wants to prepare me to put myself out there. This is good. I lean in with interest. "I look at the outfits you wear," he says. I glance down at my funky top, my miniskirt, fishnets, black hi-tops. "The short little skirts, the tight little dresses. And your hair."

"My hair?" I say, unconsciously twisting a strand of my longish mane.

"It's inappropriate for a woman your age to have long hair. You're projecting a certain image. A sort of . . . little girl, slash, whore." Whoa. Is it okay that he said that? I guess it's good he's being so honest, right? Right? Professor?

"Huh!" I say, flipping back my hair. "I *think* I know what you're saying."

"When I see how you dress, it upsets me. It actually enrages me. It really does."

I don't like this. I don't want to enrage him. That wouldn't be good—would it?

"No," I say, "I appreciate your feedback, I really do." Because I do. Even though a voice in the back of my head wonders where the fuck he gets off.

"You know what I want to do when I look at you?" he asks. I shake my head, smiling innocently, taking a sip of ice water. My glass smells like Clorox. As a matter of fact, the whole damn restaurant smells like Clorox. "I want to, I don't know, I just want to . . . I want to . . ." He seems so *aggravated*, like we are intimately involved. Like we've been married fifteen years and I am still putting his socks in the wrong drawer. How powerful I must be to provoke him to this degree, to the point where he needed to invite me out, off campus, in a cab he paid for, to a lunch I hope he'll pay for, just to sit across the table and say to me, "I look at you and I just want to . . . I want to . . . I want to strangle you with my cock."

Yes. He really did say that.

He can't say that—can he? He's my teacher. I've come to him for help and now he wants to *strangle me with his cock*? Is he *serious*? That's disgusting. And hostile. Hostile with a big side order of misogyny. I should be open. I should trust him. After twenty-five years of therapy (which he often holds up as a badge of honor) he should know not to talk to students this way—right? But maybe this is exactly what I need to hear. Maybe this exchange will prompt me to finally grow up and stop expecting other people to save me, stop wanting daddy's approval. Maybe this is the key to quitting sugar.

Or maybe he's just a nut job.

Our food arrives. My bowl of soup is so deep, the noodles and chicken strips look like they are drowning. *Save me . . .*

"Here's the thing," he says. "If you really want to improve your writing, if you're really serious about it, I suggest you get yourself into therapy."

"Oh, well, I've actually been in therapy a lot," I say. "I just think maybe I haven't found the right one."

"I'm seeing a new guy," he says. "A Jungian guy. He focuses on the early stuff, the stuff with the mother, which, as far as I'm concerned, is the only stuff worth talking about."

"No," I say, trying to forget about his strangling cock, trying not to splash my face with hot broth as I slurp up my noodles. "I totally agree. The mother thing is huge."

"You'd better believe it. My mommy complex wants to eat me alive. But this is the first guy who's made me stand up and fight for my life. I'm happy to give you his number. His name's Will. He's the real deal, I tell you. He's fucking brilliant." I should be honored. He wouldn't give out his shrink's name to just *any-one*. Like to that Joe Normal in class who's writing that stupid Disney-esque paint-by-numbers comedy. Or that cute little red-head writing that milquetoast family drama. He would never give his shrink's name to them.

Like hell I'm going to see his shrink.

When the check arrives, my teacher takes out his wallet. He'd *better* fucking pay for me after what he's put me through. "I say we go Dutch," he says.

"Oh . . . sure," I say digging into my bag for my money. I can't stop seeing his pimply white cock whirling around my head, closing in on me. In our taxi back to school I am perfectly charming, even though I keep picturing grabbing his willy, tugging it, and *snapping* it off. I'm not mad. I appreciate his help. I do. Even though I want to chop it off with an axe.

He has a point about therapy. But I don't want Jungian. I want something more traditional. The NYU clinic refers me to a nice, ordinary Upper West Side shrink. Dr. Silverman is clean-shaven and mostly bald with thick-rimmed glasses, the proto-typical Woody Allen shrink. He wears a bright, cherry-red cashmere sweater, well-pressed khakis, and shiny, hard shoes. We sit in chairs across from one another—like a normal shrink and patient. He sits up so extremely straight and stiff, when he crosses his legs he has to manually lift one up and over the other. And he speaks with . . . broken pauses . . . like how my dad sometimes drives . . . on the freeway . . . with his foot on . . . then off . . . the gas pedal, because he doesn't trust . . . the forward motion . . . of the car. Come to think of it, he looks . . . a little like . . . my dad. This . . . could be . . . a problem.

"So . . . what can I do . . . for you?" he asks.

"Well," I say. "I'm in my last semester at NYU—"

"Oh! Con . . . gra . . . tu...lations!"

"Thanks, I mean, I still have to finish my thesis. I'm in Dramatic Writing."

"Oh! Sounds . . . exciting!"

Get me out of here. Give him a chance. Tell him about the sugar. His response will determine our future.

"So . . . the main reason I need help, along with trying to finish my writing thesis, is—well, I have this problem with food. Mostly with sugar. It's gotten better, but it's still hard."

He exaggerates a look of shock, abruptly pressing his back up against his chair, and gestures to my body.

"But . . . you're not . . . fat!"

That's it. I'm outta here. I don't want to hurt his feelings, so later on, I leave him a phone message explaining how I need to see a woman instead. That woman ends up being Catherine, a fiftyish eating-disorders therapist recommended by a friend of a friend. Perfect. Except . . . while I talk she munches Triscuits from a box. Oh, and she smokes. She seems disgruntled. And depressed.

Next.

Then there's the city social worker. Nice and cheap. If I don't have to ask my dad for as much money for a private shrink, I won't feel as guilty and I'll improve faster. Only . . . her office is decorated with about a hundred ducks. Stuffed animal ducks, rubber ducks, big plastic ducks, small glass ducks, paintings and prints of ducks. Ten minutes in, she gets a call from her mother. I know because she says, "Hello, Mother," and sounds annoyed. "I can't talk right now," she tells her mom. "Because, I'm in a session!" Then she proceeds to pull the phone into the closet for a private conversation. I hear her berate her mother for not taking her meds—at which point I climb over the stretched phone cord and tiptoe out the door, then make my run for it. Only as I hear myself mouth the words "fucking quack" do I realize the significance of all the ducks.

And so, alas, it comes down to brilliant Will, whose number my professor is more than happy to provide. Brilliant Will's office is on East Twenty-Third Street, six doors down from a bakery window with an obscene amount of pastries. I feel sorry for all the pastries. How will they keep from going stale? What happens to the ones not purchased? Will they be euthanized?

Will looks like a young Burt Reynolds playing the role of a shrink, with salt-and-pepper sideburns and a handlebar mustache. His office is in a dance studio, with a wall-length mirror. I hope I won't have to look at myself. We sit face to face on the carpet and he asks me about myself. I gather from his garlic breath and bag of rice cakes on the shelf that he's a crunchy-granola type who understands about health and food, so I tell him straight off about the sugar. He nods. He gets it.

"Tell me about your mother," he asks. I knew it was coming. Just not this fast.

"My mom? Oh, well, my mom is . . . She's amazing. She's totally supportive of me. She's always wanted the best for me." I pause, looking down.

"You look sad," he says.

"I just—I miss her. I don't know how I'll ever live without her."

"Is she alive?"

I look up in shock. How could he even ask me this?

"Oh my God, yes! I mean, she gets sick all the time. She doesn't exercise or take care of herself. But yeah. She's fine. I just miss her. I feel like I'll never have enough of her. She's kind of like . . ." No. Don't say it. Don't fucking say it. "She's kind of like chocolate." He is predictably impressed with my metaphor. Great. Now I'm in for it.

Will places a straight-backed wooden chair in the center of the room and motions me over to it. I walk over and he positions me so I am facing the chair. "I want you to imagine this is your mother," he says. Why do I always end up with these freaks? I picture the chair with thick black hair and bangs, dressed in a classic black Anne Klein linen pantsuit. "Here," he says and hands me a stick with an oblong stuffed pillow attached to it. "I want you to hit the chair with the pillow. Feel free to say whatever comes to mind. You're safe here. Take your time." I hold up the pillow stick and prepare to strike. It's like I'm going to hit a piñata. Like candy will fly out in every direction. Now I want candy. Great. I can't do this. This is stupid.

"Sorry," I say lowering it. "I don't think I can do this."

"Don't judge," he says. "Just let it out." Let *what* out? My mother doesn't deserve this. Not after all those delicious school lunches and driving me to ballet lessons and buying me outfits and predicting my greatness. How can I do this to her? "Here," he says, taking the stick. "Let me show you." He stands before the chair, spreads his legs slightly, juts his jaw forward, and begins to yell, each time taking a methodical swat at my mother. "I'm *angry*," he says. Strike one. "I'm *angry* and you won't see it!" Two more strikes. "You're *killing* me with your *sweetness*! You're *poisoning* me!" He gnarls angrily beneath his elongated mustache, curling his upper lip and bearing his pointy fangs like a rabid schnauzer. "Stop *poisoning* me with your *sweetness*! *Stop it*!" He takes one last, hard swipe at my mom, then he stops, bows his head, inhales deeply, exhales loudly, then looks up and hands me the stick. I pause, take a breath, and assume the position.

"I'm angry," I say, gently striking the chair.

"I don't buy it," Will says. I can see him in the mirror, pacing behind me, arms folded over his chest, worriedly fingering his mustache.

"I'm angry, and I can't stop eating sugar." Another strike.

"Come on, lady, don't bullshit me." Lady? Did he really just say *lady*?

"I'm angry, and I want you to accept me. Accept me as I am."

"Still not buying it. Look, I don't know who you're trying to kid, but what I *do* know is you're angry." Who *is* this guy, anyway? He's probably just goading me to make me mad so I'll think I am getting my money's worth. I lower the stick and turn to him.

"But what if I don't *feel* angry?"

"Bullshit. You're enraged."

"Well . . . what about my father? I'm *definitely* mad at *him*."

"I know he hurt you," he says. How does he know? Now he's a psychic? Maybe it's some sort of therapy given. Fucked-up females are always hurt by their dads. Is he wise? Or is he just another know-it-all wheat-grass murderer? "I know this is hard. But I want you to stay with your mom." Ugh. I *hate* this. I don't *want* to be mad at my mom. I *hate* this. But I should try. I should. If nothing else just to get him off my fucking back. Besides, she's three thousand miles away. Maybe she'll never know.

"I'm angry!" I yell, clocking the chair a good one.

"That's more like it," Will cheers. "Keep it coming."

"I'm angry!" Another swat. "And I can't stop eating sugar!" *Swat! Swat! Swat!*

"Good. Let it out."

I hate that "let it out" shit.

"I know you think I'm perfect, mom, but I'm *not!*"

"Good! That's good! Try this." He starts feeding me lines. "You're like candy to me!"

"You're like candy to me!" This is ridiculous.

"I can't get enough of you!"

"I can't get enough of you!" *So* embarrassing.

"I'll *never* be enough for you!"

"I'll never be enough for you!" That's it. I can't take his manipulative bullshit anymore. I let it out. "Why are you *looking* at me?" I yell at the chair. "You're always *looking* at me! What are you *thinking*? You think I'm not good enough, *don't* you? You have *no* idea what I've been through, Mom! *None!* And you don't *want* to know! You just want me to be *happy*! *Happy* and *healthy*!" I'm shaking. But I continue. "But what about me? You want me to be some perfect person, but I'm *not*! I'm not perfect, Mom! All I want is sugar! Do you understand? That's *all* I fucking *want*! And I *can't fucking stop*. I *can't fucking stop*. But I can't even tell you *any-thing* unless it's *great*. Well this isn't *great*, Mom. This is *shit*. I feel like shit, and I hate myself and I want to die, and I wish I could tell you that."

I stop. Can't look up. Can't.

Silence.

I look up. Will is smiling in the mirror, the proud papa. He steps up and places a warm, fatherly hand on my shoulder. "How do you feel?" he asks. I'm sure he wants me to cry. Or ask him for a hug. I can't do it. Or won't.

"I'm fine," I say.

"Good work," he says, nodding. "Very nice."

"Thanks," I say. Eyes averted. I already know, I'm not com-ing back. Even if everything I just said is true, I can't come back. He brought me to the edge. I've seen a glimpse of the gorge of pain I carry inside. Maybe I am just not ready to take the leap. But I've had a look. And for now, maybe for now, that is enough.

CHAPTER 17

CAKEWALK

I follow closely on the heels of my parents as they cautiously enter the dimly lit vestibule of my Sixth Street tenement apartment building. This is their first time visiting me on my turf since I left home nine years ago, but it took this epochal event to compel them to make the trip. After eight cities, three colleges, four performing arts programs, two mime companies, and an incalculable number of chocolate bars, I am finally, finally going to graduate—with something like 348 credits. That's 218 more than the minimum number required to graduate from my program. I actually have more if you count all the extracurricular courses in dance, drama, and macrobiotics. But we'll let those go for now.

We begin our ascent up the severely slanted stairwell. I look around nervously, hoping none of my freak-of-the-week neighbors will appear. Like Geri, the fiftyish alcoholic, mild by day with her lipstick-smudged coffee mug and her house slippers, rip-roaring drunk by night, often passed out in her apartment doorway. And Lani, the bulimic painter who helped me get my lease. Her apartment emanates a constant waft of turpentine and tobacco. And Donny, my neighbor across the hall, the stand-up comic with the severe stutter. His apartment vestibule is decorated with romantic, sepia-toned portraits of himself and his German shepherd "Nancy," both costumed from the Old West.

My parents and I reach the top floor landing and huddle together outside my apartment door. My hand shakes slightly as I reach to unlock the entry to my hovel. The door swings open and I watch my parents as they silently take it all in. The low, slanted ceiling with the brown water stain. The uneven shelves chaotically stuffed with books, props, and piles of writing. And the very urban view through my rusty gated window of all the other gated windows and tenement roofs.

"Where do you eat your meals?" my father asks, looking for the kitchen table. I never even thought about a kitchen table.

"I'm not really sure," I reply, wondering if I should feel bad about my lack of domesticity. "I don't really eat here that often." My mother is staring at the fridge door. Since when did it turn yellow? As she swings it open, a rock-hard lemon rolls forward. I never noticed the mold along the interior rubber lip of the door. "Anyway," I say, trying to sound in control, "the East Village has lots of really great, cheap takeout." Emphasis on the word *cheap*. I don't want my father to think I've indulged.

Just then a roach's antennae poke out from one of the stovetop burners. Fucker! In a sudden, sharp move I flip my hair back over my shoulders to startle him and he scurries off.

"Well, I hope you're getting your proper nutrition," my mother says.

"I'm fine," I reassure her, conjuring up the humongous brownies from Brownie Points on Second Avenue. Toss on a scoop of their vanilla ice cream, a dollop of hot fudge, a squirt of whipped cream, and a handful of nuts and you've got yourself one helluva calcium- and protein-rich meal for less than five bucks.

"Daddy and I will give you money for a table and chairs," she offers.

"Oh, you don't have to," I say, guilt-ridden over her endless generosity, yet scared of the gravy train finally coming to a stop. "I'm fine—really."

"Where do you watch TV?" my father calls from the bedroom. I dread that he is in there. He might know I've been with men.

"I don't!" I call back, hoping to appear virtuous. And virginal.

"We'll buy you a television set as well," my mom adds.

"Okay," I say, "but just a small black-and-white one." Most normal parents cut their kids off after college. I may have to be the one to cut *them* off. I hope I have the nerve. I haven't so far.

Graduation morning, the bright June sun shines down from a flawless blue sky. It must have been a harsh awakening for all the sleeping homeless who were literally swept out of Washington Square Park in preparation for the annual NYU graduation ceremony. Who *are* the people under all the tarps and blankets, anyway? How did they end up sleeping on a park bench? Where are their families? Do they even know? My parents have no idea how scared I am about supporting myself. I fear I could end up sleeping over a subway grate, picking away at a discarded, half-eaten bag of cookies. I could never have reached this day without their help. Maybe if I had been cut off earlier, if I'd had to put myself through school, I'd have cleaned my act up long ago. That makes me sad. I shouldn't be sad. I should celebrate. I am finally graduating—with honors, no less!

Seated in the hot sun as the endless list of graduate names is called off, I worry if Café Luna was a good pick for our post-graduation lunch. It isn't the cleanest and the waiters can be harsh. But that's part of its charm. My mother always says she wants to go to Italy. She wants to live in an Italian villa. At least that's what she says.

When the last student's name is finally called, some of my fellow matriculators and I dash across Fourth Street, into the Student Center, and up to the roof to gaze down over the park-wide ceremony about to conclude. The crowd rises. I visually comb the massive throng of families and friends, looking for my parents. I hope they are okay without me. And me without them. Then I see them, standing in the bright sun. My mom looks glamorous in her wide-brimmed Sophia Loren–esque navy-blue sun hat, and my dad, so dapper in the beige Brooks Brothers linen suit my mother no doubt selected for him. They came here for me. To celebrate me. They are looking for me. I am looking down on them. Watching them. Seeing them. Separating from them. They look so small from up here. Suddenly my father is not the all-powerful monster I always imagined him to be. My mother is not the solid statue of perfection. They are just tiny human people, here to see their youngest graduate.

Too bad the only table available at the very busy Luna Café is in the rear, next to the kitchen. My mother doesn't like sitting near the kitchen. Or the bathroom. Or the silverware tray. Or the front door. We once changed tables four times in a Chinese restaurant. She didn't like the aquarium fish staring out at us while we ate.

"I was here with some friends from school," I say as we scan our menus. "It was pretty good."

"It looks tarrific!" my father nods. Sometimes his obliviousness comes in handy. He is a cheap date, even if my mom isn't.

We put our orders in with the sweaty, brusque Italian waiter and immediately my mother's ritual Wash'n Dri's are handed out. "Your mutha," my dad remarks, as usual. "Awl-ways prepared. I should have bawt shares in Wash'n Dri yeahs ago. I'd be a millioneah by now!" My mom shoots him her look as she innocently drops her balled-up wipe under the table.

"Want some bread?" I ask, sliding the basket of crusty Italian bread her way. I'm so glad I don't want any bread. Once I start, it's hard to stop. "It's *really* good." She delicately places a slice on my father's bread plate, then reaches for one herself. She tears off a small hunk and daintily pops it in her mouth. As she chews, she holds her lips pinched tightly together, barely opening them wide enough for the next mouthful, probably to screen out the waft of Pine-Sol emanating from the bathroom.

"Now," my father asks, chewing his bread. I brace myself for the inevitable. "What are your plans for the immediate future, if I may ask?"

"Well," I say, suddenly dying for bread, "I'm definitely going to keep working the record-store job while I start trying to get my stuff out. They're going to increase my hours, too, so that's great."

"What kind of 'stuff' are we tawking about heah?" my father asks. He still doesn't get me. He probably never will. Not the way I want him to. Why can't I accept that? Why do I still have to react to him like I am five?

"My stuff. My work. My writing. I mean, I definitely know I want to perform, but I also know I have to work. . . ." Silence. Eyes to my dad. To my mom. Back to my dad. The food arrives. Praise the Lord.

"Wow, look at this!" my father exclaims as a veritable Mount Vesuvius of chicken parmesan, pasta marinara, and Italian broccoli is slapped down before him. My mom's gigantic bowl of gnocchi looks like a village of delicious, round pasta people, and my linguini is just the creamy dream I hoped it would be.

"I hope you guys like it," I say, spinning up a forkful of linguini. My mom delicately forks a cheese gnocchi into her mouth and chews it slowly, cautiously, like she is afraid of what she might find inside. Maybe she's chewing slowly because she has so many thoughts in her head that she has to concentrate. I flash on my last session with Will. I remember yelling at the chair and I feel terrible. *Am* I mad at her? Why am I mad at her? What do I want from her? She's just a person. A person with likes and dislikes. I just wish I could make her happy.

"It's delicious!" my father offers. "And such generous paw-tions!"

"I'm so glad," I say, trying to keep the mood up. "Do you like it, Mom?"

She nods, smiling slightly, and then finally opens her mouth to speak, softly, with great control.

"Just, please, whatever you do, make sure the job doesn't keep you from doing what you're really here for."

"Oh, don't worry, Mom. It won't." I pause. "Could you please . . . pass the bread?"

My father pays the bill and we make our way up Mulberry Street to a pastry shop I hope my mom will love. Sugar cures everything. Nibbling a cookie, I watch the euphoria melt over her face as she daintily slides a cream-filled cannoli into her mouth. It's the Good Ship Lollipop taking her away. It's her momentary sabbatical at the Italian villa. I wish I could make her bliss last forever. I'd feel so much better about separating.

I want cheesecake. Tiramisu. The chocolate-chip gelato looks amazing. I could eat the whole tub. "How about a bag of cookies to take home?" my mother asks as the waiter hands my father the check.

"Oh, no thanks, Mom."

"Let's get you a box, just to have."

"I'm *fine*," I say. She still doesn't get it. I'll eat the whole box, feel like crap, and have to cancel my plans to go dancing later tonight with my friend Jenny. But if I *don't* take them my mother will feel hurt. Rejected. Why can't she get it? She can't help herself. It's like she *has* to give to me in this way. It's the only way she knows.

"I really don't need them," I say. "But thanks anyway, Mom."

She buys me an assortment.

At the corner of Canal and Mulberry I flag down a cab for my parents. "How will *you* get home?" my mother asks.

"I was just going to take the subway." She looks at me like I just said I am going to hitchhike. Naked. With Charles Manson.

"We'll give you money for a cab," she says, digging in her purse.

"It's not necessary," I say. "I take the train all the time."

"Then we'll drop you off on our way."

"You don't *need* to. I'll be *fine*."

"Please, let us drop you off," my father chimes in. "It'll make your mutha happy."

I sit flanked by my parents in the back of the taxi as we race up the Bowery.

"Why don't you just come back to the hotel with us?" my mother asks.

"I can't," I say. "I'm actually . . . going out."

"Out where?" my father asks, like I've never been out in my life.

"Just . . . dancing," I reply, flushing with guilt, then add, "with my friend, Jenny," so they won't worry.

"Please be careful," my mother pleads.

"I hope you lock your door at night," my father warns. I laugh to keep from screaming.

"Well, we still can't get over you," my mother says, smiling and shaking her head.

"What do you mean?" I ask, knowing full well, but wanting to hear it again. Wanting to see if I can take it in this time.

"You!" she exclaims. "You're incredible."

"Thanks," I say, looking down. "Thanks to *you* guys."

"Don't be silly," she insists. "You did this all yourself. You can do whatever you put your mind to." I love it when she says this. I love it, and I hate it. It tastes so good. It can kill me. It's the ultimate sweet.

The taxi makes a right on Houston. My stomach clenches. They'll be leaving early in the morning, so this will be it—that is, unless I get up at the crack and hoof it to their hotel for one last good-bye. Or give in and go back to the hotel with them after all. Fuck it. Maybe I should just go back to Hillsborough with them. Erase my life. Start over. Finally put my mind to something.

"We're very proud of you, deah," my father says.

"Thanks, Daddy," I say. I will take it. A simple, uncomplicated compliment.

The driver makes a left on First Ave. heading north. Only six blocks left.

"You *sure* you don't want to come back to the hotel?" my mother asks.

Suddenly, I remember. In a wave. Right from my gut. I am ten. They were visiting me at summer camp. I wanted to leave with them, go back home, but I had to stay. They expected it of me. As we said good night, I longed to go back to their guest room with them. I longed to go home. But I had to return to my cabin with the other girls. My mother slipped me a white, foldedup shopping bag, and I knew what was in it. We both knew it was against the rules, but I took it anyway. Alone in the darkness of my sleeping bag, I quietly indulged in my See's. Guilt and shame enveloped me. What I really wanted was them. What I really wanted was home.

"You sure you don't want to come with us?" my mother asks. "We'll get housekeeping to bring you a cot." The taxi rattles up First Avenue. "What do you think?" I should go with them. I wouldn't even need a cot. I could lie between them on the giant bed and watch TV. Sneak some items from the mini-bar. Quietly finish the box of cookies my mother bought me. But eventually you have to put down the cookies. Put down the cookies and *walk* the fuck *away*.

"Let her go, Mim," my father says.

We pass Fifth Street.

One more block.

I lean forward to address the driver. "Could you pull over at Sixth Street on the right, please?"

"Don't be ridiculous!" my mother scolds. "We'll take you to your door!"

"You don't *need* to, Mom. It's only half a block down." She huffs and she puffs, but the driver has already pulled over. He keeps the meter running as my father exits the cab, holds out a hand for me, and then for my mom. She follows us out, looking disgruntled. We stand at the corner. The taxi waits. We stand together, trying to say good-bye. Behind me is my corner deli. I wonder if they have those Häagen-Dazs bars, the ones with the milk-chocolate coating and the chopped almonds.

"G'bye, Dad," I say, reaching to hug him.

"We love you, dah-ling," he says. I turn to my mother, and she quickly shoves a wad of cash into my hand.

"That's okay," I say, pushing it back.

"Just *take* it," she demands through her clenched jaw. I sigh and pocket the dough. *Just go with them*, I yell inside. *You know you want to. Just fucking go.*

"Well, thanks," I say, reaching my arms to hug her from the waist up. Maybe one day I'll be able to hold my body fully up against hers when we hug. Feel her belly and her breasts engulf me like a real mother and a real daughter. "Love you, Mommy," I say, damming my tears as I watch my dad hustle her back into the cab. Then he climbs in and pulls the door closed.

I see him lean forward to tell the driver where to go, and then he sits back. The cab starts to move. There is a sudden commotion in the back seat. My mother looks agitated. She is shaking her head in that trying-to-get-my-father-to-do-something way. The cab jerks to a sudden stop. My father rolls down his window and holds out the white bakery box, shaking it wildly to get my attention.

"Your cookies!" he shrieks. Oh yeah, the cookies. The wonderful Italian cookies. I want those cookies. I should take them. Like a normal girl. A normal daughter. Oh God, I want to be normal. It's just a box of cookies, after all! Just a nice, clean, crisp, white bakery box with a couple dozen harmless, buttery cookies. Such a sweet gesture. So generous. What is my problem? My problem is, they still don't get it. *I* still don't get it. Maybe I don't need to get it. Maybe I just need to accept.

"You take them!" I call. "Enjoy! Love you guys!" The box disappears inside the cab and off they go. As they speed up the avenue, my mother cranes her neck to look back and wave one last time, then blows me a kiss. I catch the kiss and send it back, keeping my eyes glued on her anguished face in the rear window of the cab. Her face grows smaller, and smaller, eventually disappearing into the blur of traffic.

CHAPTER 18

PSYCH MAJOR

Labor Day afternoon I am doing my laundry at my usual dive laundromat on Avenue A, looking forward to an afternoon of writing accompanied by some cheap falafel and a pint of chocolate chocolate-chip when I see a guy loading up a few dryers. Despite his Mick Jagger lips and his cute, wiry, athletic, rock 'n' roll physique, there's something unassuming in his posture. He looks—I don't know—nice?

"You gonna use all three dryers?" I tease. He looks up through his wire-rimmed glasses, embarrassed, surprised by my brazenness.

"Four, actually," he says with a smirk, then turns back to his clothes.

Okay. That's that. I've sworn off men, remember?

When my load is dry I gather it up and automatically wander over to fold at the table where he sits reading the *New York Times*. I don't read the *Times*. But I notice his section has a Japanese image on its cover. "Oh, is that about the Japanese dance company?" I ask, hoping to impress him with my cultural prowess. He looks at me like, huh? Upon closer examination I see it is actually the *Book Review*. "Oh! Right! The *Book Review*! Sorry, it's just, this director I'm working with told me about some Japanese dance company, and I thought that's what it was about!"

"So, are you a dancer?" he asks.

"No," I say, pulling the chair out across from him, sitting and starting to capably fold my stuff to overcompensate for my idiocy. "I mean, I was. I'm an actress. A performance artist, really. Not like you'd think. I don't get naked or pee on stage, not that I wouldn't get naked or pee if the work really *called* for it. But I wouldn't do it just for the sake of doing it, you know what I mean?" What *do* I mean?

"So, what do you perform?" he asks.

"More like theatre pieces. One-woman shows."

"Wow. Sounds cool."

"Thanks. I mean, I'm also a temp. But it's just . . . temporary." He laughs. That's good. Not that I am ashamed of temping. I can make up to twelve bucks an hour, no strings attached, and there are all those free reams of paper for my writing, free photocopies of my one-woman scripts and grant applications, and the occasional free roll of toilet paper when I'm really hard up. Of course, my biggest challenge as an office temp is avoiding the leftover donuts found in the coffee room, and staving off the three o'clock slump by taking a bathroom break and actually dashing to the lobby newsstand for a couple of candy bars.

"Well," I say, stuffing my folded piles into my tattered, blue-satin laundry bag. "It was nice talking to you!"

"Yeah," he says. "It was . . ."

I pause, waiting for him to make a move. He doesn't.

"Well, bye!" I say, rising and hoisting my sack over my shoulder.

"Bye . . ." He smiles up at me, a bit pathetically. I am not going to chase him. No way. This is the new me. I wander next door to the Korean deli and buy a coconut juice. Something healthy. Just in *case* I run into him again. And in case I don't—I go back in. To the laundromat. I march directly up to him with absolutely no idea as to what I might say when I get there. What's one more humiliation?

"Hi," I say.

He slowly looks up, sees it is me and smiles. "Hi!"

"I . . . thought you might want some company while you fold." He looks pleased, so I take a seat. "I'm Lisa, by the way."

"Gordon," he says. Gordon from Ohio. Twenty-three-year-old Gordon. Four years my junior. A recent Harvard grad. A psych major. Sells oldies music for a catalog and lives on Seventh between A and B, just around the corner from me. As we step out onto Avenue A, each clutching our sacks, there is that awkward moment.

"So . . . ," he says. I hold my breath, trying to remember that I don't want a man. I don't need a man. "My parents are coming to town this Friday to see the new show with me at the Met." Oh. My God. Is he about to invite me to join him and his parents? No. No way! And which Met is he referring to? The museum or the opera? *Which fucking Met?*

"That's so *great!*" I nod enthusiastically like I know which Met. Like I know which show. Yeah, that's right, I know all about it from reading the *Times*. Cover to cover. Especially the book review.

"They're really into art," he says.

"That's so cool!" I say, relieved I had the wherewithal to hold my tongue for five seconds and not ask which Met. And happy he is on good terms with his parents. Guys who hate their parents are dangerous. Not to generalize.

"If nothing else," he continues, "we could have dinner. Say, Thursday?" *If nothing else.* Whoa. His sentence structure makes me swoon. But the *piece de resistance* is the small, black address book that he then takes from his back pocket. Most of the guys I've been with never had an address book—let alone an address.

We plan to meet Thursday night at seven, corner of Seventh and A. Thursday night at 6:55, I dig out his number and give him a call. "Hullo?" he says. Obscure rock music blares in the background.

"Hey! It's me, Lisa?" Silence. "From the laundromat?"

"Oh, yeah!"

"I was just calling to make sure we're still on."

"Oh—well—yeah!" God. I am such an idiot.

"Okay, cool! See you soon!" I hang up before he can change his mind, wait three minutes, then grab my keys and go.

As I round the corner of Sixth and A, I see him a block away. Waiting. He looks awkward. I like that. It's human. I feel confident in my Bundeswehr tank top and worn-out jeans. I have no idea what "Bundeswehr" means. Just that it is German, and right now German is in on the Lower East Side. And that I look good in it.

He is happy to see me and suggests getting a drink before dinner. How civilized. He leads me to one of the many too-cool-for-school art bars on Avenue A and buys me a beer. I don't really drink beer, but tonight I do.

"So," he says, looking amused. "That was funny when you called me."

"I called you?"

"Just before. To make sure we were still on?"

"Oh, right! Oh, God . . . did you think that was weird?"

"No, I actually thought it was funny. I mean, kind of neurotic, but funny." Words. I like his words.

Over Japanese food we talk about where we come from. His hometown in Ohio sounds like mine in California. The owner of *Hustler* magazine lived across the street from his sister's girls' high school. Patty Hearst's kid sister was in my high school mime troupe. Despite our privileged upbringings, we both embrace spare, artistic existences on the gritty Lower East Side. Similar backgrounds. Similar parents. Artistic moms and professional dads. I've never been able to talk to a guy about parents. Acknowledging your parents makes you real. Can the guy handle it? He's definitely young and with a streak of the Angry Young Man. Music is his passion, though he says he's never had the guts to actually play. He's smart. And perceptive. What a change after my long line of candy bars. Finally, something seems right. Wholesome even. But what if he's just another sugar high?

What if he's not?

After dinner, we walk outside and Gordon suddenly grabs and kisses me. It's abrupt. It's awkward. But it's a relief. There.

We stroll down Second Avenue. "What should we do now?" he asks, sniffing around.

"I don't know," I say. I know. Say good night. Do not stop at the deli. Go straight home. Do some writing. Go to bed. *Alone.* See what happens. Take it slow. Keep control.

"You want to take a walk?" he asks.

"Sure," I say.

Walking east on St. Mark's Place, our arms brush against one another, sending electric shocks of desire into my chest. I must not cave. The only way to know if this is real is to hold back on sex. Start out as friends. Keep it light.

"So, have you been in any long-term relationships?" I ask, keeping it light.

"Ah, not really . . . I've seen some different women . . . but I, uh . . ." He starts to laugh. "I actually just decided I was through with women."

"Oh, man!" I exclaim. "That sounds familiar!"

We walk on. He stops in front of a boxy, gray apartment building on Seventh and Avenue A.

"So, this is where I live," he smirks sneakily.

"Oh, okay! Well, it was really nice . . ."

"Look, I know we're not gonna, you know, but do you just want to come up and see my record collection?" Is that a line? He may be a rocker, but he seems too innocent for a line.

"Okay," I say. "But then I really should get home."

"I know. Don't worry." I try not to worry, even when we are hit by the aroma of Lysol as we ride up the building elevator. But hey, an elevator! Very upscale! I try not to worry when he unlocks his studio door at the end of the hall and we are met with the bachelor stench of dirty sheets and newspaper. Or when I look around, taking in the room, which looks like a tornado has passed through, leaving in its wake a line of open kitchen-cabinet doors, scattered sections of the *New York Times*, socks and belts, and takeout menus. Maybe I should run. I can't bear another romantic disappointment. But there's something about this guy. I can't put my finger on it. There's a framed Rothko poster. A map of the world. And—oh my God—a cutout wooden head of *Mad* magazine's Alfred E. Newman with that wide, impish grin hanging on the wall. Oh, yeah! I *forgot* about *Mad*. I used to *love Mad*. My brother had that head on his bedroom wall growing up. And then it hits me. My brother. Granted, Gordon is completely different from my brother, and yet he has a similar modesty, a kind intelligence, an integrity. He feels . . . familiar. Familiarity has always bred contempt for me. And yet, how I've longed for the familiar. . . .

"So, here it is!" Gordon waves his arm self-mockingly at a shelf filled with hundreds of record albums. The one place in the apartment where absolute order exists. "What do you like?" he asks, flipping through record jackets.

"Oh, I don't know, I mean, I like a lot of things." I plop down on the oatmeal-colored couch. He puts on R.E.M.'s "Green Grow the Rushes" and joins me. "So," I ask, cautious but curious. "Where do you sleep, anyway?" He indicates the couch beneath us.

"It's a pull-out," he says, repressing a naughty smile. It doesn't take long for our full-on make-out session to commence. I attempt to put on the brakes.

"I gotta go . . ." I mumble seductively.

"You sure?" he moans longingly.

"I'm sure . . ." I hold firm as he holds me firmly. More kissing. More grinding. More stroking. "I should go . . ."

"Okay . . ." he says, kissing me so hard my lips might break.

"I *reallllly* gotta go!" I heave him off and fly up from the couch.

"I'm sorry, let me walk you home." We part with no definite plan, but he says he'll call me Saturday. That's two days. That's a long wait. Thanks to the ole hold-out-for-sex insurance, I am pretty sure I will hear from him. Not to say I am not a nervous wreck until my phone rings.

Saturday night, following a scrumptious meal at a Chinatown dive, we grope our way back to my place. He presses his body into my back as we ascend my severely slanted stairwell, his lips pressed hot against the nape of my neck. We tumble into my apartment, past the books, the plays, and the props I've strategically laid out to impress him along the way (just in case we end up here), into my bedroom, and onto my futon where, all night long, in the glow of my tiny black-and-white TV set playing classic old movies, we make love four times. The movies provide a soundtrack of hushed voices, bombs exploding, and tragic, romantic music, while we play out our own epic feature in full Technicolor.

The morning light barges in through my poor-excuse-for-a-curtain bedspread that hangs over my window gates. Sugar. I want sugar. I don't want to separate from this boy, but I can't wait to be alone so I can get my fix. It will take truckloads to tow me back into myself.

"You know what we should do?" Gordon asks after making love yet a fifth time, just to top ourselves off. My mouth and face are so sore from making out, I can barely speak. A kissing blister has formed on my chin. "We should go to the Ninth Street Bakery, get some poppy seed pastry and coffee, then go sit in the park. What do you say?" Eat pastry with a guy I've just had sex with? Now, that's decadent. Although . . . it does seem like a wonderfully *normal* thing to do.

"That sounds great," I say. Maybe I can do it. Maybe I can be normal. I've never braved the Ninth Street Bakery. It's run by Orthodox-looking rabbi types. I have always been afraid that if I went in there to load up, they would know with the wisdom of their forefathers that I was bad.

In Tompkins Square Park, I watch Gordon attempt to balance the *Times* sports section in one hand, a coffee in the other,
and a slab of rich, black poppy-seed pastry on his left knee. He
looks up. "Sorry," he apologizes. "I kind of have to read the sports
section first thing. Long-time tradition."

"Oh, that's cool!" I chirp. I nibble delicately on my sweet,
rich slice. The angst of our impending separation takes hold.
When will I see him again? How will I hide my various ailments
and insecurities? How will I keep from wanting him too much?
This time I will do it. Hold onto myself. Keep some distance.
Have some trust. Show some restraint. I will do it. I should do it.
I can. I must. I will.

And then, ten days later, our third time together, I tell him I
love him.

CHAPTER 19

SUGAR MOUNTAIN

You can say a lot of things on a third date. You can say you snort heroin. You can say you want to murder your boss. You can even say you did. But you can't say "I love you." You just can't. Everybody knows that. I couldn't help it. The words just slipped out. It felt so real, I assumed he felt it, too. But no three words probably ever made the color drain from the guy's face faster than these.

We continue hot and heavy after my little blooper, but it seems to set off a pattern of weirdness between us. We'll have two good, neurosis-free weeks. Great conversation. Great sex. Then his angst creeps up like a fast-moving mold. I don't even have to see him in person to know it is there. We'll be talking on the phone, making our plans, when a putrid cloud of unease rises up through the receiver. I tell myself everything is fine. It's all in my head. I'm just not used to a man really wanting me. Leave it alone.

"Are you okay?" I always succumb to asking, even though I beg myself not to.

"Yeah. Why?"

"I don't know. You seem kind of . . . worried."

"I'm *fine*."

"Are you sure?"

"Yes! But if you keep asking I may not be!" His anxiety makes me anxious, which makes him more anxious, which makes me quietly hysterical. What does his anxiety *mean*? I realize he's only twenty-three, and I'm almost twenty-eight. He hasn't been with a lot of women. Maybe we found each other too soon and he needs to sow his oats. I try to pull back. Give him some room. I can't. I push 'til he caves. A discussion ensues. He admits he feels nervous. He doesn't want to, but he does. Something to do with his mom. How she hovered when he was a boy, like something terrible was going to happen. It messed him up, especially around women. Now he doubts his natural instincts. Apparently, just because a guy goes to museum openings with his parents doesn't mean he doesn't have issues.

I certainly have mine. I'm clingy. I'm insecure. I have high expectations. How can I not, when my mom still sends me five cards on my birthday. When Gordon presents me with an un-wrapped XTC record album and no birthday card, I try to hide my disappointment.

"Wow, thanks . . ."

"I knew you liked the band," he grins, self-satisfied.

"I do! So . . . this my birthday gift, right?"

"Yeah—why?"

"Nothing, it's just, my mom always made such a huge deal out of our birthdays. She even celebrated our *half*-birthdays."

"Jeez . . . that's a bit excessive," he says. I shouldn't have said anything. I'm going to fuck this up. "So, are you disappointed?"

"No! I'm not!" *Yes!* I *am*! But I shouldn't be. I feel trapped in my brain. What is ever enough? "It's great. I mean, thank you!"

"Birthdays just weren't a big deal in my family," he says. "I usually had to remind my mom it was even my birthday at all." We agree that a compromise between the two parenting ap-proaches would have been healthy.

They say the first chunk of a relationship is supposed to be roses and chocolate. There is plenty of chocolate on my end, but our first year together is pretty thorny. Not that we don't have fun.

Saturday nights we usually see a movie, a rock concert, or a play. Then dinner out. Mexican, Japanese, or, most often, Indian, just down the street. Gordon always orders something exotic, like lamb vindaloo. I play it safe and stick with tandoori chicken. He likes his food so spicy, tears run down his cheeks and his nose runs out the door. He cools the flame with nan bread smeared with mango chutney, which I happily partake in. I watch myself eating with this man. This is what lovers do together. They enjoy good food, then they go home to fuck it off. Gordon loves our sex, and I love his love of our sex. I also love our sex, but I am mostly in it for the love. Though I haven't dared to use that word again.

Sunday mornings we pull on our clothes, tear across Avenue A and into the gritty Odessa Café with barely a minute to spare before the end of the 11 a.m. breakfast special: coffee, freshly squeezed orange juice, and two humongous slabs of challah French toast, all for $2.99. I won't eat the rest of the day . . . or so I tell myself. Until Sunday afternoon, alone in my apartment, my loneliness strangles me. I do my best to hold out until dinner, then I inevitably venture out for my regular Sunday night fix: a bag of Gummi Bears and a Häagen-Dazs bar. I live in fear of him seeing me while I am out on a sugar run, so I always take a circuitous route to the corner deli in case he is out with friends or, God forbid, another woman.

No. That won't happen.

I want to tell Gordon about the sugar. I want to make sure he still wants me. When he stays at my place (which he affectionately dubs the "chamber of horrors"), I leave ice-cream and candy-bar wrappers on top of my open garbage can instead of burying them beneath the empty lettuce bag, hoping to be caught. He doesn't notice. Or, if he does, he thinks nothing of it. I finally tell him, "I have this problem with sugar. It's better than it used to be, but it's still an issue."

He doesn't really get it. He tells me I have a great body. That I am beautiful. I love that he doesn't seek out my imperfections the way I do. He doesn't see *me* like I do. He also loves my work.

He edits my scripts, picks out the music, and records the voice-overs and sound effects for my shows. And he is my emotional sounding board when it comes to dealing with quirky club owners and hipper-than-thou performance artists. Despite everything, despite myself, the guy believes in me. And I believe in him. I encourage him to play music. Take him to buy his first guitar. Write songs. Form a band. We believe in each other. I can't believe it.

I am scared. What if it doesn't work out? I already know we both have a lot of growing up to do. What if he decides he's not ready? Some days he's ready. Some days he's not. I never know. I hate not knowing. We should slow down. I can't slow down. And so—my body does it for me. I get sick. It's another upper-respiratory infection. Gordon shows up at my apartment after work with a bottle of rubbing alcohol. He says his mom rubbed it on his chest when he was a kid. I love that he wants to take care of me, though I hate to be vulnerable. He says to lie back. I remove my pajama top and lie back, squeezing my upper arms into the sides of my chest to prop up my boobs. I have to look good, especially if I am sick. At least in this position my stomach is flat.

Gordon burrows his face into my neck. When I don't respond he pulls back. "I know . . . you're sick . . ."

"Well . . . maybe I'm not *that* sick . . ." Not that I'm horny. I'm just afraid not to please him.

"No," he says. "Let me take care of you." He unscrews the rubbing alcohol and begins to pour it on my chest. His hand slips and he pours the entire bottle over me. I laugh to conceal my annoyance. He wipes it up and then I lure him into fucking me so he won't know I'm annoyed. We start to have sex when I am interrupted by a bolt of searing pain through my lower gut. "I'm sorry—my stomach!" I dash to the bathroom and turn on the faucet to mask the sound of me crapping my brains out. I should be so lucky. I'd be much better off without my tormented brain.

Gordon does a double take as I emerge from the can, depleted and pale. "You okay?"

"Yeah—just—my stomach—sorry . . ." Then I actually try to get him back into bed.

"I want to," he says, "but I think you should probably rest."

I don't want to rest. I don't want to lose this one.

Over the next two days everything I eat turns to shit. My stomach becomes concave, which I love. But what good is that when I am too sick to flaunt it? Things get so bad, there is only one place left to go. Maybe the hospital will be the break I need. From my constant fear of losing Gordon. From never knowing how he's going to feel from day to day. From our roller coaster of emotions. It's also a break from having to take care of myself. But Roosevelt Hospital is no Club Med. It's drafty, dirty and the nurses are downright mean. Still, I am relieved when the doctor admits me overnight. Maybe he will find the answer. Maybe he will find *it*.

The doctor runs all the tests. He says it is one of three things: a hernia, an intestinal virus, or an ectopic pregnancy, which occurs outside the womb and, basically, if left untreated, can kill you. I think he says *octopic* and picture an eight-legged creature attached to my uterus sucking me dry. Unfortunately my aunt Selma from New Jersey is in the room when the doctor announces my list of possible conditions, and she takes it upon herself to call my father in California and relay them to him—or just the one about my possibly having a life-threatening pregnancy, anyway.

"You're not *pregnant*, are you?" my father blasts me on the hospital room phone. He must know from my mom that I am seeing someone. He must know I am having sex. How embarrassing. Our bodies are not for pleasure. They are for reproducing. And health. In my family there is no shame in sickness. But sex? Sex is self-indulgent. And shameful. Sugar is the only acceptable physical pleasure in our house. The only place I can express my sexuality guilt-free is on stage. As long as I am performing I feel I am worthwhile in the world.

"Because an ectopic pregnancy is a very serious thing!" my father shouts through the receiver.

"*Daaaaad!*" I hiss back. The old, cracked-rubber hospital phone cord writhes like a snake. "I *know* that, Dad!" I don't know that. I can't take my health seriously. Or won't. I still want someone else to do it for me.

"What was *that* all about?" Gordon grills me when I hang up and lie back down.

"My father . . . he's just worried . . . he's always worried. It's just his nature. Nothing to worry about."

Turns out it's not an octopus pregnancy. Or any of those things. Just another case of my body trying to remind me of my limits.

That spring Gordon gets his own taste of my father when we fly to California and he picks us up at the airport. I am bringing home a boy. This is *huge*. "You have awl your geah?" he yells from behind the wheel as Gordon and I load our bags into the trunk and climb into the car. Me in the front, Gordon in the rear.

"Yep!" I reassure him. "That's everything! So, Dad, this is Gordon!"

"Hello, Bert," Gordon says.

"Hello, young man. Because I'd hate for you to forget anything! Please be sure you have it awl."

"I'm *sure*, Dad." I crane my neck to look back at Gordon. "We have it all, right?" He gives me a nod, half-smiling with a what-the-fuck expression. My father drives out of the airport and up the freeway ramp. "So, Dad," I say, trying to connect. "You look really—"

"Hold on a minute, deah!" he barks. "Let me get my bearings heah!" Freeway merging is one of his most feared and loathed activities. Someone will crash into you. Even if they don't, they still could. "Now, I know you were sick. I hope you finished up awl your medication."

"I did. I finished it all."

"Because otherwise you have to start it awl over again."

"I know, Dad. I finished it. I promise." I am mortified.

"Did you stop your mail while you're away?"

"Yes, I stopped my mail." So embarrassed.

"I hope so. You don't want people to see you're not home."

"I promise, Dad. I *definitely* stopped my mail." I look back at Gordon again—who is now scowling. He's getting a taste, all right. Oh well. He can handle it. I hope.

My mother adores Gordon, the cute, bright, intellectual but artistic and very cute goy. We follow her into the kitchen where the table is laden with bagels, cream cheese and lox, sliced onions and tomato, and a giant bowl of fresh fruit, freshly squeezed orange juice, and French roast coffee. I watch Gordon's face as my mother lowers a gigantic platter of pastries in front of him. Cheese and apple Danish, bear claws, cinnamon rolls, brioche, and croissants, plain and chocolate. There must be thirty pastries on that platter. Seriously, you could hide a body under that pile. All I can see of Gordon are his blue eyes peeking up from behind sugar mountain, wondering what to make of it all.

The minute my mom leaves the room I turn to him with my usual "are you okay?"

"Yeah," he laughs, shaking his head in disbelief.

"What?" I ask, smiling and cringing.

"All these pastries," he says, reaching for a croissant. "Now I get it."

I am smiling inside. My ally has arrived.

CHAPTER 20

FREEFALL

It's a warm Friday evening in July and I haven't even ripped off my temp stockings when the call comes. "We have to talk," Gordon says. "Can you come over?" My hands go damp. My throat tightens. I know what this is about. It's about that girl at work. That broken bird. That's how Gordon described her when he first admitted his little obsession with her. He said she was like a wounded bird. "I guess I have a neurotic thing for women like her," he explained. "They make me want to save them." What about *me*? Save *me*! I guess her neurosis is sexier than mine. Hunger. Not sexy. Plus, I get jealous. Plus, I'm insecure. But I've given him so much in our year and a half. I must be good. Too good? Shit. He's going to leave me for someone more fucked up than me. How did I become the sane one here?

I hear the drum roll of death as I descend my stairwell, walk outside, and head east on Sixth.

I can barely even write her name. Valerie. Buxom, curvaceous, fleshy in all the right places Valerie. The temptress whose eyeballs I want to gouge out. The V of her pout points south to the V of her cleavage. The real kind of cleavage. Saggy but womanly. The kind I will never have. She speaks with a slight lisp. I would never judge someone for having a lisp. But on her it is somehow vulgar—as is Gordon's admitted obsession for her. If I had any shred of self-love, I would have walked away six months ago when his feelings for that broken-bird bitch first started. She's been a black cloud over our relationship. He insisted his obsession wasn't about her, per se. It was about his own crap. I found him a shrink and he agreed to go. He started bringing me his weekly therapy revelations, like a cat brings home its dead mice for the owner to see. I didn't want to see. I just wanted her to go the fuck away. He told me he didn't want to lose me and insisted his attraction was purely neurotic. This made me believe that if he worked hard enough in therapy, it would go away.

It didn't.

She didn't.

Here comes the rain.

Gordon paces nervously in his apartment, one hand in the pocket of his worn-out burgundy cords, the other hanging loose by his side.

"What's wrong?" I ask, feigning innocence. The wooden cut-out face of Alfred E. Newman grins at me from behind his head. Yes, Alfred! Me worry! Me worry a whole fuck of a lot!

"Well . . . I think . . ." He looks down, like he can't speak.

"It's okay." I stroke his arm but he pulls away. I understand. I do. I always understand when you want to hurt me.

"I just . . . I think we need . . . to stop seeing each other."

My teeth start to chatter. I clench my jaw. A faint white *buzzzz* shoots through my inner ear. I squint to keep from crying, then begin to sob.

"Look," he explains, like he has it all worked out. "It's for the best, for both of us."

I collapse to my knees, landing face to face with his crotch. I should blow him. I should pound his dick in. "Please don't leave," I beg. "I'm so sorry! Please give me another chance! We'll work it out! Please!" Gordon helps me to my feet, reassuring me we will both survive. I look at his face. He looks relieved, like he's just been told his terminal diagnosis is mistaken. Then I feel it. The hurt. I almost hate him.

"So, what are you doing tonight?" I ask, looking him square in the face. His guilty grin meets mine. His guilt is for fucking me. Mine is for knowing I've allowed myself to be fucked.

"I'm, ah, I'm going out," he says. I nod slowly. Okay. *Now* I hate him.

I walk zombielike down the Lysol-permeated hall, down the stairway to avoid his druggy neighbors in the elevator, out to the street, and back to my place . . . I guess . . . I don't remember, really, how I get home. I am in a walking black-out of pain. Once home, I pace my slanted floor with no thought of bingeing. With no thought of anything. And then, with only one thought.

I grab my keys and tear back down my stairs, out to the street. As I race up Sixth Street I wrestle furiously to remove Gordon's apartment keys from mine, then clench them tightly in my fist and pick up my pace. In and out of several Indian restaurants I tear, readjusting my eyes in each new, dark vestibule as I search furiously for my prey. Then I swing the glass door open to our favorite joint. The one where we've shared so many cheap and intimate meals. I always tolerated him ordering the spiciest dish on the menu, not even thinking of me, even though I always shared *my* dish with *him*.

And there they are, huddled at a table at the rear of our place. *Ours.* He is smiling, listening to her, as he takes a sip of his Taj Mahal beer. The back of her raven-haired, birdbrain head is facing me, bobbing about as she no doubt lisps away. I waste no time. Just charge down the entry steps and rush the dark, carpeted aisle to their cozy little nest. Gordon looks up in shock.

"Just thought you might be needing these!" I hiss, tossing his keys smack down into his vindaloo. I hope the sauce splashes into their eyes, blinding them both. I don't stick around to find out. I cannot get home fast enough. My apartment is just a block and a half away, but if I could take a Learjet to get there, I would.

I thrust myself face down into my futon and I cry. I cry and I cry. Soak my pillow straight through. I cry my lower back right out, forcing me to crawl from my futon to the toilet. Not that I have much left to pee after all the tears. The only plus to all my crying is all the water weight I imagine I am losing. I will look *great* once I emerge from this.

Only, I am not going to emerge from this. I am going to cry myself to death.

I have no money to pay for long-distance calls, but so what. I'll be dead before the bill arrives. I drag my phone deep into my futon to call my sister Lauren, now happily married, loving her work as an elementary school teacher, and blissfully pregnant with her first child in Northern California. She encourages me to hang on until Monday for therapy and tells me I am going to be okay. Thank God my mother is helping me with therapy. Thank you, Mama.

Monday morning, I call in sick at my temp job, then I call my shrink for an emergency session. Hobbling to my shrink's office, I wonder if an air conditioner might fall from a window and smash me. It would take at least that to stop the pain.

Doubled over in her chair, I cry and I cry and I cry, all the way down, below the cookies, the ice cream, and the one-night stands that have built up over the years, below my knees, down to the tips of my polish-chipped toenails. I cry like I haven't cried since I was a young girl. My tears are violent and uncensored. I have no words, except "I can't believe this is happening." It's not just my sadness for losing Gordon. It must be all the sadness I have ever felt, all the tears I should have shed, but instead stuffed them down and numbed them out with sugar. Because I didn't believe I deserved love, I didn't deserve to feel. I cry for all the times I was ready to separate. From siblings. Lovers. Friends. Parents. My mom. I wasn't ready to cry then. Now, I cry. My shrink is a buoy in my sea of tears. For three weeks I white-knuckle it between sessions, wearing a path from my temp job to therapy to home, gripping my hand over my heart to keep it from falling out and cracking apart on the pavement. I keep my eyes down just in case, *God forbid*, I might see him. Or *them*.

Sugar isn't an issue. It isn't an issue because I am not eating *anything*, really. I drop ten pounds without even trying. I trudge along until August, then fly home to have my right leg stripped of varicose veins. Veins that I am certain I caused with sugar. It even says so in the book *Sugar Blues*, although knowing that doesn't stop me from consuming the entire five-pound box of See's chocolate bridge mix my mother brings me as I lie recovering from my out-patient surgery. I stare numbly at the small TV set she has placed at the foot of my bed, my leg a throbbing log of pain. I reach back and forth from the box to my mouth, box to mouth, until every last chocolate-covered nut, raisin, and caramel is demolished.

"I'm sorry you inherited my veins," my mother says, perched on the end of my bed.

"Oh, Mom, don't be silly," I say. Like she could have helped it. But the sugar fix, *that* she could have helped.

Or could she?

She didn't *have* to set me up with See's. But this is how she loves me.

"The nurse said you were calling out a name as you went under," she says. "She said you were calling for Gordon, Gordon."

"Yeah . . . well . . ." is all I can say. In the dim light of my bedroom I see the pained expression on her face. Hearing her half-drugged daughter call out the name of the man who broke her baby's heart was way too much information for my mom. She can't stand to see me suffer. Me, I am agony incarnate, all jacked up from sugar with no place to go, except for limping to the toilet, or to the family room phone—my lifeline.

Lauren invites me to spend a week with her very pregnant self and her husband. I am tempted but afraid. If I go there, I might feel. If I stay here, I will stay numb. I choose to feel.

My first night, the crickets outside my sister's house keep time with my brain as it backs up and crashes over and over what happened with Gordon. I finally limp downstairs to escape the wretched movie of him and Valerie in my head. When Lauren's restless pregnant legs carry her downstairs for warm milk, she finds me seated, staring into the cold, unlit wood-burning stove. She drapes a blanket over my shoulders, tells me to elevate my legs, brings me a mug of warm milk, and sits.

"I know you're suffering," she says, letting out a deep sigh. "I wonder if you could just tell me what happened. I mean, I know what happened, but maybe if you told me it would help." She is with me, not telling me what to do or how to move on. Just asking me to share my grief, no matter how bleak.

"I still don't understand," I utter, shaking my head, keeping my eyes down. "I finally found this great guy who thought I was amazing and loved my work. I mean, I know we had problems. I know he was young, and I know I was clingy. I just thought we could work it out!"

Lauren takes my hands in hers. I never noticed how much her hands resemble my mom's. They are peasant hands. Hands that exude motherhood, worry, and care. The moment she touches me, my tears begin to fall. My first tears since New York.

"He's gone, Lauren," I cry. I still can't look up. "He's really gone."

"But he loved you," she says. "That's the thing. He *loved* you. I *know* he did."

"I know he did, too." And then slowly, I gather the courage to look up. She is crying. For me. Here is the sister who once threatened to jump from our backyard magnolia tree if my parents didn't get rid of me, now reaching a hand to pull me up.

I've always fled when something hurt. Now I sit with the emptiness, with the great big giant hole inside. Together, we sit.

———————

I have a photograph from that week of homemade pesto and rented videos, of gentle walks along my sister's wooded street accompanied by a Walkman tape of Streisand, my childhood idol, a tape my brother-in-law thoughtfully compiled for me. It's a silly photograph, but it captures a time that is the start of healing. Lauren and I are in her kitchen. In the background, with her back to the camera, she is reaching for a bag of pasta from the cabinet. The rear seam of her sweatpants is vertically torn and she's not wearing any underpants, so her naked butt crack peeks through the tear.

In the foreground I sit hunched over a typewriter, channeling my angst into a new theatre piece. I've just looked up for the shot. I'm looking smack into the camera with a goofy expression, as if to tell the viewer that I know what is behind me. My sister's behind. It's a reminder of something silly. And human. And real.

I feel joy in the moment.

Maybe I don't have to die.

Maybe I am going to be okay.

CHAPTER 21

THREE DECADES LATER
THERE WILL (STILL) BE SUGAR

I am hunkered down at the edge of the exam table in my new doctor's office. She's an enormous Greek woman with long brown hair and painted red lips. "What can I do for you?" she asks, perched on her little rolling stool across the room.

"Well, I just—I get sick a lot," I say.

"Sick how?"

"It's always the same. I'm hot, no fever, my glands are sore, my stomach hurts, I feel nauseous—I should tell you, this happens *a lot.*"

"How old are you?" she asks.

"I'm fifty-three," I say. Yep. It's been over three decades since I first left home, first started bingeing, first started feeling ill, and here I am. I should be healthy now, living in LA with all this health food and sun.

As she examines me, I tell her about my sugar history. How I don't binge like I used to but that it's still a problem. I feel self-conscious talking to her about food and hope she doesn't think I think she's fat. Then I ask the big one: does she think all the sugar could have had a long-term effect on my immune system? "Oh, sure," she says. "I think it's a definite possibility."

Oh. My. God. She thinks it's a definite possibility. Well halle-fuckin'-lujah. Somebody in a white lab coat finally gets it.

I want to jump up and hug her and kiss her, kick my heels up in the air. Vindicated at last!

She says I have a virus and prescribes chicken soup, Tylenol, and rest. "Thank you," I say. "Thank you *so* much." And then, on my way out, she shows me the kitchen where there is a stack of holiday cookies, cakes, and candy her patients have brought in. "Please," she says. "Do me a favor and take some home. Help yourself. Help me out. *Please.*"

Wow.

How am I ever going to quit sugar?

I thought that once I found a man it would cure me of sugar. Especially when that man turned out to be Gordon after all. A few months after that terrible Friday in New York, when I threw his keys in his vindaloo, he saw an ad for my new show. He called and asked if he could come. "Sure," I said. Why not? He loved the show. We talked a bit, hugged good-bye, and that was that. A week later he called again. We started hanging out. He never mentioned her. The big V. And I was not about to ask. If you don't look out the window when you fly, maybe you won't crash.

We crashed.

One month later, was the night before Christmas Eve. The night before we were each flying home to celebrate with our respective families. I was nervous. I told myself, I shouldn't feel nervous. We had just made love. We were exchanging gifts. What more could I want? I was trying on his gift to me, a hand-made bronze-satin jacket with a miniature TV pin stuck on the collar, picked out just for me, when he let out a sigh. "What's wrong?" I asked, internally cringing.

"I was just thinking about my therapy session today," he said.

"Really?" I started to tremble, instinctively pulling the sheet up around my naked body.

"I spent the whole session talking about her." My teeth began to chatter. Stop it, teeth!

"Her," I said. Say it. *Say it!* "You mean . . . Valerie?"

"Yeah," he said. "Man, *that* was a waste of money." It didn't matter that I didn't know exactly what he meant. What mattered was . . . she was still with us.

He laid back, his eyes glued to my face. Maybe my head would explode, like the guy in the movie *Scanners*. "I don't think we should talk about this right now," he said. I nodded, wanting to blow up *his* head. He suggested we sleep. It was late. We each had planes to catch. Planes I hoped will each go down in a fiery ball. If I were healthy, I'd have singled out his plane, but I still couldn't let go of that self-destructive impulse. Not yet.

The following night, in my parent's home, I sat knees-to-chest in a dark corner of the TV room, head in my hands, phone by my side, trying to get up the guts to do what I had told my sister Sarah what I knew I must do.

"Do you want me to sit with you?" she asked.

"No, thanks," I said, bracing myself. I was deeply comforted to know she was near. I felt her love. Despite all my years of craving more from my sister, what she gave me in that moment was really all I could ever want. She walked out, promising to keep Dad from picking up the phone in another room and automatically dialing out. She had my back.

Gordon's mother answered in her familiar sweet voice. When we met last Christmas, I knew both of his parents liked me. Now I was going to lose them, too. "Hello?"

"Hi, it's, um, it's Lisa."

"Oh . . . hello," she said so kindly, I half-expected her to say "I'm sorry for your loss." Maybe Gordon had told her things were not great. Maybe she didn't want to provoke more attachment from me to Gordon's family. Because all she said was, "Let me get Gordon for you. You take care now, dear."

"Thanks," I said, not moving an inch. Footsteps sounded through the receiver, then some mumbling, some rustling, then new footsteps.

"Hello?" Gordon said, sounding like he had just swallowed something. A bite of ham, perhaps. A dinner roll.

"Hi," I said. This time I was not going to wait for him. "I have something to tell you."

"I know," he said. Because he knew.

"I don't want you to call me again, okay?" Keep breathing. Keep going. "Don't call me, don't write to me, don't look for me, don't talk to me—I don't *ever* want to hear from you again. *Do you understand?*"

"Okay," he said, and I hung up before he could say good-bye.

Three months later, when I was back in New York, he did call again. I didn't call back. And again. Nope. He left a note in my mailbox. Drew a sweet picture of me and called me a tall drink of water. My heart ached. But no. Then on my half-birthday he left me a humorous and romantic card. It was especially meaningful as he'd been critical of my mother's celebrations of our half-birthdays. It's like he was showing me he could change. He could value something that had, indeed, held sentimental value for me. I cried with joy at his card. But I slipped it under my pillow. And didn't call.

The next time he phoned it was late. I let it ring. And ring. I knew it was him. Just before the phone machine picked up, I answered. We spoke. For two hours. Halfway through, he brought her up. Said he'd only ended up sleeping with her twice. They were still friends but she was pretty messed up. "Besides," he said, "I'm not in love with her." He paused. "I'm in love with you." Okay. Shit. A million shits. Shits of joy. Shits of fear. Four months earlier I would have died to hear these words. Still, I said nothing. I just lay there. Taking it in.

But the gate to my heart opened. Thus began a handful of lengthy, late-night phone conversations, like we were talking for the very first time. About everything. About nothing. There was no particular point. No particular subject. Or agenda. We just wanted to be together. "I wish I could see you," he'd say, but I held back. For once. It would have been so easy to hook up. I could have been in his bed in four minutes if I ran. Maybe three, depending on how many Avenue A posers I had to dodge to get past. But I didn't want to run. Not this time. I was right where I wanted to be. In my own bed. In my own skin. And he respected it.

I respected it.

We respected it.

I always needed my fix *now*. How many times did I blister my mouth gobbling half-baked cookies before they were cooled? I never learned to self-soothe. Giving me everything as soon as I wanted it was the best my parents could do for me. And, also, the worst.

And so I called the shots. And then—we both called the shots. Like starting over on the right foot. And now, two decades later, here we are. Married. With child.

And I still want sugar.

Well, if a man couldn't cure me, then what about theatre? After all, theatre was my first love. I knew, I just knew, if I could make it as an artist, then I would be happy. In New York I booked my shows at all the hot East Village performance art venues— The Pyramid Club, P.S. 122, Franklin Furnace, King Tut's Wah Wah Hut, La Mama, Dixon Place. My characters were born out of angst and fury. Like Melba Axelrod, the Park Avenue matron in leopard lounging PJs and two-inch red talons. She oozes resentment towards her husband, Axel, who can't—or won't—give her a child. When he takes her to Bloomingdale's for a new fur to placate her, she gets lost and transforms into a live fox. Her daughter, Owna, the pre-pubescent princess who is terrified of getting fat, transforms into a demented fitness guru and leads her imagined TV audience in "Anorexercise: The Mourning Workout," a Jane Fonda–like workout routine a la eating disorders.

And Brenda Dough, a punky suburban teen costumed in ripped, black leggings and ratty orange sweatshirt with "Mom is dead!" scrawled across the chest. When she runs away from home in search of stardom, her naive, nit-witted mother, Elma, takes a bus across country in search of her daughter. She finds her in a dive club on the Lower East Side now posing as Pretentia, the goddess of solo performance art, and mother and daughter have it out on stage.

Plus there's Audrey deBloom, a ditsy secretary with a squeaky, little-girl voice, a mini-miniskirt, and six-inch turquoise-blue spike heels. When she discovers that her boss, "Mista Peterman," whom she is infatuated with, is sleeping with a dozen *other* women, she seductively scolds him, gives him an enormous blow job, and then swallows him whole. All in mime, of course.

But despite all my work, and all the courage I summoned to put myself out there, alone on the stage; despite the favorable reviews and winning various artist grants and artist-in-residencies, I constantly compared myself to others. Compare and despair. If I could just get this one particular venue to book me. If I could just be as famous as Karen Finley—although, I could never spread chocolate all over my body. I'd have to eat it. If I could just get a great review in the *New York Times*. Or a good review. Or any review. People say you can have all the fame in the world and still feel empty. Look at all the famous artists who've drunk and drugged themselves to death. But that was not me. Once I attained a solid level of success, I would stop wanting to binge on sugar. I would.

I didn't.

I won a grant to create a show based on my life as a temp. It's a view from the bottom rung of the corporate ladder, seen through the eyes of an office temp/wannabe star—aka me. The show struck a chord. It was the first one that seemed like it might just take me there. To that sugar-free star in the sky.

Indeed, my show did take me places. Chicago. San Francisco. Santa Barbara. Baltimore. St. Louis. An independent producer saw me at the Solo Mio Theatre Festival in San Francisco and invited me to the Edinburgh Fringe Festival. Two weeks after my and Gordon's glorious wedding in Sonoma, fully orchestrated by my mom—from my bouquet of white lilies to the five-tiered apricot wedding cheesecake—I was flown to London for two weeks' rehearsal with a hired director, all expenses paid. Life was everything I'd dreamed of. *Temporary Girl* was a hit at the festival. I got fantastic reviews. Sold out almost every show. At night, alone in my room, I secretly devoured entire rolls of chocolate-dipped McVities Digestive Biscuits and told myself it was okay since they had the word "digestive" in them.

One Saturday night after the show, my choreographer and I were walking back to her room for Indian takeout and a movie. I couldn't stop thinking about my performance. I couldn't stop talking about various moments in the show, as if to keep the moments alive, keep pouring sugar in through that feeding tube. "You know that part when I blah blah blah . . ." I asked, trying to keep up with her as she trucked up the hill. "I thought that was really good, didn't you? They really seemed to like the blah blah blah, don't you think?" Suddenly, she stopped and she turned to me and she said, "God, you just can't let it go, can you? You're constantly missing out on what comes next because you're holding onto the past. You had a great night, now move on!" It stung. But she was right. It's like there was a bend in my brain that kept me from moving on. Kept me wanting more validation. I couldn't stop it. I just wanted more.

I hoped she'd ordered enough nan bread.

Bronchitis landed me in an Edinburgh emergency room. I could not stop coughing. My producer was supportive and jolly, blowing up surgical gloves to volley about the exam room while we waited for the doctor. I felt embarrassed. If I'd been a *real* professional, I wouldn't be sick. I feared I'd caused this with all the biscuits and the English chocolate, the lack of sleep and the worrying about my future.

Some of my happiest childhood days were when I got to stay home sick from school. I often faked ill just to be able to stay with my mom. It was the only time I had her to myself. Away from my siblings and my father. I did anything to stay home. I pretended I couldn't turn my head so she'd think there was something wrong with my neck. When she took my temperature I'd hold my breath, hoping my heart would stop and my fever would rise. I threw myself off my bike in an attempt to break a limb. When I was home ill she let me stay in her bed and watch *I Love Lucy* and *The Galloping Gourmet*. She brought me lunch on a special tray made to look like the dish they were serving on the show, hid candy in my backrest pockets, and served warm, homemade chocolate pudding.

Sweet Jesus. No wonder I get sick a lot.

Thanks to a heavy dose of antibiotics and some potent cough syrup, I finished out my tour. And several more in the years to come. I even got to make a movie version of *Temporary Girl*. There were more new shows: *Ms. Diagnosis. Beyond the Fridge. I Was a Teenage Mime. How to Make Love with the Lights On (And Look Great Doing It!).* More great reviews. More viruses. More sugar. But I began to develop a vague new understanding that something was wrong with me, not just in a physical way, but in a mental/spiritual way. I had my soulmate. I had my art. But there was something going on inside that needed my attention.

But I don't want to give myself attention. I want *your* attention.

After Dr. Cookie confirms my suspicions that sugar can indeed affect the immune system, I call Sarah to share the news. And to ask for help. Again. (Yep, old habits do die hard.) She tells me to watch the YouTube lecture "Sugar: The Bitter Truth." In the video, Dr. Robert Lustig claims all sugar is poison. He says sugar causes not just diabetes but heart disease and cancer. My lifelong fear. Sarah says cancer cells feed on sugar. I picture all the little cells gnawing away on a Snickers bar. She sends me the *New York Times Magazine* story "Is Sugar Toxic?" It's *amazing*. How great that the truth about sugar is *finally* coming out.

I still don't quit.

I get sick again and Dr. Cookie is out of town, so her office refers me to her colleague, a young Iranian doctor who is caring, kind, and smart. He does a blood work-up and says it looks okay, but then I get sick *again* and the nausea is unbearable and so he sends me for an endoscopy and colonoscopy. That's when they stick a tube down your throat and up your ass to see what's going on. I am sure they won't find anything. They never do. This sugar/health thing must be all in my head. I just have to *decide* to be fine.

The gastroenterologist is a fiftyish Israeli woman with gorgeous skin and a luscious French-tip manicure. It's my world tour of doctors. I can't believe she's wearing a pale pink Chanel skirt suit and leopard sling pumps while preparing to stick a camera up my ass. I need to impress her. "I have this great idea," I tell her as I lay there watching her prep my IV. I haven't eaten and I'm feeling a little loopy. "Someone should create a ride like at a water park, it would be called 'The Colon,' and it would be this amazing slide where you twist around and around and then you land, like, plop in this great big, white pool filled with water. Whuddya think?" She laughs, says it sounds terrific, and injects some drug into my IV. "By the way, I *love* your shoes" are my last words before I fall out.

Two days later I get a call from my internist's office. He's gotten my test results from the gastro doc and needs to talk. He won't tell me anything over the phone. He wants me to come in person. My heart pounds. My breath quickens. He's going to tell me I have something horrible. It's finally happened. All my years of abusing my body, feeling bad, and not taking care of myself and now the chickens have finally come home to roost. They're squawking uncontrollably. The sky is falling! The sky is falling!

"What's wrong?" the doctor asks when he enters the room and sees me trembling, clutching Gordon's hand.

"I'm so scared," I say, my teeth chattering.

"Oh, don't be scared," he says, grinning warmly. "Don't worry!" He obviously doesn't know who he's dealing with. My hands are so moist Gordon has to wipe his down. The doctor explains my test results. Apparently some of the cells in my gut have changed. "Your tissue looks inflamed," he says. "It's called metaplasia. Sometimes when cells are faced with some kind of stress, they respond by adapting, by changing." Cells. Changing. This does *not* sound good. Try not to get hysterical. Try not to go to the worst place. *Try.*

"Am I gonna die?"

"No!" he chuckles. "But—" I *knew* there was a but. I knew it, I knew it. "We have to watch it. But I don't want you to worry. We just want to keep an eye on it."

"So—what should I *do*?"

"Nothing. There is nothing to do. You go home, feel free to Google it. Read all about it. But please don't worry. I don't want you to worry. We just need to watch it is all."

Watch it my ass.

Gordon tries to reassure me on the drive home. "It's great they found it, babe," he says. "It's gonna be okay. Have some faith." Yeah. Right. Just please get me home so I can go online and find out if I'm gonna die.

I don't even remove my jean jacket or put down my purse before I am on my laptop. And there it is. There are the words . . . *may develop from metaplasia into dysplasia and then malignant neoplasia.*

I'm going down.

Just like my mom.

My mother went down just like I'd always feared she would. Cancer. Peritoneal cancer. That's the membrane that lines the abdominal cavity. In my mind, in my brain, in my sad, angry, terrified brain, it made sense her cancer was stomach-related. The stomach. That's the core. That's where she washed it all down with sugar. All the feelings. The anger. The disappoint- ment. For years I wished she'd see a shrink. I even wrote her a letter or two about it. She believed in therapy, but she wouldn't go. She did, however, try to get my dad to go, to deal with his lifelong guilt over leaving his parents on the East Coast. He wouldn't go, either.

I guess it's easier trying to fix someone else.

Once when my parents visited me and Gordon in New York, they took us to see *Les Miz* on Broadway. We were all seated in a row, watching the show, when I noticed Gordon looking over at my mom. In the dark of the theatre she had pulled out a bar of Halvah, the thick, rich candy made from crushed sesame seeds and sugar, and she was delicately gliding the five-inch bar into her mouth. Gordon looked back at me in shock. There it was.

My mother never spoke a word about sugar. But I knew; I'd received the legacy.

A few years before she got sick, I was worried about her health. She looked puffy. And pale. I got brave, sat her down, and berated her for not eating green vegetables. "Oh, I eat plenty of green things," she protested.

"Really?" I said. "What have you eaten that is green?"

She paused. She smiled.

"Pistachio ice cream," she said.

It tormented me that I couldn't get her to take better care of herself. I couldn't make her not eat sugar or exercise or go to therapy. My sisters and I were always so relieved when she went off to that health ranch in Mexico once a year. She'd come home rejuvenated, eating healthy, taking long daily walks. But life creeps up, and in a flash you're back where you started.

Along with the chemo and the surgery, my sisters and I tried to save our mom with food. Spirulina shakes, raspberries, broccoli soup. My brother, the practical doctor, gave solid support, though he stayed out of the kitchen. But my mother's illness did finally create equity and a deeper bond between me and my siblings. We held hands and ran through the fire together, trying to save our mom. The most private woman ever. Like Jackie O. private. It wasn't like in a novel or a movie, when the mom gets sick and the daughter comes to care for her and they have a big breakthrough in their relationship, and oh, the cancer was actually a *blessing*, a *gift*, as it gave the girl a chance for real connection with her mom! If I couldn't get in before, now I was *really* locked out. Her newfound frailty made my mother ever more determined not to let her guard down. I didn't care. As much as it tortured her having us wait on her, we persisted.

One time she was in bed, too exhausted to greet the day. I was straightening up her bedroom, trying to act like everything was going to be okay as I puttered about. She said to me, "Please don't decide to do this kind of work. This work is for other people. You have much bigger and better things to do." Maybe she was afraid that once she died, I'd give up my pursuit as an artist to become a hospice caregiver or something. Or maybe she couldn't let in the simple, intimate moment of her daughter taking care of her on her sickbed. We had to stick to the plan.

And what was the plan? My second-to-last visit home, I was standing by her bed. I saw her pain. She saw my concern. "Don't worry," she said from her pillow. "I can't die yet. I have to see you get your Oscar." I knew that she knew that I knew I had as much chance of winning an Oscar as she did surviving the cancer. Still, I *yearned* to believe her. All my life I strived for her belief in my talent, but I think what I really craved was just to be able to be with her. Not as a star. But as me. Her daughter. Lisa. My mom and I held a silent pact. It was a bond of sugar and stardom. It was something I had with her that none of my siblings had. But it only went so far. It left me—for lack of a better word—forgive me—hungering for more.

My addiction tells me I am nothing without an Oscar. It's an old, old voice. It's the voice that told me I could save her. The voice that told me she could save me.

I often felt as if I'd rather die than not make it.

What *is* it, really?

What is *it*?

It was at the heart of my mother's belief in me. If I could be what she thought I could be, I'd be worthy. I could rise above my shame. I would deserve to live. I picture the finest chocolate bunny flown in from Switzerland. So rich and sweet. But it's also hollow. I wanted solid. I picture my mother and me trapped inside of it. Only way out is to eat your way out.

I felt secretly, guiltily mad at her for not taking better care of herself all those years. She couldn't help it. Or wouldn't. Or couldn't. Her last words to my sisters and me, her last dying words were "Girls! Take care of yourselves! Don't let this happen to you!" Don't let this happen to me? But *how*? How would I not let this happen to me? How would I take care of myself when I *still* longed for someone else to do it? I knew what I needed to do. Clean up my food. Exercise. Go within. Want what I had. I knew. But alas, self-knowledge avails us nothing.

I don't want to die.

I call a friend who is well versed in diet and health. She knows I've been suffering, but we've both been in the dark about what is really wrong with me. "I finally got a diagnosis," I tell her. "I have metaplasia. I'm, like, inflamed inside. I have inflammation. I'm so scared."

"Oh," she says, like she knows exactly what to do about this. "Well, you *know* they're finding out now inflammation is at the root of *everything*, right? It's *all* about inflammation." She directs me to Dr. Nicholas Perricone, a dermatologist. He's called the "father of the inflammation theory." He determined that inflammation is the root cause of ageing and disease, and his "Perricone Prescription" includes an anti-inflammatory diet (scary word— *diet*) that eliminates almost all high-glycemic foods. I detest dietary restrictions. I'm afraid they will send me into a binge. But now, I am ready. I finally have my proof. My doctor says not to do anything *because he has no fucking idea what I should do*. But I do.

I quit sugar. Cold fucking turkey. Something just shuts off inside me and sugar is not an option. I'm scared straight. When I crave cookies I have . . . a rice cake with almond butter! A bowl of blueberries! I actually *want* produce. And salmon. Lots of salmon. My mouth waters at the sight of a sliced orange. It's a miracle. Friends and family can't believe it. Everyone is excited for me. I last a month. Two months. It's fantastic. Amazing. I do get sick with the same old virus or whatever it is. My stomach hurts. But it's okay. I'll get there. I don't even *want* sugar. It's *true* what they say. Once you get sugar out of your system, you won't even *want* it!

Until I want it.

Then it's a pint of cookie-dough ice cream and a plastic tin of sea-salt brownies down the hatch.

I always thought once I got an honest-to-goodness medical scare, *then* I would quit.

I didn't.

Help. I need help.

I need my dad.

But my dad is gone, as well.

He hung around longer than we thought he would after losing Mom, especially when he stood at her grave and said, "See you soon, Mim." But he lived another ten years. Until his broken heart failed him.

With my mother gone, I finally had to face the man I'd feared and hated my whole life. For shaming me. For being bothered by me. I would never be his favorite. He was never going to accept and appreciate me the way I wanted him to. On one of my visits home, I was cleaning out a drawer and found an old photo of myself from that year I moved home to quit sugar. My face was puffy and pale. My eyes looked empty and dead. I showed it to my dad.

"Who is that?" he asked.

"It's me," I said. "It was from when I moved home to stop bingeing."

"I have no recollection of that whatsoevah."

No recollection whatsoever? Of an entire chapter of my life? Proof. He never saw me. He never acknowledged my pain.

I put the photo away. It was time to move on.

And what about what we *did* share? The list was short. Like . . . our morbidity. Our humor. And a little bit of showbiz.

Over a decade ago, I'd flown home for lower back surgery so my mom could help me recover. My father agreed to film me in a short Super 8 movie about a girl who is conflicted about getting well. He filmed me leaving the hospital, still dressed in my hospital gown and carrying a fake IV pole. On camera, I walked through downtown San Mateo, to the local stationery store to send myself a get-well card, the local See's to send myself a box of chocolates (of course), the local florist to have flowers delivered to myself. We kept running into people he knew. "Dr. Kotin!" they would yell. "What's this?" He'd explain to them that he was making a movie with his daughter. They'd chat a bit, and then we'd move onto the next shot.

In the last scene, I wandered into a cemetery, set down my RIP tombstone, plopped down onto the ground, and waited to die—then I pulled out a tube of SPF 80 suntan lotion and started rubbing it all over. Just in case I lived. My dad *loved* this. He totally got it, although he wasn't thrilled about sneaking into the local cemetery to grab the final shot. I hurriedly searched for a good spot with my father running after me, camera in hand, yelling in a whisper, "It's not right! There's people buried here! It's disrespectful!" He finally took the shot. "If it helps yowr career!"

A couple of months before he died, I sat with him on the couch. He was so quiet. A faraway stare in his eye. He suddenly looked over at me, and then he placed his long bony hand on mine. The hand I'd always feared and loathed. The hand with the finger wagging in my face with disapproval and threats. But now its claws were gone. "I'm sorry I was a little haahd on you when you were a young girl," he said, patting my hand. Totally unprompted.

"Oh, Daddy," was all I could say. Because he *was* my daddy. He was the one who used to reassure me when I had a medical question (as long as it wasn't female-related). He always gave me the antibiotic ointment and the Band-Aid. Despite our conflicts, he was like Dr. God to me. He'd have the answers. I wish I could call him now. I wish I could ask him to set my mind at ease about the metaplasia. But I have to help myself.

I see a supposedly brilliant blonde naturopath who sends my shit to a lab. The results come in and she informs me I have no immunity in my gut. "You have *beyond* leaky gut," she says. What the fuck is that supposed to mean? She explains that, after all my years of bingeing, taking antibiotics, and not taking a proper shit, everything's backed up. I'm poisoning myself. *This* is why I feel ill. Makes *perfect* sense to me. As long as we know what it is, we can fix it, right? I follow her directions. I choke down vitamins and herbs with pea-protein shakes to strengthen my immune system, pop two-dollars-a-pop probiotics to replenish the flora in my gut, gobble ground flax seeds, and gulp magnesium capsules to help me crap. And I still feel like shit.

A holistic doctor in the valley has a six-month waiting list. He *must* be amazing. He sends seventeen vials of my blood and another round of my shit to the lab, then tells me I have Epstein-Barr—which only reminds me of Rosanne Barr, which only makes me feel worse because I will never be as funny or as famous as her. I spend hundreds on supplements and vitamin shots. I feel worse. The doctor waves some slides over my body and determines I have parasites. So *that's* it! Enid from the macro house was right. Maybe the worms are chewing holes in my colon—thus the leaky gut! I take some $500 medicine from Canada and immediately develop a severe twitch in my right upper lip. It gets worse. The doctor's too busy and famous to return my calls, and finally his nurse says to stop the meds, and so I stop the meds and I stop twitching. And I still feel like crap.

A nutritionist/self-declared microbiologist says I have a staph infection nesting in my throat. An acupuncturist puts me on Chinese herbs and tells me to eat buffalo, pork, and eggplant. My therapist says it's in my head. She says I need more therapy.

I am driving west on Santa Monica Boulevard. The glare hurts my eyes. I feel like crap. I can't quit sugar and I'm going to die. Then I remember. OA. *OA*? No way. No fucking way. Go back to those losers? No thanks. I can do this alone.

I can't do this alone. But I have to figure out a way. I have to. Gordon deserves it. Our daughter deserves it. Yeah, our daughter. All five years of her. And even though I don't always feel it, I know, I just know, from a place that is very real and very core, I know I deserve it, too. It's taken me the better part of a lifetime to figure that out.

My mother's words "Don't let this happen to you" haunt me as I think about my daughter. I reflect on my mother's sugar legacy to me—and what I will bequeath to my daughter. I never want her to hate her body. I never want her to cause herself pain. Above all, I never want her to feel shame or have to hide in the soul-destroying way that I did. But in order to show her that, I need to be out—and transparent—and ask for help. I need more allies.

That Saturday morning, I walk into an OA meeting. It's been thirty years but it's like it was yesterday. There's that same churchy-coffee 12-Step program smell. Yuck. Get me out of here. The room is packed. Everybody's sitting in chairs, facing forward, fully engrossed in the speaker . . . who is . . . a man. A young man. A young *thin* man. "Hi," he says. "I'm Josh and I'm a compulsive overeater and a sugar addict." A what? Wait. Huh? What? Wow.

I slip quietly into a chair and I face forward and I listen. "I'm so grateful to be here," Josh says. "I have to tell you, I love this room. This is the only place I know you're gonna get it. Normies, they just don't get it. People have no idea what I've done with food. They wouldn't believe me if I told them. But I know you'll believe me. Because you've done it, too. Everyone is this room has their own story." I can't believe I am here. I am back. And it feels . . . good. I fight the shame. My mother said OA was for other people. But I also know she wouldn't want me to die.

"When I first came into these rooms, I didn't wanna hear about a higher power," Josh says. "I said, fuck that. I can do this myself. I mean, I still don't wanna get on my knees. I still don't wanna pray. But when I do, I'm at least admitting I need help. That's like a higher power right there. 'Cuz I was always like, No thanks, I got this. Like the little old drunk falling off the bar stool, sayin', 'I got this!' That was me. But I got tired of falling on my ass. I got tired of denying my feelings. I know it sounds crazy, but I never got that I ate so I wouldn't feel. It's so basic, right? But I never got it." I know it sounds crazy, but neither did I.

At the end of the meeting the leader asks the OA fellows who've volunteered to talk to newcomers to please rise and state their name. A few people do, one of whom is a woman who says, "I'm Karen and I'm a compulsive overeater. If you're new or you just *feel* new, feel free to come up and talk to one of us after the meeting." There's something about her. A kindness. A vulnerability. She's not fat. She's not thin. Probably about my age. With such a kind face. So much compassion. And pain. She's had some pain. I can tell by her posture. Like she's protecting herself, wearing an oversized but neatly pressed, untucked tailored shirt with jeans, her lovely shoulder-length hair nicely styled. She's seen some hard years, but she is so present. So soft, and kind.

"Hi," I say to this complete stranger. "My name's Lisa. Can I talk to you for a minute?"

"Sure," she says with a look of curiosity.

"I just—I heard you say it was okay to talk to you, and so, I wanted to tell you, I was actually in OA thirty years ago."

"Wow," she says, now fully engaged.

"Yeah, I know, but then, I left, I couldn't do it, I just couldn't do it, and now, like, thirty years have passed, and I had this medical scare, and I have to quit sugar, I really do, and I want to, but I can't, and I'm scared, and so, I came here today, I mean, I just didn't know where else to go." Tears are streaming down my face. I've never admitted this to anyone. Not like this. Not from my heart. Not from this place of unbridled fear. Naked and raw.

"Well," Karen says, and I can see in her face she is fighting back tears. "I want to tell you, you are so brave. You've come to the right place. And you are going to be okay." She asks if I want to exchange numbers. We do, and then we walk into the bright Saturday sunlight together. It is then that I see, it is then that I understand, she reminds me very much of my mother.

"Please call me if you want to talk," she says.

"I will," I say.

That afternoon I am walking to Target for a few household supplies and thinking about the chocolate I might buy. My cell-phone rings. I don't recognize the number. It's her. That woman from OA. Calling to see how I am doing. She hopes it is okay to call. "Are you kidding?" I say. "I'm so happy to hear from you."

Karen becomes my sponsor. I don't think about the whole God thing. If I do or don't believe. For now I just . . . agree to disagree.

I get a year. A whole year without sugar. A follow-up endoscopy shows the metaplasia has decreased. I get another year. Then another six months. That's two and a half years with no sugar. A third endoscopy shows the metaplasia is gone. It's fucking gone. Vanquished. Annihilated. I reign supreme. I've licked sugar and the metaplasia, too.

And then I slip. And slip again. Then get back on track. Then slip.

Okay. I guess I'm an addict. I guess my addiction will always be with me. Like a constant reminder that I am alive. I wish I had one perfect answer. And yet—the desire for one perfect answer is like the addiction itself.

I think the answer is in the acceptance that there *is* no answer.

I think acceptance is the answer.

I'm still trying to accept that.

There are days when I hate my body. Days when I think my body is fine. Days when I can't take a shit. Days when I don't give a shit. Days when I feel like shit. Days when I think I *am* the shit.

I still hide in my humongous pin-striped overalls from time to time. But I try to show up for life no matter how I think I look. Or don't look. I try not to call in fat.

I still cut carrots on the diagonal to include both the yin and the yang in every slice—even though it might be a crock. I still attempt to chew my rice forty times per mouthful—or at least once.

As I write this I have eighty-four days of abstinence. My food is not perfect. I am not perfect. That's the hardest part. Remembering I don't have to be.

I still get sick. I still seek answers. But regardless of my health, I have a bottom line: no bingeing and no recreational sugar. That means no cane sugar. No maple syrup. No agave. No honey. It doesn't matter if it's organic or processed. Sugar is sugar. In OA I am told I have an allergy of the body coupled by an obsession of the mind. I heard at a meeting that being an addict is like this: You are standing in front of a lake and your body is on fire. You should jump in. Jump into the fucking lake! But I, the addict, believe I must understand *why I am on fire* before I can let myself jump into the lake. And therefore burn myself up and everyone close to me.

The lake is life.

Time to jump in.

Feelings come up. All the fucking time. I try to sit with it. Try not to act out. Try not to take the first bite. Breathe. Write. Make a call. Cry. Take a walk. Sit. Feel. Breathe. Turns out that's where God is for me. In the breath. In the simple act of life that I cannot control. I try to get out of my way so that I can live. Live and let live—and that means, most of all, letting myself live. Yeah, there's still a voice in my head that says I should be able to control this. I shouldn't need other people. I shouldn't need a "power greater than myself." It doesn't matter. God is my willingness to reach out and ask for help. Right now that's God enough for me.

Simple program. Not easy.
I keep coming back. Where else would I go?
It's not about the sugar.
It's all about the sugar.
Why do I crave sugar?
It's because my mother ate éclairs when I was in utero.
It's because they had four kids in six years.
It's because they fed me formula.
My sister Sarah was only fourteen months older and wished
      I didn't exist.
My father couldn't deal with me.
I was a teenage mime.
I felt ostracized as a Jew.
I had a big nose.
I left home too soon.
My grandmother was OCD.
I slept with the wrong guys.
I had food allergies.
I was dumped.
My writing professor said he wanted to strangle me with
      his cock.
My mother wanted me to win an Oscar.
My father wanted me to get a job.
Gordon broke my heart.
Gordon begged me for my heart.
It's because I wanted to get married. And he resisted.
It's because we got married.
It's because my parents passed away.
It's because I didn't want a baby.
It's because I had a baby.

It's because I wanted to write. With a baby.

A mom at school didn't hug me like she did the other moms.

My daughter didn't get invited to some kid's birthday party.

We have three fucking birthday parties to take her to this
weekend.

My writers' group didn't love my new chapter.

My writers' group loved my new chapter.

It's because I wrote a book.

It's because the book went out.

It's because you didn't buy my book.

It's because you bought my book.

It's because you read my book.

What do you think?

What's *your* list?

ACKNOWLEDGMENTS

Thank you first to the Studio Theatre Writers' Group. Your feedback and support have been invaluable. Special appreciation to Craig Sabin, Angelle Gullett, Robin Greenspan, Dallas Dorsett, Carol Ann Seflinger, and Jon Zelzany.

Profound gratitude goes to my agent, Stacey Glick, at Dystel & Goderich. Thank you so much for getting it. I am honored to have worked with you.

Thank you to my brilliant editor, Gayatri Patnaik. Your insight, vision, empathy, and humor in guiding me through the process of shaping my book have been a revelation.

Thank you to my readers: Laura Tucker, Gwen Watson, Danzy Senna, Isabelle Leon, Susie Shaw, Carol Margraf, Susan Eisner-Lee, Leah Allina, Tracy Poust, Jane Crosby, and, above all, the amazing Georgia Harrell.

Personal appreciation goes to Renee Rosen, Joseph Lee, Carolyn Abedor, Caroline Kleinman, Rob Kaarto, Kara Harshbarger, Sharon Ben-Meir, and Tracy Spuehler for all your humor, your smarts, and your encouragement.

Unqualified thanks to my remarkable sisters. My beautiful brother. And my generous and beloved parents. I know you know how much I treasure you.

So many thanks to everyone at Beacon Press for taking the risk and providing a home for my story.

I also want to appreciate the many cafés where I sat writing this book.

Thank you William Dufty for paving the way with *Sugar Blues.*

I could never have the words to properly thank my husband, Gordon. Your wisdom, friendship, humor, and patience are astonishing. Not just because you read my book at least twenty-five times and offered your brilliant criticism. But because of everything. Everything. I cannot thank you enough.

Eating disorders are a dis-ease of isolation. I want to thank all the brave and beautiful souls who share about their struggles with sugar and food. And, finally, for those who suffer silently, I hope my memoir has helped you feel a little less alone.